Social Media M
3 Book

MW00872818

Boosting your Business through Social Media Marketing on Facebook, Instagram, Pinterest, Youtube, and Twitter! Top Personal Branding Strategies!

WRITTEN BY **STEPHAN ANDERSON**

Social Media Marketing 2020 Book 1

Build Your Brand and Become the Best Influencer Using Social Media Marketing. Top Personal Branding & Digital Networking Strategies (Online Business)

WRITTEN BY STEPHAN ANDERSON

This document is geared towards providing exact and reliable information concerning the topic and issue covered. The publication is sold with the idea that the publisher is not required to render accounting, officially permitted, or otherwise, qualified services. If advice is necessary, legal or professional, a practiced individual in the profession should be ordered.

From a Declaration of Principles which was accepted and approved equally by a Committee of the American Bar Association and a Committee of Publishers and Associations.

The information provided herein is stated to be truthful and consistent, in that any liability, in terms of inattention or otherwise, by any usage or abuse of any policies, processes, or directions contained within is the solitary and utter responsibility of the recipient reader.

Under no circumstances will any legal responsibility or blame be held against the publisher for any reparation, damages, or monetary loss due to the information herein, either directly or indirectly. Respective authors own all copyrights not held by the publisher.

The information herein is offered for informational purposes solely and is universal as so. The presentation of the information is without a contract or any type of guarantee assurance.

The trademarks that are used are without any consent, and the publication of the trademark is without permission or backing by the trademark owner. All trademarks and brands within this book are for clarifying purposes only and are owned by the owners themselves, not affiliated with this document.

Table of Contents

4

Introduction

Social media has become a selling force for the marketing world and marketers are taking great advantage of it. A recent survey shows that about 75% of sales and purchase decisions are done through social media evaluations in one way or the other. Even the way we do business and maintain customer relationships has changed drastically within the last few years all because of social media. The traditional way of selling both offline and online has changed from email marketing, networking, phone calls and face to face discussions to almost complete social media selling. That been said doesn't mean our traditional ways of selling are no longer good or in use but, we rather make better use of them combining social media selling information and experiments to grow sales using social media.

Social media has exploded over the past 5 years with Facebook, Twitter, Digg, Delicious and thousands of other websites. These websites are geared toward allowing people from all over the world to communicate within a moment's notice. As social media exploded, websites like Facebook and so many others realized that millions of people were using their platform for business and adapted for those businesses.

Social Media Marketing, Truth and Lies

Social Media Marketing seems to be the latest buzz word for anyone looking to increase their online presence and sales, but is Social Media Marketing (SMM) all it is cracked up to be?

S.M.M companies are now springing up all over the place these days and they are telling anyone that will listen about how incredibly important social media like Facebook twitter and YouTube are to your business but, for the average small to medium-sized business, does marketing to social networks live up to all the hype? Is spending a small fortune on hiring an SMM company worth it? And has anyone done their research on this before they hired someone to set up their Facebook business page? Some SMM companies are setting up things like Facebook business pages (which are free) for $600 to $1,000 or more and telling their clients that they don't need a website because Facebook is the biggest social network in the world and everybody has a Facebook account. Now while it may be true that Facebook is the largest social network in the world and yes, Facebook's members are potential consumers, the real question is are they buying? Social media marketing companies are all too happy to point out the positives of social media like how many people use Facebook or how many tweets were sent out last year and how many people watch YouTube videos etc. but are you getting the full picture? I once sat next to an SMM "expert" at a business seminar who was spruiking to anyone who came within earshot about the amazing benefits of setting up a Facebook business page for small business (with him of course) and selling on Facebook. So, intrigued by the aforementioned "experts" advice I looked him up on Facebook only to find he had only 11 Facebook friends (not a good start). So being the research nut that I am, I decided to take a good look into SMM regarding selling to see if it worked, who did it work for and if it did why did Social Media Marketing work for them? And should businesses rely so heavily on social networks for sales?

As a web developer I was constantly (and now increasingly) confronted with several social networking challenges when potential clients would say that having a website sounds good but they had a Facebook business page and had been told by various sources (the ever-present yet anonymous "they") that social networks were the thing to do, but after discussing their needs it became quite clear that those potential clients didn't actually know why they needed social networks or SMM to generate online sales, they just wanted it. For small and medium-sized business I always recommended building a quality website over any type of social network, why? Well, it's simple really because social media is Social Media, and Social Networks are Social Networks they are not business media and business networks (that would be more like LinkedIn). I know that sounds simple but it's true and the statistics back it up. The fact is that social media marketing fails to tell you that Facebook is a social network, not a search engine and despite the number of Facebook users and Google users being around the same, people don't use Facebook in the same way that they use a search engine like Google (which has around half the search engine market), Yahoo and Bing to search for business or products. They use it to keep in touch with family and friends or for news and entertainment. In a recent study done by the IBM Institute for Business Value around 55% of all social media users stated that they do not engage with brands over social media at all and only around 23% purposefully use social media to interact with brands. Now out of all the people who do use social media and who do interact with brands whether purposefully or not, the majority (66%) say they need to feel a company is communicating honestly before they will interact.

So how do you use social media marketing? And is it even worth doing?

Well first of all I would say that having a well-optimized website is still going to bring you far more business than social media in most cases especially if you are a small to medium-sized local business because far more people are going to type in "hairdresser Port Macquarie" into a search engine like Google, Yahoo and Bing than they ever will on any Social Media Site and if you don't have a website you're missing out on all of that potential business. However, despite all the (not so good) statistics I still think it is still a good idea for a business to use social media just not in the same way that a lot of SMM professionals are today, Why? Because it's not working in the way they claim it does. Basically SMM Companies and Business as a whole looked at social networks like Facebook as a fresh market ripe for the picking and when Facebook started getting users measured by the millions PayPal co-founder Peter Thiel invested US$500,000 for 7% of the company (in June 2004) and since them a few venture capital firms have made investments into Facebook and in October 2007, Microsoft announced that it had purchased a 1.6% share of Facebook for $240 million. However, since Facebook's humble beginnings up until now (2012) both SMM Companies and Business have failed to truly capitalize on the huge number of Facebook users online. The truth is numbers do not equal buyers. Is it in a Social Media Marketing company's best interest to talk about social networks up? Absolutely. Is it in a Social Network like Facebook's best interests for people to believe that companies can sell en masse by advertising and marketing with them? Of course, it is. In early 2012, Facebook disclosed that its profits had jumped 65% to $1 billion in the previous year as its revenue which is mainly from advertising had jumped almost 90% to $3.71 billion so clearly the concept of SMM is working out for them but it is working out for you? Well... statistically no, but that does not necessarily mean that it never will.

I believe the major difference between social networks and search engines is intent. People who use Google are deliberately searching for something so if they search for hairdressers that's what they are looking for at that particular time. With something like Facebook, the primary intent is usually to connect with friends and family. In October 2008, Mark Zuckerberg himself said "I don't think social networks can be monetized in the same way that search (Search Engines) did... Three years from now we have to figure out what the optimum model is. But that is not our primary focus today". One of the biggest problems businesses face with social networks and SMM is perception. According to the IBM Institute for Business Value study, there were "significant gaps between what businesses think consumers care about and what consumers say they want from their social media interactions with companies." For example in today's society people are not just going to hand you over there recommendations, Facebook likes, comments or details without getting something back for it, so the adage "what's in it for me?" comes into play. So the primary reason most people give for interacting with brands or businesses on social media is to receive discounts, yet the brands and businesses themselves think the main reason people interact with them on social media is to learn

11

about new products. For brands and businesses receiving discounts only ranks 12th on their list of reasons why people interact with them. Most businesses believe social media will increase advocacy, but only 38 % of consumers agree.

Companies need to find more innovative ways to connect with social media if they want to see some sort of result from it. There were some good initiatives shown in the IBM study of companies that had gotten some sort of a handle on how to use social media to their advantage, keeping in mind that when asked what they do when they interact with businesses or brands via social media, consumers list "getting discounts or coupons" and "purchasing products and services" as the top two activities, respectively a U.S ice cream company called Cold Stone Creamery offered discounts on their products on their Facebook page. Alternatively, there is a great program launched by Best Buys in the U.S called Twelpforce where employees can respond to customer's questions via Twitter. With both Cold Stone Creamery and Twelpforce the benefit is clearly in the favor of the potential customer & the great trick to social media marketing is to sell without trying to sell (or looking like your selling) unfortunately most social media marketing is focused the wrong way.

Building a tangible buyer to consumer relationship via social media is not easy and probably the most benefit to businesses' using social media to boost their website Google rankings. But businesses need to understand that you can't just set up a Facebook business page and hope for the best. SMM requires effort and potential customers need to see value in what you have to offer via your social media efforts give them something worth their social interaction and time and then you may get better results.

Importance of Social Media Marketing In 2020

In the world of technology, communication has become easier than ever. The world has now shrunk from a vast populated land to a network of communicating individuals living in a global village. People from all over the globe have come closer together and distances have decreased to the extent that an individual is merely a click away.

In this ever-growing network of people a new theory has emerged, the idea of 6 degrees of separation. The idea behind this is that between you and any other person in the world is only a chain no longer than six people. This emphasizes the significance of online communication and the way it has made the world a whole lot smaller.

This is the power of social media and the developments in online communication. A happening in one part of the world reaches the second part in a matter of seconds. Imagine if that news or happening was about you. The significance of this technology is the ease it provides. Using this tool to your advantage can give you a large number of benefits.

Social Media Marketing brings Global Fame to your Name

This is your ticket to international level fame. Your company or your name could be known throughout the globe with millions of followers and fans. Millions of people can access these sites where people come to communicate online and express their views. Once you step into the world of social media marketing all of these people become your potential prospects. Your services are merely a single search away.

Promote your Business or Product as a Serious Product.

This technology provides you access to virtually the whole world and all its inhabitants. They are there to read and share anything that you have to say. This is your chance to establish a image for yourself that "Hey! I am here to do business" and "I am serious about the product or services that I provide".

Brings you Closer to Thousands of People Without Much Effort

Social media marketing is practically free. If you were to attempt to reach out to millions of people through physical means you would have to make a lot of investments. This technology is the way to most efficiently reach out to your potential clients, not only in terms of finances but in terms of time as well.

It gives you Feedback on the Type of Viewer you have

A interesting thing about marketing on these social websites is the level of feedback that you can expect. Using social media marketing can educate you about the people who are or might be interested in your product or service. This gives you a better chance of altering your campaigns to gain improved results. You may learn about the number of people who visit your page, or the ages of people who comment or share your posts, or even their ethnicities, localities, religion, hobbies, and preferences. You educate the world about your product and social media marketing educates you about the people who took an interest in it. You get to know them personally through the network of social media.

Established an Efficient Communication Channel between you and your Client

Your client may have some issue or he may need help or want to inquire more about your product. Your presence on social media allows you to respond to him on a personal level. This in turn, assures the client that you are responsible and instills a sense of trust.

Your Company Is Seen As A Person

Generally, people might not prefer to do business with a company or a corporation and prefer to work with individuals. This is because a person is real; he has a real presence in this world, he is someone you can relate to, he has feelings, thoughts, and emotions. Having your business on social media gives it a human personification. It appears to be more of an individual than a company; someone people can talk to; someone people can reach out to. This creates a comfort zone between the clients and your company and produces benefits for both.

It Makes you More Accessible

Social media sites ensure your presence 24 hours a day, 7 days a week. Your client can easily drop off a message and you can choose to reply as soon as you wish. This strengthens the bond between you and your customer and inspires a feeling of loyalty for your brand. This constant availability cannot be found when dealing with a physical office due to office opening and closing times. This ease for the customers to reach out to you in their time of need can only be ensured by social media.

Social Media Levels The Playing Field

Whether you are a multinational company or a single person start-up, in the world of social media you are all on the same level. Your finances and resources may not make much of a difference when it comes to social media. What does make a difference in your skill to communicate and attract people and the quality of the product or services that you provide? In the physical world, new start-ups would face immense financial difficulties in trying to promote themselves, while the marketing of giant enterprises would continue to dominate. Social media network gives you a fair playing field to show your true spirit and skill.

You Might Discover New Potential Clients or Customers

While reviewing your feedback of viewers you might begin to see obvious patterns in your business response. People from a particular region that you might never have thought of are showing a lot of interest in your product are your best clients. These patterns will also allow you to see a certain untapped market that you can exploit. You can swiftly move and make use of the opportunity.

The Marketing Campaign is Easier to Manage and Cost-Effective

Setting up a social media marketing campaign requires much less effort than actually setting out to physically execute your marketing campaign, for example, putting up banners or advertisements, etc. to get you to message across. Social media marketing is relatively easy to manage and quite frequently updated.

Your Network Grows Exponentially

As more people add to your social network, they become the cause for more people to join in. As the people keep adding the rate at which people are added grows with them. And as the tree branches out, so will your business.

People are More Receptive to Social Media

People tend to pay more attention to things on social media. The reason is that people feel that compared to mainstream marketing social media has no political agenda behind the information or the presence of any big corporation trying to sell their products. It is just people sharing their knowledge and opinions. Therefore the people tend to pay more attention to social media posts and are more influenced by them as opposed to specialized advertisements. People regularly check their social media feeds for posts that their friends and family make, and there you are, right in between all their posts with your latest news or promotion. The readers are bound to pay attention to what you have tried to communicate and then forward the news to their acquaintances and the message will spread exponentially.

Social media is the new generation of communication and information transfer. Almost everyone is keeping their presence online visible. You should not stay behind the competition and use this technology to your advantage.

Social Media Marketing Guide for Beginners In 2020

Social Media Marketing is the process of gaining attention and web traffic through social media sites. During this process, usually creative content to reach the masses through publicity coming from a third-party trusted source needs to be created for people to share the content of their interest with others and create a vicious chain that would make business cover and go beyond the market audience intended. Every online marketer needs to have a goal, a product, a service and a cause to promote through the vast and overwhelming World Wide Web. If you already have those things defined in your mind, then congratulations! That could be probably the hardest part of entering into the social media challenge, and from now on, every single effort will contribute to reaching those goals efficiently and flawlessly until you put your feet on the Social Media Guru status.

The Social Media world is wide and more extensive than ever. It is a very strategic marketing platform that reaches different cultures, ages, religions, sexes, locations, interests and such, therefore it makes it the perfect vehicle to reach and target the right audience and achieve total success. The whole world won't care about video games, for example, but only the people that video games are part of their interests. If you target male audiences with ads of high heels on sale, maybe some of them would go and buy a pair or 2 for their wives, but a pair or 2 is not exactly the kind of impact you want to have. Therefore, you focus on certain group ages and certain other factors that cause some services and products, videos and news to go "viral"

First, we need to know the basic social media sites

Facebook

Holding more than 900 million users, if you're already a Facebook user this might not be new to you, but there are lots of features worth mentioning. You can create a dedicated business page and interact directly, and free, with your customers uploading free pictures, products and videos of the service you intend to provide or the product you are trying to sell. That way, you can build a database of people that will share your posts with their friends and therefore create the never-ending chain. Most of these social media sites have seamlessly mobile integration so people whether it is a portable PC, a desktop, tablet or mobile phone get always connected with media in a way that you should take advantage of. People log in to Facebook, in any situation, while commuting, in the park, at home, at school, at work. Then you're there, promoting your business for it to be displayed in the news feeds, and you would be there, constantly doing the mind trick game to the point that people will find something attractive and worth checking according to their interests. Many big corporations like Starbucks, Microsoft, Apple, Rockstar, Pepsi, etc. are doing the same, and it works perfectly!

Blogs

Blogs are an easy way for people to communicate in a semi-professional way when it comes to the quality of content. Quality content is always the key to good writing and therefore, good blogging. There are many blogger CMS (content management service) where you can get yours up and running for free in less than 5 minutes, some of these are Blogger, WordPress and probably the most user-friendly one, Tumblr. One of the tricks here is knowing your audience, your market, who you are targeting and what you want to accomplish with that. Now, this has to do with some SEO or Search Engine Optimization knowledge, which is in other words, using the right keywords to rank as high as possible in a search engine i.e. Google, Bing. It has to be related to your posts and at the same time, you have to make sure you use a keyword search tool to chęck the competition and number of searches this given keyword has. The lowest the competition and highest number of searches it gets in a month, the more convenient for you. If you were to advertise your website holding a service of technical support chat, you would have to make the keywords very specific so people that are looking for your service would find you first.

It is, for example, technical support for Windows, then you'll have to include specific words, as going a little more straight to the point. Since the competition would be really high and Windows technical support is a wide content, you would focus and go further the specific services your product offers, therefore, adding additional keywords to go straight to the point would be the most successful way to do it and you would rank higher in a search engine and people would find your product easily. From "Technical Support Chat" to "Technical Support Chat for Windows 7 and XP" you can see how we are narrowing the concept of the service you offer making it more specific, detailed and then competition of support for mobile operating systems, cellphones, Mac, iPhone, Windows Vista, Windows 8 and such, are left behind and those sites offering the services you're not related to won't steal your chances to be found for people that are merely looking for chat support for Windows 7 and XP. Once understood the keyword concept you can proceed and create content on a blog that would be easy to find on a search engine by including the right tags.

Then we have the Social Media integration again in the blog space. There are many options to share the content of your blog. Many Content Manager Services like Tumblr have social media buttons to share and like or dislike. You need to look for the options to enable them (in the rare case they are not enabled by default) so every post of yours would have the buttons for share on Tweeter, Google+, Facebook, etc. and Reblog within the blogging network you are affiliated to. With great quality and eye-catching content, you are encouraging people to share your stories on other media sites like the ones mentioned above plus you sharing them and there you have outstanding chances to reach a wider audience.

Twitter

A fast-growing, very popular social media site. With over 340,000,000 tweets a day and around 140,00,000 users worldwide, this platform is pretty appealing to businesses and companies as well as for celebrities, musicians, actors, everybody! A tweet is a message of 140 characters maximum that one can write and post and followers can read and see any time in their news feeds. Talk about it, interact directly and start new conversations is one of the things that make this platform extremely successful. The way they follow Kim Kardashian and read and talk about everything she tweets in a day, the same way they can do with advertising and marketing campaigns about brands and products of their interest.

140,000,000 users to target the right audience might sound like a difficult task, but seen it from the other side of the coin, means more potential customers for a business. Once you get into the already mentioned vicious chain of any social media site, things just keep coming along by themselves and the first thing you'll notice is hundreds of hundreds of people engaged in your brand, talking about it, reviewing it and telling others about events, broadcast and such.

Linkedin

Possibly a not so popular platform making it boring for some people, but a very professional and strategic one for the rest. Some people won't spend long hours chatting or talking to others about silly, trivial things, instead, this social network goes straight to the point. People on Facebook and Twitter, for example, follow anyone of their interest for the sake of simply socialize as well as businesses and companies, but Linkedin is intended to filter and leave the fun behind to focus deeper on professionalism in social media.

On Linkedin, you can be part of the people looking for a job/ service or part of a company offering a job/ service. You can create either a personal profile with your professional information about yourself, studies, contact information, interests, certifications, identifications, etc. or, create a business or company page, same way as you do it on Facebook or Twitter sufficing the same purpose: share information about your brand, service, product and keep your audience and followers up to date with the latest information about your company.

YouTube

YouTube is a very interesting platform. People go watch videos of any kind or gets redirected by any website that has a backlink to it or search engines. Once people are there on a given there you have some more "Related Videos" on a column on the right side of the screen. Clicking from video to video makes you find things you never thought you would find, interesting topics, funny videos, how-to kind of videos, publicity, etc. Your chances to be seen are overwhelming and you can also get people to subscribe to your Channel, which is in other terms, your own

YouTube space where you upload your videos. Some people find it way more interesting and easier to just watch a video rather than reading a whole article. You have the resource of visuals. If you were to promote fashion clothes and that is the purpose of your whole social media marketing, you can, along with other options, upload a video with people modeling your clothes, redirect people to your main business site, recommend people to share your video, to subscribe for future video updates, to visit your "fashion blog", like your page on Facebook, follow you on Tweeter, Google+, Linkedin, etc. Close your eyes and try to visualize the Tree Diagram of the whole Social Media marketing strategy and how it gets to potentially reach every single corner of the World Wide Web. Ambitious, isn't it?

Google+

A fair newcomer on the social media site battle, Google+ offers integration of a variety of services including Gmail, Google+ Basics, Google+ Circles that let you share information or "statuses" in a way Facebook does but has less popularity so far. You have the "Stream" feature similar to Facebook's News Feed that would let you see what others are up to, an option for following very similar as well to Tweeter.

The service is was very appealing to professionals and business networks because of the exclusivity and integration of services. You create a Gmail account for example, and unless you disable it, by default you have access to all these services and a profile ready to be edited with a picture, contact information, etc. You have access to the whole Google+ network including already mention Gmail, YouTube, You+, Circles, Basics and even the well-known search engine saving and displaying results to the most relevant things to you. It is convenient to have a spare Google+ account for any Social Media Marketer because it's potential functionality and because no source is too little or too much in marketing. Might not have the same impact, a 30 seconds ad on TV than a small billboard on a bus, but the more you get the message sent the better results you will to accomplish.

Social Media Stats

According to the new 87 studies perform on social media marketing up to 2012, this approach from companies to customers called B2C or Business to Community has grown and reached 16% of customer engagement but has the potential to grow to 57% in the next 5 years. More than 30% of the worldwide population is now online permanently or have some sort of eventual access to the web. More than 1/5 of consumer's free time is being spent on social media sites, reaching an approximate of 250 million tweets and 800 million Facebook statuses updated every single day. Only in the United States, more than 80% of online active users spend theirs on social media sites or blogs. 60% of people use 3 or more digital forms of research product comparison, prices, and information about intended purchases, being 40% of those done via social media sites like Facebook or simply redirected from one of these sites leading to even direct interactions with retailers about offers posted. Around 56% of Americans have one to three profiles in a social media site being 55% of them aged between 45-55 and having at least one profile

Search Engine Optimization (SEO) Facts

70% of the links search users click on are organic. 46% of all searches are for information about products or services. Half of all local searches is performed on mobile devices. 66% of new customers use search and online research to find local businesses. There are 863 million websites globally that mention "SEO." There are 9.1 million searches conducted including the acronym each month, with the top two phrases being "SEO services" and "SEO company." More than 60,000 Twitter users include "SEO" in their bios, there have been 13 million blog posts published that include "SEO" in the title, and Amazon.com carries almost 2,700 different books about SEO 75% of searchers never scroll past the first page of results. 93% of online experiences begin with a search engine. B2B companies that maintain active content like blogging and SEO programs increased their total website traffic, on average, by 25% in the past year, while those who neglected SEO experienced an average 15% decline in overall visits. 21% of all time spent online is spent on web searches. The big three search engines Google, Bing, and Yahoo! are among the five most-visited sites on the Internet. Considering that AOL is #7 and Ask is #10; five of the top 10 most-visited sites on the web are search engines.

Social Media Marketing Trends You Should Not Ignore In 2020

The success of social media marketing lies in the right mix of fruitful strategies. The wrong combination will simply reduce the traffic from targeted customers rather than attract them. If you devise your social media strategies such as social media optimization based on current trends, you can increase profits and use social networking sites effectively for marketing.

Low Usage of Social Bookmarking Sites

According to the research reports, the use of social bookmarking sites has decreased to 10 percent from 26 percent in 2011. This considerable drop in usage indicates the fall of bookmarking sites. Even though the sites including Twitter, StumbleUpon, Reddit, and Pinterest are still popular among marketers, the majority of sites (e.g. DIGG, Friendfeed) are almost dying.

Therefore, it is not a good practice to trust a bookmarking site blindly for marketing purposes in the current scenario. Instead, check for the sites that are most popular and perform the bookmarking very cautiously.

The decline of Daily Deal Sites

Daily deal features or simply daily offerings of deals are regarded as a powerful way to attract a large number of targeted customers at a time. The research report says that around 80 percent of marketers are not interested in using the most popular daily deal sites including Groupon or Living Social for their campaigns shortly.

Now people concentrate more on the considerable amount of returns that they receive from their purchases over time. Hence, it is advisable to use social networking sites for long term marketing goals rather than daily goals.

Top Sites for Social Media Campaigns

Marketers who use social media for marketing will carry out social media campaigns (using social networking sites for promotion) for their products or services to attract targeted customers. The campaigns will be successful only if the relevant site is popular among the customers.

The research report indicates that marketers who spend more than 40 hours a week for social media marketing carry out their campaigns more intensely through Google+, YouTube, Pinterest, and Instagram compared to those who spend six hours or less a week on social media marketing. Also, around 92 percent of marketers who have five or more years of experience prefer LinkedIn than 70 percent of marketers having less than five years of experience.

Around 67 percent of marketers are planning to increase campaigns through Twitter even though it is a slight decrease from 69 percent last years. Young marketers, more than older ones prefer photo sharing sites including Instagram for launching campaigns. 62% chose to blog as the most suitable platform to master, which is the highest one followed by Google + (61%) and Facebook (59%).

Trends of B2C and B2B Marketers

Business to Consumer (B2C) Marketers use Facebook at a higher rate of 67% than other platforms. In the case of Business to Business (B2B) marketers, both Facebook and LinkedIn have an equal majority of 29% each. Given below is the pie chart showing usage statistics for each platform about B2C and B2B marketers.

B2B marketers uses a more diverse array of platforms compared to B2C marketers. Both of them do not completely utilize blogging and have minimal You Tube usage.

If you are a B2B or B2C marketer, try to encourage blogs as they are regarded as the most popular social media platform. YouTube being the second largest search engine, you can enjoy the benefits it offers by posting low-cost videos. Orabrush (B2C Company) and Blentec (B2B Company) have become strong brands by making use of low-cost YouTube videos.

As B2B marketers increasingly use LinkedIn, they have an opportunity to utilize SlideShare (owned by LinkedIn). This social media entity can be used for generating leads for B2B organizations.

Fewer Check-ins Online

As per the research reports, there is a decrease in the usage of geo-location services including Foursquare from 17% in 2011 to 11% this year. These services allow check-in to your locations automatically online. The decline in this kinds of services indicates that people are now concerned more about privacy and safety. Marketers can tackle this situation by introducing contests and rewards. This will encourage people to check-in more.

If you are still following the old strategy for social media marketing, then it is time to develop new strategies based on all these current trends. It is better to entrust this tedious task to a reputable social media marketing company that offers reliable social media marketing services rather than try implementing the strategies on your own.

10 Checklist Points Before Engaging In Social Media Marketing In 2020

Social media marketing has a phony reputation. For many an executive from the commercial department, this exercise sums up to a string of signups over several social networks randomly and from time to time, multimedia, article postings, and advertising over Facebook and Twitter. This is not the right shot!

SMM is more than just being present in the Social Media Sphere. It is a sharp commercial engagement that may just turn into total havoc if, not handled properly. The goal of Social Marketing in cyberspace is the same as the real-world thing. It's about delivering Unique Selling Points that will end up in concrete and sustained sales. It is about converting an anon into a brand advocate at best. Achieving this objective follows almost the same rules except for the fact that Social Media allows a closer, more personal and customizable, so to say Social approach of the targets. The same rules apply but with more or fewer variations. Assessing the prerogatives, context, environment, and toolsets are the essential starting point of any Social Media Marketing campaign. It implies thorough setup and clinical precision in the way messages and attitudes are to be delivered through dedicated channels. Within such campaigns, posting on Facebook, on a fan page, group page or personal page is never the same process.

Here are 10 CHECKLIST POINTS BEFORE ENGAGING IN SOCIAL MEDIA MARKETING:

- Define your base strategy. Setup a budgeted roadmap with intermediate white stones that will help at fine-tuning the campaign all along the way. The roadmap should stay in tune with what is being done or what has been done in the real world. Social Media Marketing is never an innocent act. It is time-consuming and will incur expenses. Being precise about the campaign will decrease the burden. As said earlier assess the main objective and methodology. For example, you may need to revamp your actual website to allow SM integration and SMO. Make your campaign stay SMART - Specific, Measurable, Attainable, Realistic, Relevant and Time-bound. Either go for Awareness or Sales or Loyalty. One at a time! Don't try to aim for all objectives in one go. Remember! Stick to your company's marketing and communication policy.

- Assess and understand your campaign's environment. RESEARCH and don't stop til' you get enough! One surely doesn't want to jump into dark waters without basic precautions and headlamps. So does you with your Social Media Marketing Campaign. Diving recklessly into Social Media can spell TOTAL MESS especially when dealing with building awareness and product reputation. Building an effective Online Social Strategy implies thorough knowledge of the competitors' doing's on common platforms (of course)... but above all, take a humble preview of how others from different sectors have done or are doing. Get into both successful and failed case studies. Learn more about the technical potentials of every Social Network and platform.

- Identify these platforms and toolsets that are relevant and positively responsive to your roadmap. Social Media Marketing is about delivering the same consistent message through the whole spectrum of interwoven Social Networks. The intertwined winning triumvirate is made of the Blog, Facebook, and Twitter, to which you would add a YouTube account if you would have video clips uploaded regularly. Choose strategically. For example, you might feel the need of Slideshare and LinkedIn accounts instead of a Foursquare one, if your product or service is more into pitch-intensive B2B. Your toolset should also be made up of listening and monitoring wares.

- Realistically budget and size your Online Advertising. Use the full potential of Google AdSense and Facebook's advertising platforms, but make sure to target wisely. Goal-tied

Marketing Campaigns means nothing without proper advertising. Intuitive Online advertising is now accessible through a few clicks and will unleash its power to communicate about your brand on a global basis. They can also enhance diffusion to limited zones. Think about identifying and assessing your targets on geographical grounds. This will help at optimizing your online advertisement budget. Choosing PPC or CPC is up to you accordingly to your basic roadmap requirements.

- Set up a Social Media taskforce from within your staff and look for an outsider to operate as a Community Manager. The web never sleeps. Social Media Marketing is a 24/7 perpetual roll-on. As such it is time and resource-consuming. One should never expect to be capable of handling a Social Media Marketing campaign alone, especially if other primary company duties are at stake. Instead, invite some of your staff to engage in social networking on your business's behalf. Be choosy though! Those indulged in such a sensitive and interactive task must write well, be tactful, creative and loyal. Outsider Community Managers are seldom biassed and are limited to the sole responsibility of consolidating your taskforce's activities over relevant Social Networks. In any case, you should build a team whose main goals and capabilities are to listen, learn and reply tactfully.

- Prefer influential relationships. Get your team to identify major Bloggers and mainstream Social Media activists who fringe with your zones of interest and industry. This task is one of the hinges of success for your campaign. Getting to talk to Social Media heavyweights is like hiring evangelists when relationships get entrusted. Getting Lady Gaga to like your pair of boots is like tapping straight into a sea of opportunities as wide as 9 million individuals who would just follow Gaga's recommendations. Getting her to buy one would mean immediate success. CAREFUL however! The adverse effect is also proportionally as big as your contact's notoriety. Be sure of what you sell to him or her. A successful Social Media Marketing campaign starts here.

- Identify relevant measuring and benchmarking tools. They are proof of your campaign's success or need for fine-tuning. For example, the increase in the number of likes on Facebook or followers on Twitter is a indicator of your campaign's health. Getting to know how many times your brand is mentioned across the web and rating these comments help at fine-tuning the campaign. You should also be able to keep track of your on-growing relationships and traffic that comes from Social Platforms. Identifying prospects for future opportunities helps in developing better strategies. Beware! At the actual state of affairs,

Social Media Metrics can be tricky! You will need a very wide array of results coupled to trending reports to be able to depict the exact snapshot of your on-going campaign.

- Identify offline components that will be needed to complement your Online Social Marketing. Offline events are powerful conversion tools when geared the proper and relevant way. Offline components may also mean socializing with people of the web, in the real world, offering real-world prizes and gifts, organizing rallies, bar camps, conferences, and seminars... etc Determine how these components can enhance your target's brand experience and how they will relevantly fit into your Online Marketing Scheme.

- Urge for quality relevant content when posting articles, multimedia, and comments. Praising your 270hp 1974 red Corvette when you advocate for ecological products on your blog isn't the best of strategies. Be sure to lay editorial rules that will define consistent cross-platform content production both in terms of easy-reading literature and technical specifics. Should an uploaded video be in HD both on YouTube and on Facebook? How long should be an article? Should an article contain a generic common byline for multiple authors or should it bears the actual author's name and on what grounds? One should always define this lines accordingly to the targeted audience.

- Urge to stay HUMAN at every stage! Putting up a Social Media Marketing strategy is about building your brand's Social Media presence where your quality accessible content will be delivering values of your organization. Social Media is about... Socializing first! People are touchy when it comes to attitudes and postures. They don't like to bullied or taken as immature consumers. Being too techy, too commercial demotes the social experience. Simple language and "real-worldlike" politeness are the bases for the best of approaches. It is sometimes more fruitful to start a discussion that may seem miles away from your product and its campaign objectives. With the will to listen and the power to communicate clearly, high conversion rates are never far ahead.

3 Mistakes in Social Media Marketing That May Come Back to Haunt You In 2020

You order an item online and it takes way more time to arrive than it should. Plus, a few items are missing in the package. Frustrated, you take to the vendor's Facebook channel to voice your concerns and expect to be compensated.

And despite repeated prodding, there is complete radio silence at the other end.

The experience didn't feel good, did it? You think maybe this business doesn't care about you - how you trusted it to give you a good experience and it shattered this trust instead. So you do what any frustrated individual would - you vow never to order anything from here again and hit the "unlike" button.

For social media strategists, there is a lesson to be learned here. A social media marketing strategy can eventually falter with a few unlikes and negative comments.

As a business owner, social media gives you limited chances to make a good impression. How you take advantage of these changes might make your business or break it.

The proof is in these states:

- 71% of users who have a positive social media experience with a brand are likely to recommend it - Ambassador
- According to a study, hardly 20% of social media posts hardly generate any emotional reaction on social media - Havas Media
- 42% of Twitter users expect to expect a business to respond to their inquiries within an hour - Ambassador

As a social media marketer, the best way to improve your social media strategy is to first find why it falters in the first place. Here are some mistakes that you might have overlooked:

Being careless with negative feedback

If you have ever dealt with a salesperson, you wouldn't expect him to become defensive when you have a complaint or be careless about your concerns.

So why would your followers on social media?

Keep in mind, whenever anyone says something negative about you on social media, the rest of your followers can see them. And they will be as interested to see how you respond.

For businesses, this is a nail-biting scenario. But it is avoidable. Here is how:

- **Put Someone Competent Behind The Wheel:** Experienced professionals like social media experts will take an unbiased approach to the negativity and know that being careless about it serves no purpose.

For example, they know that being unresponsive to comments like "your service sucks! I want my money back" doesn't help anyone. A well-worded reply, on the other hand, helps both your reputation and appeases rising tempers.

To illustrate, your reply should go something like, "We are sorry that you had a bad experience. Can you tell us exactly what happened so we can make amends?" This way, you are more likely to ease frustrated customers.

- **Become Alert To Mentions By Using Online Tools:** It's easy to forget about something you don't encounter every day. Comments on social media are the same. You can't track every one of them. No one inboxes them to you and there is no guarantee that followers will tag you.

To keep track of all comments, you can use tools like Google Alerts which notify you when anyone uses your keywords on their social media fields.

Using Social Media Management Tools To Schedule The Same Posts On All Platforms

Social media management tools allow marketers to post the same content on several social media platforms at once. Many businesses use it to schedule posts. And it has worked for them too, freeing up the time they need to focus on other tasks.

But oftentimes, people use these tools as a shortcut to schedule the same posts on several platforms. It's a lazy tactic and shows that you don't care how your content is received by audiences.

Keep in mind, what works on Facebook or Twitter won't necessarily work on LinkedIn. Every social media platform was created with specific target audiences in mind. A 140 character tweet, for example, won't sit well with LinkedIn audiences who expect more comprehensive posts.

Use tools to schedule optimized posts

To make the most of social sharing tools, improve your social media strategy first. Take the time to learn about the unique capabilities of each platform. Limit yourself to two or three platforms if that is what is takes. For example, posts that are rich in imagery are more successful on Google+.

Hootsuite and HubSpot are two of the many social media management tools that you can use to automate posts and even see which channels are driving the most engagement. In addition to automated content sharing, these platforms also offer free online social marketing training courses that can help you make the most of each platform like optimizing your posts for different social media channels.

Skimping on social share buttons

Business owners usually reserve their best content for their websites. Content like informative blogs, for example, establish them as experts in their niches.

It also gives visitors a chance to stay longer on these websites. Perhaps they would like to look around to see what else is on offer?

Unfortunately, you could feature content that everyone would love to share - but if visitors don't have any way to share it, it isn't going to get the exposure you are looking for.

To make this work for you:

- **Make your social sharing work on mobile:** Statistics show that over 15% of tweet mentions are from the tweet buttons that are embedded on your site. This also proves to show that people share a lot on mobile devices.

- **Tools to create social share buttons for WordPress:** You can use online tools to create customized social share buttons for different audiences.

When selecting appropriate plugins, a good rule of thumb is to select those that allow you more freedom in the type of social share buttons you can create for different platforms.

For example, to improve engagement with mobile audiences you can tell your developers to download WordPress plugin tools like Simple Share Buttons Adder to create customized share buttons for your web or mobile audience and add them to all of your social media posts. Another plugin tool is Addthis.

- **Have a Social Budget**: If anything is worth doing, it's worth doing right. Tools like Simple Share Button Adder are free to download and use. But if you want to make your share buttons shine, it's best to have a budget for it and use it to purchase their pro or premium packages. These offer more customization options and retail for around $10 to $100.

- **Select Shareable Content Wisely:** If you want to take advantage of social media, your content must be something that people would want to share. Image rich posts, for example, are shared a lot more than text-based content.

To illustrate, consider infographics. Studies show that infographics are shared and "liked" on social media 3 times more than any other type of content.

Use tools to keep yourself alert to negative comments and rely on professional help. Avoid taking the lazy way out by ditching the auto-posting strategy. Pay attention to the type of content you post, how your followers share content on your social platforms of choice and optimize it for mobile to expand your reach. It's a mistake to regard society as a quick and easy solution to market your brand. It takes time, effort and patience. Learning about the mistakes and pitfalls can help you avoid them.

5 Effective Social Media Marketing In 2020

Social media is here to stay. As an entrepreneur or small business owner if you're not using it to grow your business you are missing out. I am sure you have seen the statistics by now. In 2015, 73 percent of U.S. Americans had a social network profile, representing a six percent growth compared to the previous year according to Statista. The numbers do not lie. Social media is a way of life all over the globe.

As an entrepreneur or small business owner if you're not using social presence on-line to grow your business you are missing out. Below I've listed my easy 5 step process for developing a strategy for social media marketing.

Identify your Goals

For every company, there should be a mission. Your company mission should have a mission statement. For every mission, there must be a goal. What is the positive outcome or end goal that you want to achieve? You may want to become internet famous, you may want to get speaking gigs, you may want to promote a book or training program or you may just want more customers. Whatever it is you must write down your goals and the logic behind them. Understanding where you want to go and how you're going to get there will help you devise the best plan and route you should take.

Get Brand Clarity

Get clear on your brand before you put it out there. Answer these 3 important questions. What do you do? Who do you help? what do you want to be known for? Once you can clearly articulate the answers to these questions, you can communicate this on social media or in front of anyone. You must be able to clearly and succinctly say in one sentence what you're all about and describe your business model in a way that makes sense.

Master the Art of Pull Marketing

Pull marketing is about client attraction. When you create core messages with a strong call to action statements, you are setting the stage to have people in your target audience self qualify and respond with, "me too" or "I need that" or "where can I learn more?" Your goal is to have ideal prospects able to see themselves in your business model. They need to be able to see that your company offers exactly what they have been looking for.

Social platforms are a great tool for utilizing pull marketing tactics. Whether you run ads or create a poll, survey, or contest you can get targeted leads using social media advertising and messaging. The key is crafting messages that your target market will respond to.

To sell anything to anyone, you need to have a trusted relationship. This concept holds on-line as well. You must truly connect, converse and engage with people on social media before they begin trusting you. One of the best ways to engage with people is by using groups inside of social media platforms like Facebook, Google+ and LinkedIn. In this group, you can converse and have electronic conversations with people and demonstrate your expertise. On social sites like Instagram and Pinterest, you have to use hashtags. On Twitter, you use hashtags and lists to engage with others.

Whatever platform you're on, make certain to showcase what is unique about you. You must be able to clearly articulate your unique sales proposition. When people do not understand what is different about you, they reduce your product or services to price.

Another great way to build relationships with people on social media is to follow, comment and share their content. On every social media platform, there is an opportunity to provide feedback by sharing, commenting or clicking a button to like the message. When you show up on that person's social media page, they are sure to notice you, sooner or later.

Create an Action Plan And a Content Marketing Calendar

Using social media can be overwhelming. That's precisely why you need a social media action plan and a content marketing calendar. How are you going to mix social media in with your overall marketing strategy? You must understand that marketing works best when you have a few strategies complimenting each other and working together.

The number one reason why you need to put together an action plan is that your ideal customers are searching for you on-line. For example, You're a health & wellness life coach specializing in nutrition and teaching people how to lose weight without dieting and have a better relationship with food. Your prospect is on-line searching for keywords like weight loss, healthy foods, life coach, diet and wellness. As an entrepreneur in that space, you must show up in the search when the prospects go looking for a solution to their problems.

For every industry, people are looking for answers to specific problems. You must create messages for every problem that the people in your target market has. Social media gives you a unique opportunity to communicate frequently with your target market on a wide variety of topics. As you can see, using social media as a method to grow your business requires you to go back to the basics and understand marketing 101. Once you complete each of the steps above, you will have a better handle on how to incorporate social media to grow your business.

Brand creators have one goal - to make a brand that will stand out and stick in people's minds. To do this, it must have a distinctive look that sets it apart from other companies. It must be consistent wherever it appears - online, in its website and social media and offline, on billboards, flyers and other traditional media. It must carry the message of the company clearly and concisely, using words or images that are simple and easy to understand. More importantly, it must have the ability to connect emotionally with people through the message it delivers. Brands represent the company's values and principles, and when people feel the connection to these values, an affinity is formed that creates a bond between them and that certain brand.

Benefits of Brand Marketing

The next step after the brand building is its marketing. First, define your target audience. Much as you are tempted to cater to everyone, focusing on a niche market betters the probability of success. Defining your target market is best done by market research and analysis. A brand is represented by a logo or a slogan or both. There are certain rules for making a logo or slogan, based on people's general preferences and the attraction-grabbing factor. Whatever logo or slogan you finally decide on, the fundamental guideline for both is the embodiment of the message it aims to deliver, using simple and clear language and images.

It is unwise to disregard the role of a brand in the marketing strategies of a company. When you have built a successful brand, sales and profits increase and your company gain a foothold in the industry you are in. Hence, the effort of doing extensive market research and identifying your target audience will be all worth it when you harvest the rewards of brand marketing.

Here are the Advantages You Get From An Effective And Compelling Brand:

- It can influence the shopper's choice.
- It can create a loyal and regular following.
- It can command a premium price.
- It can spread to extensions in the form of new products.

New Trends for Building and Marketing a Brand

Building and marketing a brand will never go out of style. After all, it defines and identifies the business. However, factors that affect brand marketing are constantly changing to adapt to people's behaviors and the prevailing sentiment. With consumers now possessing a higher level of discernment and enlightenment, the following trends in brand marketing have been observed. It's your call as a business owner to take a second look at your current brand and reposition it to meet the challenges and seize the opportunities that the market presents.

Brand Accountability

Be prepared to respond to issues regarding your brand. The unstoppable popularity of social media has its positive and negative aspects, and any mistake your business makes becomes common published knowledge. Make sure you have plans in place to protect your brand's name.

Brand Credibility

Confirming what your brand is promising to its buyers has never been easier today with social media. A large percentage of potential customers look to Facebook or Twitter for product or service reviews and comments. Leave up to what your brand promises, and deliver.

Brand Flexibility

Technology has given rise to many changes and your brand should be resilient enough to adapt to these changes instead of resisting and looking outdated. Being flexible yet remaining true to its core values and promises keeps your brand and business current and modern.

Brand Visualization

As attention spans keep getting shorter, people turn to images for instant comprehension. This accounts for the success of Pinterest and Instagram. Re-evaluate your brand and shift your focus to visual content for a more compelling come-on.

Why and How to Build Better Brand Awareness?

When you want to eat French fries, do you go to a fast-food restaurant or a McDonald's restaurant? When you want to search for something online, do you search it online or Google it? When your friend wants to buy something online, where do you think he or she will go? An online shop or Amazon.com?

As these brands have become so well-known, we have already replaced the generic terms for the product name. Manufacturers use names, terms, designs, symbols or other features to distinguish their products from others'. The brand is no longer just a trademark for customers to differentiate one manufacturer from another. It is the personality that identifies a product, service or company like a combined character under a person's name.

It's necessary to do it among consumers for keeping your businesses grow. And it is also fundamental part of any SEO strategy. Imagine a customer typing your brand name as the keyword and search for things, the search result will greatly favor the site of the brand in the query. If it is done right, your marketing will turn some customers to your brand advocates who will actively tell others about your brand and we all know peers' words are always trustworthy to people; as a result, you will see a large increase in revenue from the marketing.

No matter you are a business owner or a marketer, one thing shouldn't be forgotten that getting more people to know and care about your brand will have more benefits in both the long-term and the short-term. If you have ever taken a teenager to shop, you can get the point why researchers always say that young people nowadays tend to be deeply affected by the power of brand awareness. They are not just taking the design or the flavors of a product, the information which can reflect the philosophy of a brand influence them a lot. If they have taken a brand as his or her favorite no matter what product the brand produces in the future he or she will try it at least out of interest and trust. Yes, one can never afford to lose such loyalty customers.

Ask yourself this question, to what extent are you willing to make the brand of your product be recognized by its potential customers and most importantly, to be the one in the first thought or correctly associated with this kind of product? As long as a product is produced or a service is prepared, how to sell it to the right customer in the right market is stuffed with every manager's mind. And every step of the business is aiming to make this happen better and perfectly. If you want to get to the level to the top of the mind awareness for your brand, you are coming to the right place.

Know Yourself As Well As Your Customers

The process of building awareness of your brand is creating value to costumers', they can feel, know and experience about your product through your marketing. The more valuable to the consumers the more loyal they would become. Define your brand, create a checklist of its core strengths and broaden them to social, environmental and economic well-being aspects to get customers who value those ideas. And you also have to try attracting attention and stand out from competitors by differentiating your brand. Unique advantages will save much time for your future customers and mostly yourself to avoid wasting life, energy, and money on buying and producing things you already have. Wrap up your brand with an independent character by personalizing the product to reasons to spend time and engage with your brand for a lifetime, luckily for both customers.

get to know your customers? It's wise to broaden the communication channels of your brand to take advantage of the Internet and social media. Writing blogs or having your brilliant ideas published into books would be a great help in building trust between you and your future customers. Platforms like Facebook, Instagram, Pinterest, and Twitter, etc are easy to increase exposure, build brand credibility, and boost traffic, search engine ranking and most of all, increase sales of your product in a very cost-efficient way. Create a piece of content you know your ideal audience/customer would want and advertise it in their newsfeed. This will lead to better visibility and leads by sharing content, and most people can't resist it!

The Power Of Story

For decades storytelling has been known as one of the best and powerful forms of communication. Think of what kind of story you could relate to your brand - something genuine, heartfelt and transparent. Think about that kind of story you expected to be told along with 3 questions to ask yourself, you will begin to think about the value of your brand story: Do you have an obvious audience in mind? Does your brand have an origin? Does your brand feel authentic? As we people all need something to believe in, you have to give your future customers something to believe that your brand stands for, fights for. Building emotional connections between your brand and your audience by sharing your common values, hopes and dreams in the story you create.

Speaking The Same Languages Of Your Customers

It won't work at all if your target customers couldn't understand your language. Then it would be a waste of your efforts on every part of your marketing. For a company wishing to expand the customers across the world, the brand should first re if it has a global image and view, some basic messages can be adapted for international markets. You also have to prepare for localization for your different local markets, and that asks for reflections on every part of the marketing, even the way of telling your brand story. For some brands with great stories, a good translation or localization would give you a better brand image already.

There is one more way to better brand awareness: never give up. Use your wisdom to create; there are thousands of opportunities waiting for you.

What Kind Of Content Should Your Brand Post In Social Media?

You are ready, you have a plan, you can see it in your mind... but how do you start making this a reality? What kind of content should your brand post speak to its followers, and offer relevant information to keep them coming back?

The first step in understanding what to post/share, etc., it is important to understand the WHY and HOW of Social Media.

Before social media, there were newspapers, TV, and radio. All three are part of an important marketing mix, all three have entertaining and useful content that keeps readers coming back. These advertising mediums have shows, articles, and programs that do not pay the bills, all they are is an attraction. Once they have the attention of your customers, they are primed and ready to market your product or service.

Social media is very similar. All your pages, whatever they are, have content, the information you provide, your point of view things happening, your take on a subject - in other words, your shows, your articles, and your programs. If you post and create relevant, unique content, then you are offering something worthwhile for your clients to return and continue returning over and over again to your Facebook, Twitter, Pinterest, LinkedIn, Instagram, Blog... which serves your brand effectively. Emotion plays an important role in the choices customers make. Social media helps your brand communicate with customers. It builds rapport, a connection, friendship, trust, and a care factor. Clients connected emotionally to a product have an easier choice. A loyal emotional client will listen to your marketing message with open ears.

Content is not about only posting different things every day. The best method of finding out what's right for your brand is by trying different things and monitoring their success or failure, tweaking based on your fan's and follower's reactions. Consider different subjects, sharing or creating, questions or polls, what time of the day to post, what day of the week to post... all have influence.

Sharing is good, but sharing everything you find and of similar-minded brands can be counterproductive. If you are a hotel brand and are constantly sharing the content of travel magazines and travel sites, your consumer, at some point is going to better off checking those sites directly, since they are richer and probably offer more information. Share but do not over-share. It is important to share and express your opinion, open a discussion about a topic you are sharing and vary the topics and pages you share. Do not become the conduit for other brands to publicize their message on your page.

At the end of the day, the ideal method of communication is to create and post unique content. By doing so you can be sure that nobody else is offering what you are. You are now probably wondering, what can say uniquely and regularly? Plain, Simple, and Fun... anything you want. Social media is made up of day-to-day things that happen which fall in the world of mundane, fantasy, and rush. So have a blast with it!

Just imagine - you are the social media guru at your Hotel in Curacao and you also live on that small island. You eat at local restaurants, go to local coffee shops, go to local art galleries, you know the beaches, island transportation, where to go and where not to go, the best and the worst night spots. For you, it's your day-to-day... boring... but to anyone looking to travel to Curaçao? To someone who has not had a vacation for a year and eats lunch while sitting at its desk, drives an hour to get to work? It's Magic.

You probably think that talking about your lunch on the beach restaurant at your hotel, in January under 86 degrees scorching sun, or posting an Instagram of a Caribbean Coconut Shrimp Soup you are having for lunch is boring! Tell that to people in Boston during a cold front and suddenly your posts are the most interesting thing they have seen, your brand ROCKS!

Followers love fan discounts, promotions, deals. Some can offer them, some cannot. How far can you go? Are you an independent business or are you a franchise? The answer to this depends on the success and what you can do or not.

If you are an independent business your horizon is open to many different promotions and discounts. If you are a franchise and do "Fan-only" promotions with added value (free rental car, a bottle of wine, park entrances, etc.) for a sweeter and more effective deal. According to studies, 40% of fans "like" pages for their discounts and deals. So give your followers discounts, deals, promotions, simply put SOMETHING SPECIAL that makes them feel good.

Content is not only information. It can also be photos, coupons, RSS feeds, charitable causes, video, feeds from other social media channels, etc. All this can be posted directly on your wall or as part of a separate tab. You might be asking yourself what are tabs and how do I create one. Leave that to the professionals or at least use existing templates from tabsite, wildfire, offer pop, or any other that can be found on the Internet.

At the end of the day create unique content in any shape or form. Use photos of events, photos of winners of contests you create, posts to engage your fans, sales messages, fun facts, etc., about or related to your brand. This is about social media it is not about a brochure. Entertain your fans. Success!

Influencer Marketing: Deep Understanding and Its Basics

We know that in the Celebrity Industry, everything is a buzz, every move a celebrity makes is a huge gossip. Well, in Business and Marketing there's also what we call "hot issue", there are lots of effective methods spreading online and "Influencer Marketing" is the one who raised and outstands among them.

Today, we are living in a world full of marketing and business. When you think of doing an advertisement? What comes to your mind? Magazine headlines? TV Commercials? I'll tell you the truth, they may not be as effective as before. Time changes, effective advertising changes too. Now, Influencers simply speak up some magic sentences on their 1-3 minute video and then Voila! Sales do come true! These influencers with their extensive and large number of followers can make you outstand from that chaotic and old-fashioned advertising methods out there, on the other hand, it will also bring ultimately massive value to your brand.

So what is Influencer Marketing? This article will answer almost all of your questions about influencer marketing.

Before we dig deep into its understanding and insights. We first define the two words:

Influence is the ability to affect the behavior, development, character, and decisions of someone or something, and even the effect itself.

Marketing is an activity of a business promoting or selling products and services.

So when the two words combine, Influencer Marketing is a type of marketing that utilizes "influencers" who can influence others to buy what are they promoting or selling. There are two forms of influencer marketing:

- **Social Media Marketing:** Refers to the series of actions of gaining traffic and attention through social media sites.
- **Content Marketing:** Refers to a type of marketing that involves creating, publishing and sharing of online material such as videos, blogs and social media posts. It doesn't promote a brand to generate interest in its products and services.

Both have different definitions, but they seemed to be connected.

Influencer marketing might be a hot issue right now, but it is not new at all, in fact, influencer marketing has been alive since the time we discovered social media sites. Celebrities, Sports Enthusiasts, and Leaders were our first influencers in their particular fields and brands would partner with them to promote their products and services.

Here Are Some Good Characteristics Influencer Marketing Is Armed Of:

Influencer Marketing is Unique

Social media communication has already allowed everyone to voice out their perceptions. Anyone who can speak, and has an internet connection is welcome to share their content. Anyone who owns a smartphone could produce high-quality photography and share it with the world with their social media accounts. And who among them has the great and most intriguing engagement will rise and might become an influencer.

Influencer Marketing is Authentic

Yes, you read it right. Have you seen an advertisement online regarding the easiest way to lose those sloppy fats on your belly? Have you ever felt a single cell in your body that believes those advertisements? Or, have you seen an advertisement on TV regarding a soap which could immediately whiten your skin after just one wash? How possible is that? No offense but this is why and what makes Influencer Marketing authentic and more effective than those traditional advertising you see through online, TV commercials, etc.

Influencer campaigns are more organic and genuine than those traditional advertisements you encounter, why? Firstly, Influencers are visible and had experienced or used the product or service that has been offered. They are seen as scrutinized role models and leaders. Investing your time, effort and money on fertilizing their audience and connecting with their following is much worthy as these influencers are more trusted and had become the most trusted sources for the consumers. Meaning, people listen and believe in them.

Influencers Help You With Your Brand Image

Social media can drive traffic to your website. It can create a much stronger bond between you and your customers, boosts your SEO and could generate media coverage. Influencers are your "Superman" when you needed a hand to boost up your brand's name and create a big buzz on various social media sites. They will help you target the right demographic, grow your social media network, share ideas regarding creating your content and boosts your SEO.

Influencer Marketing is Cost-Effective

If you are tired already from posting some flyers anywhere in your area but did not get any sales at the end of the day. Influencer Marketing is the best method for you. Although there is no fixed price when it comes to Influencer Marketing, either you offer them free item, pay them by performance-based, or others suggests a "flat rate" pricing. But I tell you, influencer marketing has the best ROI. A lot of research had already proved that it is bound to be more affordable and effective than traditional advertising.

Influencer Marketing is not about celebrity endorsements and paid gamblings. It is about the authenticity of the influencers, uniqueness, and the genuine relationship between the influencer, the brand and the audience/customers. That is exactly the reason why influencer marketing is different from other marketing strategies.

Social Media Influencers: A Skin-Deep Industry?

An advertisement by local micro-influencers agency, Faves Asia infuriated many for a few reasons but none of the offenses were as great as misrepresenting the influencer industry as an easy road to fame and wealth. The video was taken off within days after overwhelming lash backs.

While one spends hours incessantly scrolling through social media gawking at the picture-perfect lush lifestyles of influencers, it can be hard to refrain from thinking that a pretty face and a little bit of luck are all that it takes to be one of them. However, the reality is often much more different from our wishful imaginations. So, what are the three fundamental qualities of a successful social media influencer?

Identity

> If you want to be known for everything, you'll be known for nothing. - Dan Schawbel

To move beyond merely being a forgettable pretty face on Instagram, one needs to establish a distinctive online persona. This requires the influencer to have a clear sense of direction in content creation and to establish a reputation as the reference point for a single or a collection of interests. As such, a true influencer also creates waves and not merely ride on fads with generic content. This requires an intricate balance between being avant-garde and attuning to current market preferences.

Likability

> A good influencer maintains their likability by putting time and effort into building trust and rapport among followers, clients, and other influencers in the industry. - Copyrise

On top of looking good and being creative, it's important to have an amicable personality. When it comes to monetizing the influence, influencers need to establish a healthy working relationship with brands and businesses. With the mushrooming of micro-influencers, it's a buyer's market. Given the same extent of influence, businesses and agencies will always go with those easier to work with over divas. It's commonsensical to have common courtesy, especially when an influencer's key criteria is to be likable.

Integrity

> At the end of the day, I'm selling my taste and my eye - if I do things off-brand I will lose respect. - Camille Charrière, Instagram fashion influencer, 529k followers

However, being likable does not mean being a yes-man or yes-woman all the time. For social media influencers who means business, while paying the bills is crucial, integrity should be the constant guiding principle. Influencers must genuinely like a brand and its products to be able to 'sell' it and for the followers to 'buy' the post and to buy the product. A mismatch of brands and influencers at best does not lead to significant sales and at worst, debase the reputation and following of the influencer. Camille has even turned down a contract worth £100,000 from fashion giant, Macy's because the clothes were not of her style and not what her followers would appreciate.

Wielding significant persuasiveness in their domains, influencers may choose to monetize the influence, use it to further causes close to their hearts or simply remain as a gratis entertainer. To be able to choose among these options, an individual must meet the necessary pre-requisites. While appearance does help to pave the way, true influencers are certainly more than genetics and cosmetics.

Why Your Business Needs Social Media for Influencer Marketing

Influencer marketing can be considered as an effective strategy to attract and engage with the potential and existing customers. Read on the article to find more information about social media and influencer marketing.

You can no longer question the significance of social marketing. Everyone is using the social marketing agency or channels for personal and professional purposes. Recently, business organizations are taking advantage of social networking sites to increase their influence and stand out in the competitive market. More than just having an online presence, businesses need to extend their digital storefront to social marketing networking sites to take advantage of this powerful technology fad. The majority of marketers place high hope and value on social marketing optimization and marketing. Not only social marketing features levels the playing field but it also brings more attention to your business.

The rise of social networks has reignited interest in influencer marketing. In the digital age, celebrities are not only the influencer's services, but also a popular blogger or an industry expert can have the strongest influence on the buying decisions of consumers. Any individual with established credibility and a large audience can be an influencer. Their trustworthiness, expertise, and authenticity can persuade consumers to engage with your brand. And that is why it is recommended to establish a potential relationship with them and orient your marketing activities around them.

Tapping into the emerging marketing tool is not easy though. Choosing the right social marketing channel is a crucial yet challenging task. The problem is that you can find an overwhelming number of social media sites. Even though they might share similar features, each site demands a unique strategy. Most of us will think about popular social media such as Facebook, Reddit and Twitter marketing services. But there are other networks that you should take advantage of such as YouTube. Flickr, Instagram, Tumblr and Pinterest for business marketing. According to the latest facts and figures, Pinterest, Google+, Facebook, Instagram, YouTube, and Tumblr are the fastest growing social marketing sites. Pinterest, being a leading referral source for organic traffic, is an impeccable choice to achieve higher search rankings and returns. Carrying out detailed research and analyzing the objectives can help you pick the relevant channels that best suit your brand. No matter whichever industry you are in, make it a point to use social media to your advantage.

How Socia Media Influences How We Do Business Today

When you are working your business and it could be any business:

- Connect with ALL the people you know.
- Connect with the friends of your friends.
- Connect with the people you want to know.

It doesn't matter what business you are in because the same techniques work whether it is your own business and you need a sales force to help you build your sales, whether it is affiliate a relationship marketing where you will look for people who have similar interests and would be interested in the product you are selling.

When you are looking for people to help you grow your business you should also consider:

- People that share your values and interests
- Ambitious people who are looking for more
- People who traditionally use what you sell
- People in transition: divorce, relocating, life change, job change
- People in depressed industries: real estate, banking, construction, interior design, insurance, and retail sales
- People suffering job burnout: teachers, nurses, and anyone on the job too long
- Unhappy disappointed network and affiliate marketers, which consists of over 20 million people

Why is this important in today's workplace; because the job market has changed and more and more people all working from home. In general, the general public needs to change their concept of what a job is. For many years, people have gotten comfortable working for someone else in an office. Those days and jobs are gone forever. Companies are looking for ways to lower their costs, therefore, instead of going through the middleman and selling their products through retail, they are going right to the consumer and using both affiliate and relationship marketing or multilevel marketing to sell their products through word-of-mouth marketing.

Word-of-mouth marketing works this way: a company will sell its products through affiliates or distributors. In some cases, you can join for free and then upgrade later where you pay a nominal fee and as an affiliate or a distributor you can earn a percentage of the sales depending on what the company is offering. For the manufacturer or software designer, this means they can keep the overhead low by working from home themselves and using websites and replicating websites to market their products through their sales force. This is where word-of-mouth marketing comes into play. For instance, social media such as Facebook, LinkedIn, YouTube, and Instagram are growing in popularity.

As an affiliate or a distributor with a company working from home, you need to consider branding yourself as opposed to branding the company. The life span of working with a multilevel marketing company may not be more than two or three years. By branding yourself as opposed to the company, then someone will learn to know and trust you, therefore whenever you change companies are products you sell, they will follow you into any business. The best way to do this is by offering training. With the use of say Google hangouts where you can invite people to eight presentations where you are educating them on a specific topic and then offering them your opportunity which just happens to be incorporated into your topic then you are gaining their trust and their belief in you.

You can also use the opportunity of being an affiliate or distributor as an opportunity to generate income for yourself while you build your own business. We have come full circle from where we were at the beginning of the 20th century back to the small businessman, but technology has helped us to become a global marketplace where we can build contacts and a following anywhere in today's marketplace. Bite working for ourselves we have the opportunity to make an unlimited income, as opposed to, working for someone else when they limit your potential income.

Influence Marketing in Social Media: Is It All About Social Rank?

One of the greatest criticisms (or even challenge) of social media Is its return on investment or lack thereof. The problem lies not so much in its inability to have a high return, but its nonexistence. There is no framework for return on investment because its nearly impossible to track it. I could have 100 Facebook fans and even have 1000 friends on Twitter, but is that considered return? And how exactly am I benefiting from this? Yes, I may be better branding my company and exposing my brand more, but I have yet to sell the money roll in. These are the questions which business executives are asking when considering using social media as a way to influence consumer behavior.

In social media, it is all about ranking: how many contacts one has on LinkedIn, how many Twitter followers, or even how many mentions a company gets. And while this may win a popularity contest, does it actual constitute as a return? And where is the real influence? And the plot (more like the challenge) thickens.

So then is ranking just a number? It might be. Take for example blogger Suzy Q: Imagine she has an enormous following on Twitter and is a social butterfly in the social media world. Granted she has many friends, but does this mean she is an actual social influencer? The answer is unclear. And if she, it would be difficult to determine how influential she is. And the reason is that anyone can rise to the top as far as popularity but not anyone has the ability to influentially market to their "followers".

So while social rank is a number, it isn't the type of numbers that investors are aiming for; they are looking for the numbers that follow a dollar sign, and until they see those numbers, the challenge of return on investment will continue.

Top Benefits of Influencer Marketing

Over the last decade, social networks have brought remarkable transformations in our day to day life. The rise of social media across the globe have revolutionized the way we communicate and share information. Not just personal lives, but social networking applications have made their way into the business world. Marketing through social media channels is the new trend and every business organization is jumping onto this bandwagon. Influencer marketing revolves around the surging popularity of such social media channels. Before we delve into the details of this innovative marketing strategy, let us find out what an influencer is.

A person who is an industry expert and is respected for his opinion is known as an influencer. More than that, they are active online and have several followers. It can be a celebrity, journalist, bloggers or analyst with in-depth expertise and credibility on the subject matter. When these respected individuals post anything about niche subject matters, then it will be followed by a huge number of people. It can even influence the purchase decisions of many customers. And that is why business organizations need to incorporate influencer marketing techniques into their marketing mix. Platforms like Facebook, Twitter, Instagram, and YouTube have led to the increasing popularity of new generation influencers. A large number of people have amassed huge followers by uploading informative videos, online tutorials, easy hacks and more. When you hire the professional services of a reliable influencer marketing agency, they will help you out in connecting with your targeted audience easily.

What are the major benefits of launching an influencer marketing campaign for your business? The primary advantage is its effectiveness.

Word of mouth recommendations is the best marketing tool for any business at any point in time. Influencer marketing is a type of digital word of mouth recommendation. So it can leave a great impact on the targeted audience. A blogger outreach tool and other techniques used by the influencers can grab the attention of your intended customer base easily. An increase in the search engine rankings is another important benefit. Building your brand through innovative brand management techniques and social media optimization strategies can increase the online visibility of your website. Last but not least, the influencer marketing method is trackable and targetable. Digital marketing techniques let you keep track of the activities and retrieve valuable insights about your advertising performance. These are only some of the major advantages of the influencer marketing method. But make it a point to find the right influencer to avail successful results.

5 Important Strategies Big Brands Implement With Influencers

Traditional forms of advertising just aren't cutting it anymore. Commercials and online advertisements are easily overlooked, skipped, and muted, leaving budgets with little to show in regards to customer acquisition and brand awareness.

This is 2018 and people are searching for information from those they trust or see as experts. That's what makes influencer marketing so valuable. It opens the door for authentic stories and experiences to formulate around brands in a way that can't be accomplished through other types of advertising.

If you've been hesitant to take the plunge into influencer marketing, then hopefully these five strategies that big brands implement will change your mind.

Celebrities or No Celebrities? That is the Question.

It makes sense to think that if a brand hired a celebrity with millions of followers, their campaign would be more successful because it would reach a larger audience.

But this couldn't be further from the truth.

Recent research has shown that engagement starts to decrease as follower counts grow. After evaluating over 800,000 Instagram users, Markerly discovered that those with 1,000 or fewer followers had an 8% engagement rate, while users with over 10 million followers only had a 1.6% engagement rate. The research goes on to show that hiring influencers with 10,000 to 100,000 followers gets you the best results. One of the biggest reasons for this is because micro-influencers tend to build a following based on what they share on their blog or social channels. If someone consistently posts about being a mom, odds are that other moms are going to follow along and relate to that influencer's content. With each new post, more and more credibility is built, and eventually, this influencer may become their audience's go-to expert on the topic.

By the time that influencer publishes a sponsored post about a product they're raving about, they've already built the trust of their audience, and those followers will want to try the product as well. This is a win-win situation because as more followers begin to talk about the product or buy it, the brand should experience a lift in their follower counts, as well as their sales.

Aside from having better engagement rates and a more targeted audience, micro-influencers also cost significantly less than celebrities. Hopper HQ recently shared that a single Instagram post from Selena Gomez costs $550,000. In contrast, it costs $214 on average to hire a micro-influencer in the United States to post on Instagram. That means a brand could hire approximately 2,570 micro-influencers in exchange for one Selena Gomez post.

Bigelow Tea, in collaboration with Walmart, realized their money was better spent with micro-influencers, so they worked with Collective Bias on their Tea Moments campaign, and the results were stunning. By hiring influencers in the healthy living and wellness verticals, the product fit authentically into their blogs and social channels. The content was so well received by the influencers' audiences that Bigelow Tea experienced an 18.5% sales lift and over 44 million impressions from the campaign.

Creative Freedom - What It Means and Why It's Important

A common mistake brands make when first working with influencers is trying to have too much control over the process. If you chat with an influencer, odds are they'll tell you creative freedom is one of the most important things they look for before agreeing to participate in a campaign. They understand what their unique voice is, and if they aren't offered the ability to keep that voice, odds are they'll decline to work on the campaign. Or worse, if they participate in the campaign and their followers don't respond well to it because it appears inauthentic, the brand may develop a negative conversation amongst their target audience.

While it may be difficult for brands to give up control of the creative process, influencers need to be trusted to do their best work. This is why hiring influencers who are on-brand with your values and style is so important.

DSW's 12 Days of Converse campaign found five influencers that fit their ideal demo and hired them to design two to three pairs of Chuck Taylors, then announce to their followers that they could win a pair of their own. Those simple details paved the way for influencers to unleash their creativity, and the response from their followers was insane. For less than $15,000, the campaign generated over 3 million impressions and over 100,000 engagements.

DSW continues to be an active participant in influencer marketing campaigns, and its revenue has steadily increased year after year. For the fiscal year 2016, DSW company revenues were at $2.7 billion, and they are now at $2.8 billion for 2017, which is a record high for the company.

Exist Where Your Audience Exists

Ten years ago, blogs and websites were some of the only online ways to tell audiences about your product. Today, there are several social platforms available to advertise on, like Facebook, Instagram, Pinterest, and YouTube. So how do you know which platform is best to have influencers post on?

With social media constantly changing social, it's difficult to pinpoint exactly where you should have content going live so that your ideal target audience sees it, so an alternate strategy is to have influencers post on multiple platforms.

Bertolli hired nine influencers to publish blog posts, social amplification, and videos about their olive oil products so that no audience was left out. By doing so, their campaign generated an estimated 6.8 million total views and $14.37 in earned media revenue for each $1 they spent on the campaign.

The blog posts were great for sharing recipes that called for using the product, and those recipes were, in turn, easy to pin on Pinterest. Instagram was a useful platform for showcasing one of the final recipe images, and to direct readers to get the full recipe on their blog.

Airheads had a similar strategy. In their campaign, the anchor videos lived on YouTube and were amplified on other social platforms to generate more traffic. This strategy resulted in over 1.3 million video views from just three influencers, and over 44,000 social engagements across all channels.

Think Numbers Are Everything? Not So Fast!

It's easy to get caught up in the numbers you see from a viewer's perspective. For example, if your campaign goal is to get over 20 million impressions and 10,000 engagements, it may be very tempting to look for influencers who have a high following and lots of comments or likes on their posts.

The unfortunate reality is that numbers don't tell the entire story. Many influencers participate in Instagram pods and Facebook threads where they share their content with their influencer peers, and everyone then likes and comments to help make it seem like that influencer has an engaged following.

On the outside, the numbers look solid, but on a deeper level, the goal of reaching the target audience isn't achieved.

One way brands can avoid this pitfall is by hiring influencers who consistently create quality content and fit the brand's image. According to Jonathan Long, Market Domination Media's founder, small accounts often outperform the larger ones, sometimes up to 300%. That's right - 300%.

When brands stop looking at numbers, they are forced to look at each influencer as an individual instead. What does that person bring to the table? Do they regularly interact with their followers? Are their photos telling a story?

These are all questions brands should ask before launching an influencer marketing campaign.

Subaru understood the importance of quality over quantity and hired influencers to post a total of 58 sponsored posts for their Meet and Owner campaign. Since almost everyone owns a car, Subaru found relevant influencers in a variety of verticals, like fitness and art, to share their stories.

1.9 million likes and 9,000 comments later, Subaru not only received increased brand sentiment and awareness, but they also positioned themselves to have another standout year in the auto industry. Influencer marketing is to partly thank for their 10% sales growth in 2016.

Surface Data Doesn't Tell the Entire Story

Once a campaign has wrapped, it can be easy to walk away from it and start on the next big project. But to continuously execute a solid influencer marketing strategy, it's important to revisit the data and take a deeper dive into the analytics of each campaign.

For example, knowing how many referrals are being sent your way, how many new leads you've gotten, what sales growth you've seen, and customer acquisition costs are all measurements that should be assessed on a deeper level.

Charmin partnered with Mavrck to help track clicks to coupons, product reviews, and sign-ups for an entire quarter so that they could look for trends in data, like the ones mentioned above. Over that quarter, Charmin was able to see that they received over, 5,300 coupon clicks, 1,800 product reviews, and an average product rating of 4.82 out of 5. If you aren't sure how or where to look to analyze your results, Social Media Examiner has some great tips for how brands can analyze on their own with a little help from Google Analytics.

One final takeaway to consider is that every influencer marketing campaign is different. What worked for one brand might not work for another, and that's why following these five strategies are so important. They help outline the basis for a successful campaign but avoid getting too far into the weeds.

Anyone who is looking to improve their marketing approach should consider implementing these five strategies the next time they work with influencers. As mentioned previously, influencer marketing continues to grow and be a powerhouse for brands big and small. By putting these five strategies into practice, you can set yourself up for a successful campaign that reaches your ideal audience and builds your brand sentiment.

Instagram: A Great Small Business Marketing Tool

Small businesses can always use any edge they can get, especially when it comes to marketing. It is not always easy fighting the competition, and for that reason, creativity can sometimes be the best solution. If your small business has been doing well on social media up to this point, you may want to consider one of the relatively new kids on the block, Instagram.

In essence, Instagram has become a widely popular social media platform that focuses on visual content. Given the nature of this, it can be a fantastic way to spread the message about your company or brand and captivate a new audience. It is essential to make sure this platform is right for your business so you don't end up talking to a metaphorical internet wall.

Got Something To Show?

So how do you know if it is right for your business? A good first test would be to ask yourself, do I have something that I would like to show my market?

This is a great way to begin since it forces you as a marketer to immediately try to come up with an idea for some content. Using a service such as Instagram will be a lot more seamless if the content or images presents itself for you and there is no need to hunt for it.

Your audience will be much more obliged to follow your business as long as it's not struggling to find and create content.

Simply put, if captivating images of what your brand takes part in or represents are easy to come across, then Instagram is likely for you. Because if you're having trouble now finding the right picture, then you'll likely still be having trouble 4 months down the road.

Does your target market, or even broader potential markets, fall into the demographics that use Instagram? This is another one of those questions that avoid the pain of talking to a wall online.

It is essential that your customers, past, present, and future, are people who are using the service. If they are not, you will do yourself a great favor by allocating your time and resources to where they are present elsewhere online.

Instagram's users are all those who have been raised in the age of technology. Social media sites such as Facebook and Twitter are already second nature to them, hence the extensive use of hashtags with this platform. Users range in ages from young teenagers through adults in there 30's and even 40's, given that they are technologically savvy at that age.

Given these demographics, Instagram is used by a large number of individuals. Not just in the United States, but on an international scale since it has an Android app too. The total downloads are well over 40 million as of the new year.

Leverage Its Visual Nature

Businesses can leverage using Instagram in a variety of ways. Regardless of which you choose, it's important to note that it should be a complementary extension of an established social media or digital marketing strategy as a whole.

For a company or brand with a lot of visual content to show its audience, it can be hard sometimes to other common platforms without overloading them. Use Instagram as the best source to show a constant stream of visual content and suggest your followers from other social media sites follow you here.

Provide them with exactly what the platform was made to do, showing visually interesting pictures. This direct visual marketing is direct in the sense that it is solely visual, but indirect because you do not want your Instagram to be a full-on advertisement for your brand.

Make It Personal

Think beyond straight promotion and more about the experience of your company's products or services create for the user. Take pictures of things you make, places you go, people, you meet, new products, happy customers, the benefits and uses of your product or service, community outreach, the list goes on.

Keep your hashtags related to your company as well as those that are popular or trending at the time for maximum exposure. If your followers enjoy seeing what you have to offer they will undoubtedly share it.

An alternative way to use Instagram is through the use of promotions. This works especially well for consumer goods brands or if you are offering a valued service to your followers. It allows for much more engagement with your audience and helps unite them as a community.

Require your followers to take pictures related to your business or promotion and use a common hashtag to be entered ingot he contests. This way they must engage to win and have an incentive to take a great picture emphasizing your company in it or through the hashtag. It is also a great way to build your audience on Instagram.

By promoting the contest on Facebook and Twitter as well, more people become aware that you are present in this space and will seek you out. If you also take part in more traditional forms of advertising, don't hesitate to emphasize your presence on Instagram there as well.

See Results And Connect

Once you have things in motion, it's important to monitor your progress. This will let you know if it's worth your small time commitment. Likewise, if it is leading to more potential customers or followers on other social platforms, then it is having a great secondary influence. This is still a great benefit of using the service and should not be overlooked.

Continue to connect with customers on there and keep them informed of everything going on with your business down the road, they will key to your ongoing growth online.

How Powerful Is Instagram Influencer Marketing?

The increasing growth of social media has triggered the rise of influencer marketing, all platforms in social media are already engaging in influencer marketing and so far, it is the most effective way to market your products and services through social media, online.

Instagram, one of the most billed places to showcase your product. It is looking for more methods and strategies to monetize the platform and the increasing users and consumers it has. Instagram is the place where you can share your moments with your friends and followers and that is why Influencer Marketing has germinated itself to grow inside Instagram.

Engagement

As we all know, Instagram's engagement rate is higher than any of the other social media platforms at 2.3%, the fact that it's organic, we can't deny the fact that Instagram has many more engagements than Facebook or Twitter. In this case, it is clear that Instagram has proven itself that it is the best place to build your influencer campaign (aside from YouTube)

Growth

Instagram is one of the fastest-growing social media platforms. This year, it is predicted that Instagram will grow by 15.1% than 3.1% of the other social network as a whole. Then, over the next four years, Instagram will add 26.9 million users far more than any other social platform. Impressive! Why? Instagram usage is exceptionally intense among millennials.

Suitability

Influencer marketing is about displaying a certain lifestyle and promoting a product or service through lifestyle. With this, those followers of yours might turn to potential customers who can participate and spread the word by using the product or service.

Personality

Influencer marketing helps influencers be able to be genuine and showcase their colorful personalities. Influencer marketing is not just about paying for product promotion, by engaging with this marketing method, you are given the chance to impress engage the audience with your product and service. It's not just paying someone with a lot of followers to broadcast your brand's message, it's about hiring and collaborating with them to experience your product and tell their followers what do they think about the product.

Right Influencer

Of course, your Instagram influencer marketing would not work unless you got the right influencer working with you. Keep this in mind: finding the right influencer is the beginning and there are more numbers of moving parts that need to be assigned in their right place.

The first thing to identify which influencer should you choose is to identify the pertinent individual for your brand who have the knowledge and influence to affect the decision of their audience when it comes to purchasing.

Instagram Influencer Marketing can have a powerful effect, but, it does need to be done right. So decide what you want to benefit from it, as long as you and your influencer are doing teamwork, and with engaging influencers, don't be afraid to accept criticism and suggestion both from your team and the audience.

Instagram Marketing Tips for Your Business

Millions of people globally are now using Instagram. Instagram has made it easier to take pictures and share them with friends and many people enjoy doing this. Apart from networking, you can use

Instagram in a more efficient way of marketing. Instagram is a great promotional tool you can use to promote your business online.

Tell the story using photos and videos

Photos are worth a thousand words and Instagram is all about pictures. If you are into Instagram for marketing purposes, then you ought to understand that random photos do not work. You need to post pictures of your product constantly. Posting pictures of your products is one of the best ways of increasing your brand awareness and boost sales of your products. The pictures do not necessarily need to be very professional. The key thing is having the pictures highlight the main features and functions of the goods you are promoting. The pictures should appeal to a vast audience on Instagram.

Videos too are important in Instagram marketing. You can create and share a video with your employees to promote the product at hand. You can also opt to do a live product review video and share it on Instagram. Pictures and videos are more appealing to many people than text files. Media files stand higher chances of going viral as people share them. They are also more memorable than text files. Create photos and videos that show your brand story and values. So images and videos are important if you want to improve your brand and sales.

Use Quality Media

To improve your visibility, you need to make and share high-quality photos and videos in your feeds. Where necessary, seek professional assistance or advice from a photographer. However, you can use a great camera to take sharp pictures. Try to get your images at best angles. Edit your photos for better results. Nowadays mobile phones are equipped with photo editing tools for this purpose. Instagram too has several photo editing tools. Apply these tools for your Instagram marketing purpose.

Connect With Our Followers

Maintaining contact with your customers is vital, particularly for developing business with a small market share. You can start by showing your clients that you are concerned about their feedback. You can achieve this by replying to their questions and comments. This will improve user-generated content and credibility as well as promote the visibility of your products and business. Your Instagram followers can significantly influence the success of your enterprise, and you should never underestimate them.

Use Hashtags

Hashtags are relevant to Instagram marketing. You need to use them because Instagram users interact using hashtags. Hashtags allow users to make their content searchable and are important if you want to increase your followers. Has tags like media can create a viral effect which is beneficial to your business. You can also take advantage of trending hashtags especially if the hashtags are related to your product. This is important because Instagram users can use hashtags to search for posts.

Use Branded Hashtag

You should include your business name in your hashtags. Use unique hashtags for a particular promotional campaign you run. Not only does this promote your campaign, but it also provides a unique hashtag for your clients to connect and share with other participants.

Have a Friendly Attitude To Everyone

While carrying out your Instagram marketing, you need to understand that Instagram is a community composed of people with varied ideas, emotions, and background. Always be friendly to everyone and appreciate their time to connect with you on your page. Always ensure you listen to your clients.

Be Active

Post at least once daily to keep things up to date and ensure your followers updated with the current happenings. You can experiment posting at varying times of the day to see which time your posts do best.

Consistency

Consistency is crucial in Instagram marketing. Be consistent in your postings and develop a theme that is prominent in your posts. Let your followers know what to expect from you.

Link your Instagram and Facebook accounts

Connect your Instagram and Facebook accounts to improve your marketing power. Nowadays, you can have an Instagram tab on your Facebook page. This allows you to share your Instagram posts to your Facebook followers if you have a fan page.

You can network with friends and the world via Instagram. Instagram can be used for marketing purposes. Instagram marketing can improve your brand's visibility, increase sales, and consequently revenues. Consider the above mentioned Instagram marketing tips to achieve success.

- There are more than 300 million Instagram users worldwide.
- Approximately 70 million photos are uploaded per day.
- The account is 'free' to set up so there are low barriers to entry.
- It is a medium that allows for easy sharing of content 24 hours a day.
- What sort of success have businesses achieved using Instagram?
- Businesses such as Levis, L'oreal and hundreds of others have been able to use the tool to:
- To increase awareness of their products and services.
- To increase brand recognition.
- To showcase their community and pro bono work to inspire and attract prospective customers to engage with their product, service or brand.
- Run successful promotions, competitions, and giveaways.

4 Brand-Building Tips on Using Instagram for Your Business

One of the most powerful marketing tools marketers have today is social media. From Facebook posts to tweets on Twitter, sharing your products or services on social media platforms is a great way to increase brand awareness, engagement, sales, and leads.

However, many people are left scratching their heads when it comes to marketing with Instagram.

Many of us use Instagram as a personal account to post photos of our family, friends, vacations, and food - but how can it tie into business? And should it? With the speed of which Instagram is growing, don't underestimate its value to boost your brand and marketing efforts. It has grown into an incredibly valuable marketing platform and even though the 18-29-year-old's are still prevalent users, the higher age groups are catching on and catching up fast.

Some 2018 Instagram stats from Sprout Social are telling:

- 7 out of 10 hashtags on Instagram are branded
- 80% of users follow a business on Instagram
- 65% of top-performing Instagram posts feature products

If you feel the tug to explore Instagram as part of your social media marketing strategy, check out these initial pointers to help you get started:

Use Hashtags Wisely

You don't need to cram every hashtag you can think of in one post, but you do need at least a few. A hashtag is the # sign followed by descriptive words about your image as in this example, I used #marketing and #ctaconf, which was the conference I was attending at the time. When a user clicks/taps on a hashtag or types a hashtag into the search box, it brings up all images that use that hashtag. The user can even subscribe to continue to follow that hashtag.

The hope is the user will see your photo, head to your profile and best-case scenario, follow you and get engaged with more of your posts! However, when hashtags are extremely popular, the competition to show up in the results is fierce. Similar to SEO keywords, the more popular a term is, the harder it is to stay at the top of the search results. Thus, my example of using #marketing was futile if I wanted to get any traction from that post. You want to make your hashtags relevant to your business and location, but also engaging enough that a user would type them into Instagram's search box.

For Instance:

- Say you have a pizza joint in Vancouver. You post a pic of your Pepperoni pizza with the hashtags #VancouversBestPizza #NicolosRestaurant #DeliciousDeepDish
- Or you're a Toronto wedding planner. You post an image of a bride and groom's first dance with the hashtags #TorontoWeddingPlanner #LoveWins #WinterWedding

Holidays and special events are an excellent time to promote your business and gain Instagram followers. Whether it's a sale on Black Friday, a Thanksgiving-related use for your product or a product shout-out on National Dog Day, they are all ideal opportunities to showcase your business brand in a non-salesy way.

Thank Your Audience for Showing Up

You don't just post a bunch of photos and hashtags and wait for the likes to roll in. To gain Instagram followers, engage with your audience and grow sales or leads, you need to put in the time.

See an example here from video expert Michele Moreno where she responds to each of the comments left on her video post. So if someone leaves a comment or question on one of your posts, take the time to reply and thank them/answer their question. Take a look at their profile, and if you like what you see, follow them.

Businesses often follow commenters first, in the hopes that they might return the favor. You can also look for people who might be interested in your product, then comment on their photos and/or follow them, but don't spam them with an ask to follow you right away.

Influencers are Instagram users who can influence your target audience because of their popularity and/or social media following.

Danielle Bernstein is a good example of an influencer who worked with a brand. You may not recognize her name, but the 1.8 million followers of her Instagram account WeWoreWhat do. Bernstein and FIJI Water worked together to create BodyWoreWhat, a marketing campaign offering 8-minute workout videos with her and her trainer.

That may be an extreme example, and unless you have deep pockets you probably won't be able to attract an influencer with almost two million followers. But don't despair. From mommy bloggers to local foodies, you can always find someone who your target audience follows, likes or admires. Maybe they'd be willing to review your product or take a photo using it - use your imagination!

Don't Just Shill Your Products

Instagram is not the place to simply share product shots all the time. Think of the experience people have using what you're offering or the benefits it gives people. Even better, show real-examples. Asking for user-generated content from your audience is one way to do this. That means that users share their photos using a hashtag you provide.

The online furniture store Wayfair.com does user-generated content very well. They have a user-generated campaign that lets customers share photos of their stylish Wayfair-filled homes using the hashtag #WayfairAtHome. Be sure to let people know that their images might be featured on your page and you can increase your Instagram content big time - for free!

No matter how you use Instagram for your business, be authentic and true to your brand. It's what the platform is all about, and it's going to help you grow your business, gain Instagram followers and attract sales or leads.

Branding Made Easier By Social Media

Social media has achieved a strong position and has powered the world in many ways that we could've never imagined before. Branding that's effective yet subliminal when it's made available to its targeted market can do wonders in marketing your brand. This advantage is not just limited to companies; it also applies to an individual item, a group or a single person.

A great way when you're showcasing your products, services, and talent to the world or meeting new people telling them about your specialties. The social networks like Facebook, Twitter, Instagram, LinkedIn, Pinterest and Google all help you to develop a particular space showing your digital presence and some even provide an interpretation of yourself.

When businesses use social media to promote their brand they get a much stronger response compared to just having a website. Small businesses must have a social media presence to grow at a faster pace. As the first notable difference, they'd get to see is the large market share.

It's not just the hype as the staggering figures indicate that social media websites contain the largest number of connections and command top attention from their user-base. Building real-life connections from networking with others has a lot of potentials.

Brand Exposure through Social Networks

From a branding perspective, you can say what you need to say about your brand and embrace your quirks! As consistent reputable information about brand credibility on current and future profiles, brand marketing is a long road and takes time and effort and when you've got a following from over 5 various social networks it becomes important for you to manage and maintain your online position.

Personal Branding: A Complete Manual

One thing for sure, we all have a personal brand. You have a personal brand and you have been sharing this brand with everyone that you have ever come in contact with. The way you choose to portray yourself is your brand. Now, the question is do you agree with this brand? Is it a true representation of who you are?

Your brand is what people say about you when you're not in the room" - Jeff Bezos, Founder of Amazon

A brand is absolutely anything, the mere fact that you know that one thing is not the other is branding. Therefore a brand is a name, an idea, design, symbols, attributes, reputation, and quality that differentiate one feature from another. That is why Apple's identity is different from Samsung's, even though they sell, essentially, the same idea. Same ideas, but different methods of presenting them. That's what makes each one unique.

What About Personal Branding?

"All of us need to understand the importance of branding. We are CEOs of our own companies: Me Inc. To be in business today, our most important job is to be head marketer for the brand called You." - Tom Peters

It is the same concept, the only difference is that it is now on a personal scale. Your name is your brand name. You look different from everyone else, therefore your appearance is your brand design. You have different parents, fingerprints, values, personality, voice, qualities, perception and elements than everyone else. Therefore, you are unique.

This is what personal branding is about, being your original authentic self and presenting yourself as such. You do not see Apple and Samsung similarly showcasing their brands, even though they are essentially selling the same idea.

You too might have the same qualifications, experience and you might even have gone to the same learning institution as the candidate you are competing for the job with. Who then gets the job? It is all up to your brand.

"Personal branding is about managing your name - even if you don't own a business - in a world of misinformation, disinformation, and semi-permanent Google records. Going on a date? Chances are that your "blind" date has Googled your name. Going to a job interview? Ditto." - Tim Ferriss

Why is a great personal brand important for your career?

Top Tips:

- CVs or resumes are no longer enough. I predict that in the years to come, resumes, as we know them today will cease to exist.
- Be consistent in the manner you sell your brand.
- Showcase your talent and become a leader in your area of expertise.
- Sell your unique promise.
- Communicate your true values, principles, ethics, and integrity effectively and consistently.

Focusing on these strategies will help you get, not just any job, but a job that is best suited for you. How is that? Because how you communicate your brand is specific and unique to you. And you might have the exact qualifications with your job competitor, however, your attributes would be different. This way, you are not a duplicate of another, as that can be viewed as boring and predictable. Furthermore, this strategy allows you to attract the right employer that appreciates and values your brand promise.

So what would make your brand stand-out? What makes you different from anyone else? And why is it crucial to build your brand? This guide will help you build an authentic and marketable personal brand. Listed below are the tips to help you be unique in the face of competition.

This is an important factor in personal branding. It is not an idea only centered on your perceptions, but also of those who know you well.

Those with a solid personal brand, know who they are and what they want in life. They are crystal clear on that. This is where you get to understand and describe your unique selling points. To help you with this important task, I have compiled several questions for you to help keep your focus on identifying your true strengths:

- What was/were the highlight/s of my career, and why am I so proud of these moments?
- What was the most fulfilling task or project I have ever worked on, and why was it fulfilling?
- What role do I always play in group tasks, and how do others in the group view me?
- How do I overcome the most challenging obstacles? What tools do I use?
- What do I enjoy doing the most (business or leisure)
- If I were to talk to someone about the subject that I enjoy the most, what would it be?
- If I were to accomplish something of great significance to me, and there would be no obstacles of any kind to stand in your way, what would it be?
- Now, try to think of 10 one-word descriptions of your strengths e.g. creative, compassionate and so on
- Choose people who know you, your friends, family, and colleagues and ask them to each give you their insight into what your strengths are. After doing that compare your lists with theirs. Share your list with them and see if they perceive you the same way as you view yourself.

"Emphasize your strengths on your CV, in your cover letters, and your interviews. It may sound obvious, but you'd be surprised how many people simply list everything they've ever done. Convey your passion and link your strengths to measure results. Employers and interviewers love concrete data" - Marcus Buckingham

Now that you know what your strengths are, use them. Utilize them as part of your strategic plan in your daily activities as well as with prospective employers. Let the right target audience know these gifts. Communicate them effectively using every relevant resource available to you. You can use your CV to highlight your strengths, online profiles and you must unquestionably have a personal website as your digital CV. Just remember your values and ethics when communicating with your audience. This will set you apart.

We all have weaknesses, but it is not always easy to acknowledge them. It is in your best interest to be completely honest with your self about what your limitations are or you will put yourself on the spot for major disappointments. Remember that weakness is anything from being utterly uninterested about anything in life to have limited skills to do anything of interest.

 "My attitude is that if you push me towards something that you think is a weakness, then I will turn that perceived weakness into a strength" - Michael Jordan

Let's help you identify these weaknesses:

- Which aspects of my career/ education that I like the least, and why?
- Am I someone who believes completely that I deserve more and better?
- Do I become debilitated by the thought of having to perform certain tasks? What sort of tasks?
- What were the low points in my career, and why?
- In a group situation, which role/s do I like the least?
- What was the least fruitful task/project I have ever worked on, and why did it fail?
- In the face of obstacles, what makes me give up?
- What is the most uninspiring subject to talk about for me?
- What do I think are my 10 weaknesses? Be honest with yourself.
- As on question 9 in strengths, only substitute weakness for strength.

Do not waste your time with weaknesses that do not hinder your professional goals. Establish what limitations you can turn into strengths to jump-start your career. Learn the skills that will help you progress. Put yourself in uncomfortable networking situations if you need people skills for example. Remember to mainly focus on weaknesses that hold you back from achieving your potential.

Top tip: Your strengths are what gives you an edge and you must use them to your advantage.

Values

Knowing what your values are, is knowing who you are and what you stand for. Having strong values, help you establish and navigate your thoughts so that they are in synergy with your passion and essence. In other words, before you involve yourself in anything at all, ask yourself, "Is this in sync with my values and what I stand for?"

Values are essentially a set of principles that you live by. They define the codes that determine your personality, attitude, actions, reactions and so on. Look at it this way; perhaps the reason you are unhappy at work is that your values are not allied with what you do. Having values, therefore, is standing up for what you believe in. It is crucial to align who you are with what you engage yourself in.

"Love is the expression of one's values, the greatest reward you can earn for the moral qualities you have achieved in your character and person, the emotional price paid by one person for the joy he or she receives from the virtues of another." - Ayn Rand

Define your Values

There are several places on the internet that have great resources on how to establish your values for your brand. These are in the form of a list of adjectives that describes your values. Find a list most suited for you and by a process of elimination, choose the top 5 words that ring true to you and who you are. Establish why you chose these particular words and define what they mean to you. Use them to build your mission statement and hold yourself accountable if you are not respecting your values. These values should be communicated in your CV, website, social media platforms and blog posts.

Passion

Have a passion for what you do! That is the biggest secret. It might seem difficult to reconcile the idea of passion and work. However, do establish that which you enjoy doing. That which gives you joy. Furthermore, consider topics that fascinate you, that keep you inspired and wanting more.

If you are still confused about what your passion might be, think about a time when you could not wait to do something or read about something. Think about the time you could not wait to get out of bed, and about the things that moved you to tears. Don't forget the projects that made me feel creative and had you filled with ideas. When you feel stimulated and motivated to do something, then you are passionate about it.

Ask yourself:

- What do I 4like about my current job?
- If I were to volunteer, which charity would you choose? Why?
- What do you spend most of your time doing?

"There is no passion to be found playing small in settling for a life that is less than the one you are capable of living." - Nelson Mandela

Your job-related interests should be in more or less of the following areas:

- Research
- Problem-solving
- Analyzing

- Planning
- Managing
- Planning
- Mentoring
- Creating
- Counseling
- Coaching
- Writing
- Listening

Attributes

What words would you use to describe yourself? Also, consider the words that others might use to describe you. Deliberate on the following words without limiting yourself; creative, thoughtful, visionary, ambitious, resourceful, risk-taker, negotiator, ethical, connected, compassionate, animated, worldly, diplomatic and so on. Find attributes that best describe your personality and use them to communicate your brand essence.

Positioning

Once you are clear about your values, attributes, and passion, it's time to now position yourself. What does that mean exactly? It simply means that you should consider how others perceive you based on your strengths, values, mission, attributes, and passion. Remember, this is about authenticity. In the place of work, you have to be consistent about who you say you are.

Create a positioning statement. This statement you can use during interviews as it is more powerful and fresh than going on about your monotonous career past. It captures your essence and uniqueness.

Target Audience

At this point, you should have everything you need to attract the right audience. You must first determine the industry in which you wish to work, then search for ideal organizations you wish to work for. Conduct extensive research on these organizations and establish what problems they are faced with; you might be a match for them based on your unique strengths, values, passions, and attributes.

With your homework done, create a personal brand strategy using the keywords in job descriptions to attract their attention. After all, they want to hire good talent and someone that matches their standards. However, remember to never give everything you have, reserve some of your good selling points for the interview.

"In Social Media, the "squeaky wheel" gets the oil. You have to put yourself out there, to find people who will relate or even debate with you, depending on what you are looking for."

Remember to stay true and be consistent with your brand. All the elements discussed in this article should be communicated effectively in digital media. You should remember that in this age of information and technology, you have the power to make or break yourself. Utilize the platforms that are now available to communicate your brand successfully.

The 7 Wonders Of Social Media Marketing To A Brand

The universe of digital marketing is wide and varied, but the one factor that is dominating it is social media. Through online platforms, companies can reach a global pool of customers that are in billions. Any corporation that is not utilizing this source is not only skipping on a fantastic growth window but a cash cow of profitability.

Be it mere PPC services or sharing content on social media, when a company utilizes any platform, they spread awareness of their service or product. Furthermore, they indicate to search engines that the brand is reliable, valid and consistent. Let's take a look at how else social media affects an establishment, positively.

Get the Customer Engaged

Marketing is about winning the attention of a person and then conveying your message. Social media is the easiest and ideal way of interacting with customers. It is the one path that allows for two-way communication at lightning speed. Catering to the wishes or interests of the patron is fast-paced with online platforms. When more consumers are engaging with your brand, there is a bigger probability of conversion.

Get More Customers Aware

Facebook, Twitter or Instagram are not just avenues to converse with current customers. They are pathways to reaching an added audience in real-time. Unlike most other marketing stratagems, social media is a hassle-free way to enhance the visibility of a brand. Just a few hours every seven days has shown, in more than 90% of companies, a greater awareness of product or service in customers.

The gist is to create all social media profiles, use them regularly and begin networking to generate a wide audience

Without a shadow of a doubt, the one benefit social media has for customers is the ease with which they can find brands. The convenience of connecting heightens user experience and benefits the company. How? A patron becomes loyal to a brand when they receive satisfaction. When a customer can communicate with the corporation within minutes of facing an issue or wanting to know more about a product through social presence, it ups satisfaction. This, in turn, leads to brand loyalty.

Gain an Understanding of the Marketplace

The reason social media is considered the MVP of digital marketing is not that it gives brands the freedom to introduce their products to a broader audience but because it offers comprehension of the marketplace. When a company can talk with their patrons through online avenues directly, they get to know precisely what is needed.

Over and above, a brand can observe the online activities of the consumer and get to know their opinions and interests. This would not be possible without pages and handles on social media. Think of social media as a research tool that can be employed to know the demographics when the brand following becomes large.

Be more Economical

Advertising, in the traditional sense, is not an inexpensive strategy. But promoting through social media marketing is hugely cost-effective.

- Creating an account on any platform is free.
- Developing a brand through your handle costs zilch.
- Even paid advertising is dirt cheap on social media.

To top the cake with a cherry, a company can invest the smallest amount and get a high rate of return. Significantly raising conversion rates is not hard with social media adverts, you need a little capital and the right time.

Gain a Brand Voice

Through an online platform, a brand can create a voice that speaks directly to patrons and generates a healthy brand image. When a customer receives a tailored reply to their query on social, instead of a cookie-cutter reply, they appreciate it more. It shows that the company values the consumer enough to make the effort to write a personal response. A brand voice, therefore, allows for effective communication, networking and healthier satisfaction in clients.

Every time a small or big business posts original content on social media or each time, they resolve a question posed by a customer, they establish authority. As more and more original posts go up and resolutions occur, in the eyes of the patron, the brand becomes an expert on the subject or topic. Just like satisfaction and loyalty affect the bottom line of an organization, authority touches it too. Why? Because it leaves an optimistic picture in the mind of the consumer. It makes them more probable of buying a product and talking about it to other potential customers.

A Succinct Layout

No marketing guru or entrepreneur can deny that media is a magic wand. It creates miracles for budding and established businesses. When you post consistently, the benefits the trade accrues are:

- better SEO
- increased traffic
- improved brand loyalty
- healthier customer satisfaction

Remember, chances are the competing businesses are already exploiting social marketing to reach probable patrons. Don't miss out on the opportunity.

7 Steps to Automate Your Online Business and Increase Sales

Today's entrepreneurs care about being passionate about work and knowing that it has a larger meaning. As entrepreneurs, we like our work to make some impact and help to make the world a better place. At the same time, however, we like our work to be successful. Doing well by doing good. With the worst recession in decades in our rear-view-mirror, today's entrepreneurs need to be extremely creative and do things efficiently. These 7 steps to automate your online business will increase sales and simplify your operations.

Automation is the key to building a successful business with fewer resources. To create awesome companies, as a team, and to use technology, ultimately to better the world is a common goal of today's entrepreneur. But at the same time, today's entrepreneurs don't have the financial resources available to hire a team of workers. So the more that today's entrepreneur can accomplish solo, the better.

Finding the formula for entrepreneur success is not going to be an easy journey or a simple task. You need to work at it. However, if you use these 7 steps to online business automation, you can start finding success and building the future you have always wanted.

7 Steps to Building an Automated Online Business:

Here are seven steps that you can take on your journey to becoming a self-employed, free and highly successful entrepreneur without breaking the bank.

Build a WordPress Website

The most popular content management system available today is WordPress. As today's entrepreneur, you will want to select the right content management system to build your website. WordPress fits the bill. It's free, it's secure, it's customizable so you can implement these automation tips into your website and get close to reaching your goal of building an automated online business.

Choose a professional WordPress theme that is clean, fast, and responsive. We recommend StudioPress WordPress Themes. They are powered by the Genesis Framework, which in layman's terms, means that the behind-the-scenes nuts and bolts of your website will be search engine friendly, responsive with instant updates and airtight security. Don't waste time with the wrong WordPress theme. Choose a state-of-the-art framework and one that will update with the click of a mouse. Many sites are hacked (or just don't use WordPress to the fullest) because they have not been updated and with StudioPress themes, the act of updating your code to the most recent technology takes just a click. Updating to the current version of WordPress and Genesis a snap. Everything is integrated, so you don't have to call your developer. Save time and money.

First Impressions Count: Your website is only as good as your design and your web hosting company.

Build your Email List

Email marketing is a powerful tool that can extend your reach beyond your website and create new sales opportunities. If you're not building an email list, you're making a huge mistake, so get started right off the bat with your new business and begin building an email list.

Any networking event provides excellent opportunities to collect business cards, which can then be manually added to your email list. But if you are like most entrepreneurs, there is not enough time in the day to attend every Chamber of Commerce event. So, to build your email list, you need to automate it. The easiest and most effective way to automate your email marketing efforts is with Aweber Email Marketing. I have tried them all and I always come back to Aweber.

First, you need to determine who is your target audience. This simple exercise will help. First, answer these questions:

- What do your ideal subscribers want?
- What's the main problem they have that you believe you can solve?
- What's your method for solving that problem?
- What do you love to talk about more than anything?

Once you're done, you simply combine them all. These are the people you are catering to. This is your target audience.

Write Compelling Content

The most effective way to grow visitors to your website or blog is to write compelling content. Yes, that's right. The time you spent in English class in high school will finally come in handy. When you're writing content, you will want to think about the audience you're trying to reach... and call them out. Write evergreen content that helps, informs and satisfies your target audience.

Evergreen content is timeless content that is still relevant. You could go through your archives, or you could also use a WordPress plug-in like Revive Old Posts to simplify the process. There is also a killer tool that I use called MeetEdgar that allows you to publish a post and then automatically recycle your top posts several times on a schedule.

The number of subscribers you have is directly related to...

- Your ability to drive highly-targeted traffic to your blog.
- Your ability to convert that traffic into FIERCELY LOYAL subscribers.
- Your ability to get your readers to promote and refer you to friends.

Now it's up to you you to take action and build your email list with compelling content.

Build your Social Media Profiles

When it comes to online personal or business branding, the creation of social media profiles is essential. Think of each social media profile you create as a landing page for your brand. This landing page is possibly the first encounter that someone is going to have with your brand, and you will want that first impression to be golden and make the visitor want to know more about you.

10 Steps you need to follow to Create a Successful Social Media Profile:

- **Your name** - Be sure to enter the name you want to be found under.
- **Your username -** Think about what people will search for you, and make sure that your username is included in the URL.

- **Your profile pic** - Use a professional photograph, but not so much that you don't illustrate some personality. Be sure to stick with the same picture as your default photo from one network to the next. This way people easily recognize you across all social networks.
- **Your link** - Make sure that your link is front and center so that people can find it quickly and click through to your website.
- **Your bio** - Take advantage of this to share only the best about yourself and your brand. And always - always - link to your website or landing page.
- **Your interests** - Look at these fields as an additional place to get some great keyword value. Find books, documentaries, and profiles of influential people in your industry and add those in these additional fields.
- **Your background** - A customized background will allow you to share additional information that may not fit in the fields of your profile.
- **Your privacy settings** - These vary from network to network, but you will want to make sure that the information you would like to be public is viewable.
- **Your activity** - Once your profile setup is complete, your on-going mission will be to maintain a healthy level of activity on your main social networks, which for most will be Twitter, Facebook, and LinkedIn. Automate this! We like Buffer. It's inexpensive and a great way to keep your social media activity at peak performance.
- **Your promotion** - your website!

If you are short on time, concentrate on the Social Media Big Three:

- Facebook
- Twitter
- LinkedIn.

Don't forget to interlink your profiles to each other. If you can share multiple links on a social profile, make sure some of those are to your main social profiles.

Sync your Blog or Website

Add social share buttons onto your page or automatically post on social media whenever you publish a new article. Additionally, with Step 2 (above) you will have the ability to create a blog broadcast with Aweber so that each time you publish a new blog post to your WordPress website, Aweber will use your post to create a dynamic newsletter and broadcast your content to everyone on your email list.

Why? Because research shows that the lead nurturing process today takes seven to eight "touches". These seven to eight touches that it takes to qualify a lead are crucial components of the lead nurturing process, allowing marketing the opportunity to educate and inform prospects as they move through each stage in the buying journey. These touchpoints are opportunities to prepare leads for the final stage in the buying journey, the point of decision-making.

Sync your social media profiles to landing pages that are specific to your visitor. Our favorite automation tool for conversion optimization is Thrive Leads Landing Pages. Build an automated sales funnel that runs a highly optimized.

Sync your website with an opt-in form so that your visitors can easily subscribe to your newsletter:

- Aweber has many templates that you can use to add an opt-in form to your website.
- ThriveLeads has many different "triggers". Trigger options can be the following:
  - Show on page load
  - Show after a certain period
  - Show when the user scrolls to a specific part of the content
  - Show when the user scrolls to a percentage of the way down the content
  - Show when the user is about to exit the page (exit intent) - this trigger option does not work on mobile devices.
  - Show when the form enters the viewport
  - Show when the user clicks an element
  - Displays on click.

Customize which opt-in form displays, when and where with ThriveLeads. You can organize all the forms you want to display automatically on the site into different Lead Groups. Within each Lead Group, you can create and edit multiple opt-in forms at once, set them to appear in multiple places, and set up A/B tests.

We "connect" our ThriveLeads form to Aweber's API so that when a visitor completes the opt-in form, their email address is automatically added to our master email list at Aweber. And from within Aweber, we have a blog broadcast set up so that when a new blog post is published, a nifty newsletter is automatically created using their templates and sent to addresses on our list.

And finally, we use Aweber's form templates to display a static and well-designed, professional opt-in form in the sidebar of our blog. Again, when a visitor completes the form, their email address is automatically added to the master email list managed with Aweber.

Get insights into your competitors' strategies in display advertising, organic and paid search, and link building. SEMRush Online Marketing Tools automate your research and optimization efforts. SEMrush will make your job a lot easier by taking the guesswork out of researching the market and your competition. It takes the guesswork out of your digital marketing time and helps you to know before-hand what works, and what is a waste of time.

Fill your Orders

If you are selling products online, you will soon discover that filling orders are time-consuming. Automate your order fulfillment with Order Fulfillment by Amazon. With FBA, you store your products in Amazon's fulfillment centers, and Amazon will pick, pack, ship, and provide customer service for them. It's a tremendous time-saver for you as you grow your online store. Keep these steps in mind if you are looking to gain the freedom that most entrepreneurs want. These steps may just be your path towards a more successful online business. The better the experience and the more valuable each of these important steps is, the more ready your leads will be to make a buying decision, and the more likely they are to convert to paying customers. The result is a highly organized, efficient buying journey that runs like a well-oiled machine. And one item that cannot be automated is you! Your leads and customers will want to have interaction, of some type, with you - the company owner. Be professional and always follow telephone and social media etiquette when communicating with the public. Remember, you are building your brand. And your brand is an asset.

Digital Marketing - Incremental Revenue

Social media advertising can have a big impact on a brand. Digital marketing ads may encourage people to try a product, a free trial could lead to a purchase, and a purchase could lead to a person using a product. During this process, brand-centric conversations usually develop on social networking websites, which can be discovered through search. These conversations become a vital factor when it comes to making purchase-related decisions, as most buyers usually check out comments on social networks like Facebook before coming to a buying decision.

These digital marketing conversations are usually driven by two factors, which are both controllable. The first is product design, and the second is the communications between customers and customer service agents. There is a strong connection between ROI and customer service. For instance, if an internet marketing professional takes the time to understand the relationship between the number of fans and the number of 'likes', together with conversations on Twitter between customers and service agents, they will get a true picture of the impact of their digital marketing campaign on social networks.

A simple way to get such an understanding is to connect customer service actions with incremental 'likes', by tracking responses of customers to the digital marketing messages of your customer care agents. You may also begin tracking incremental revenue, either directly through your Facebook business page or other social media profile. So, what is incremental revenue? Incremental revenue can be in the form of subscription renewals, product up-sells, and the customer saves collected through the actions of social care agents.

Incremental revenue can also be calculated from the expense side, just like a phone interaction. Once you track the shift of call deflection, you will get a measure of the change in expenses connected with your digital marketing effort, together with its cost. Your digital marketing program on social networks will now be connected to real money, offering a great way to calculate ROI.

As an Internet marketing professional continues to build its marketing program on social networking websites, they need to think beyond marketing. A social media profile should also link to other functional areas of a business, which also take part in social media-based conversations, such as customer service. Take into account revenue, expense change and directional KPI's, before setting up various ROI goals. Therefore, there are several ways in which you can also improve product promotion through Social media.

How to Build a Successful Digital Marketing Strategy

Social media advertising can have a big impact on a brand. Digital marketing ads may encourage people to try a product, a free trial could lead to a purchase, and a purchase could lead to a person using a product. During this process, brand-centric conversations usually develop on social networking websites, which can be discovered through search. These conversations become a vital factor when it comes to making purchase-related decisions, as most buyers usually check out comments on social networks like Facebook before coming to a buying decision.

These digital marketing conversations are usually driven by two factors, which are both controllable. The first is product design, and the second is the communications between customers and customer service agents. There is a strong connection between ROI and customer service. For instance, if an internet marketing professional takes the time to understand the relationship between the number of fans and the number of 'likes', together with conversations on Twitter between customers and service agents, they will get a true picture of the impact of their digital marketing campaign on social networks.

A simple way to get such an understanding is to connect customer service actions with incremental 'likes', by tracking responses of customers to the digital marketing messages of your customer care agents. You may also begin tracking incremental revenue, either directly through your Facebook business page or other social media profile. So, what is incremental revenue? Incremental revenue can be in the form of subscription renewals, product up-sells, and the customer saves collected through the actions of social care agents.

Incremental revenue can also be calculated from the expense side, just like a phone interaction. Once you track the shift of call deflection, you will get a measure of the change in expenses connected with your digital marketing effort, together with its cost. Your digital marketing program on social networks will now be connected to real money, offering a great way to calculate ROI.

As an Internet marketing professional continues to build its marketing program on social networking websites, they need to think beyond marketing. A social media profile should also link to other functional areas of a business, which also take part in social media-based conversations, such as customer service. Take into account revenue, expense change and directional KPI's, before setting up various ROI goals. Therefore, there are several ways in which you can also improve product promotion through Social media.

Digital Strategy Is Changing - Cultural Anthropology Is Now Your Brand Strategy

The South African shoemaker selling sandals in an open-air market in SWATO competes with other shoemakers locally or even manufacturers globally, but what makes his business unique is that his handcrafted product is made from rubber tires at the local garbage dump. The tires are free, and his business concept is easy to template from shoemaker to shoemaker without legal restrictions or permissions to prevent duplication of products. Such open transfer of intellectual information and process can be compared to the openness and power of social networks, and how conversations can freely stimulate the flow of ideas such as crowdsourcing (free outsourcing), thus empowering people, particularly those in economically challenged emerging communities around the world. For more on this kind of innovation read Steven Johnson's Where Good Ideas Come From.

So what do the emerging nation and online social platforms have to do with the "right" practice of digital strategy? The rapid increase and use of social networking platforms, mobile platforms, and available online access are challenging traditional digital strategy concepts, replacing them with new global ones. These new strategies require a broader understanding of global cultural and behavioral norms.

For example, a World Bank report recently stated that the number of mobile subscriptions in the world is expected to pass five billion this year, according to the International Telecommunication

Union. That would mean more people today have access to a cell phone than have access to a clean toilet, says the United Nations. This increase is being fueled by mobile technology growth in developing countries like Kenya, India, Brazil, South Korea, and even Afghanistan.

Your digital campaign strategy may be missing its full market potential if you do not consider the growing influence that many emerging global communities have over brand adoption. Without considering these influences, a community's global feedback loop can disrupt your campaign strategy. For example, in the US, a large percentage of the Latino and Indian population have strong ties to their country of origin.

Regarding social network strategy, South Africa, for example, has approximately 3.38 million Facebook users, or 64 percent of its online population. This translates into a much higher number of people with an Internet connection using Facebook, than countries such as Germany, where only 23.07 percent have a profile on Facebook. So while many strategists are integrating communities in Europe into their strategy mix, they may be overlooking emerging markets such as South Africa.

Around the world, including countries with a variety of different economic conditions, people using the Internet are increasingly logging on to social networks, and younger users are leading this trend. Earlier this year, Pew Research concluded that "while involvement in social networking is relatively low in many less economically developed nations, this is large because many people in those countries do not go online at all, rather than having a disinterest in social networking in particular."

As Internet and mobile availability increases over the next five years, countries such as South Africa, India, and China will embrace social networking and mobile technologies for personal and quality of life improvements rather than recreational use; the influence this audience will have in driving brand strategy will be powerful.

According to a recent poll, approximately 53 percent of Americans say they do not believe that the spread of affordable broadband should be a major government priority. Would this percentage change if this poll were taken in India, with its population of approximately 1.15 billion, and where 80% of its population is living on less than $2 a day? I think it would.

With the potential for huge financial gains by the private technology sector and political pressure placed on government officials by voters, changes in government-supported and privately funded Internet access will happen. Increased access to online social communities will also translate into consumers having even more control and influence over brands.

So where does this leave the practice of digital strategy today, and going forward? It will require you, the strategist, to build a campaign strategy with a keen understanding of consumer and cultural behavior in the local niche and global online communities. This process will replace some current strategies that treat consumers as if they are one homogeneous group or market.

Social networks such as Facebook make this process easier because of their unique advertising platform which allows for hyper-targeting. Analytics tools produce valuable data about country- and city-specific user activity, providing intelligence for audience development strategies. PR campaigns can ramp up their page view numbers more rapidly by targeting bloggers globally, which also increases viral opportunities and early brand adoption. International SEO (search engine optimization) techniques can also be honed for international strategy effectiveness, along with social media sites.

For example, in Korea, 77.7 percent of the population is online and searching, with Naver (the fifth most used search engine in the world), not Google, as its leading search tool, commanding approximately 77 percent of all search traffic.

Finally, you can increase the viral possibilities of your content by including global affiliate and blogger strategies as part of your plan.

Because digital strategy is rapidly evolving into a specialization that encompasses various disciplines, including digital strategy, cultural anthropology, intelligence, business analytics, data specialization, brand planning, etc., you must stay "on trend" and relevant. Understanding the differences and similarities in cultures domestically and globally will greatly affect your brand campaigns' success and your career.

Internet Marketing: Tips For Starting A Successful Online Business

According to Forbes magazine, 79 million people are planning to start their own business in the next 3 to 5 years. It is estimated that almost half 1 million new enterprises were founded every month in the USA in 2005. This represents a huge desire amongst the general population to start a new business and increase their worth independently and outside of the traditional job structure. One of the most lucrative ways to make money starting your own business is through network marketing. You may be surprised to hear that many people in network marketing keep their business activities to themselves. It is estimated that over 25 million people have been involved in network marketing in the past 20 years so you will probably know some of them. Unfortunately, many of these don't make any money because they don't put in the required amount of work which is a shame because there is the potential to make a huge amount of money. This is, of course, a very sad and worrying fact and you will surely be keen not to join the 97 percent this makes no money online at all. You must be willing to start a proper online business and reject the mindset of an opportunity seeker who is looking for the fantasy of turning a quick buck by pressing some shiny button. There is no magic trick to making money online. You have to learn proper business practices and strategies to be successful and it is lucky for you that these are easy to pick up and understand.

Another fabulous way to make money online is called affiliate marketing. You can make money by promoting other people's products and when someone makes a purchase, you make a commission. This can be a fast route to earning a very good amount of money online as it saves you the hassle of having to create your product or service. You can find a huge library of affiliate products to promote quickly and easily on a site called ClickBank.

Many people who try to start their own online business lack the correct mindset required of a modern digital entrepreneur. They become stuck in the mindset of an employee rather than an independent entrepreneur. It is easy to lose a sense of purpose and not know what to do next when you start working for yourself and you have no one to tell you what to do. You may soon start to flounder when you realize that there is no boss there to instruct you or guide you in your business activities. Most people stay in their traditional job with their traditional employee mindset all of their lives and never become an entrepreneur making their own money independently. If you truly want to be a successful online entrepreneur you must be able to choose your destiny without the guidance of a boss figure. With that said, it might be a good idea to connect with someone who has been there and done it before you. If you are lucky enough to meet somebody like that, they can help you to avoid the mistakes that they made when starting. You mustn't expect them to build your business for you. They will not be your new boss. As an entrepreneur, you must work this out for yourself and create your routines and processes. You should learn to take responsibility for both your successes and your failures.

10 Powerful Digital Marketing Strategies

It is prudent that any organization, regardless of type or size need to continue adapting the best marketing strategies for them to have any relevance in this ever dynamic market. In other words, the organizations need to ensure that they recognize the online nature of modern customers thereby introducing and then establishing a formidable Digital Marketing strategy.

Without the best Digital Marketing Strategy, your business may end up missing some very potential and essential sales as well as online sales opportunities. This is a significant problem especially bearing in mind that the highest number of vital customers in the modern world will start their search for a product on the internet.

Below are ten top Digital Marketing Strategies that need to be followed by all the serious entrepreneurs and they will remain relevant in the market today.

Studies have shown that most web users will determine whether to stay or to leave a web page within just 10 seconds after the page has opened. Today, web users no longer go through paragraph to paragraph in search of a text. This implies that if you were so much focused on communicating your message only through your linguistic prowess, then you may have no chance of showcasing your skills.

To combat such problems, it is paramount that you follow what other web users are doing to retain customers whom they have struggled to attract through the Optimization of their websites. The use of images together with videos is today essential for effective website communication. More can be communicated through the visual communications and within just a short space of time. This is very essential especially in the retention of the very impatient users who have visited your site for the first time.

Remember that 90% of all the information that is transmitted to the brain normally is visual. In the brain, the same visual messages are always processed sixty thousand times faster than texts. Decrease the website bounce rates as you increase search engine rankings by posting visual-centric homepages.

Make Your Message Mobile Friendly

The number of persons accessing the internet has constantly been on an increase in the last few years stretching back to a decade. Those accessing the internet via their smartphones have also been on a constant increase especially in the last five years or so. This increase will keep on being on the rise hence the need for businesses to factor the mobile devices in their strategies. In a nutshell, to remain relevant, you must have a mobile responsive website.

Focus on Content

It is worth noting that advertisements or rather marketing through traditional methods such as magazines, newspapers, TV among others is becoming irrelevant. It is therefore important that you divert a lot of your resources to ensure that your websites give the customers and potential customers the very best. Ensure that you give the desired content to the latter. There is some specific information that customers will always either need or be attracted to. Ensure that you capitalize on that. It is also worth mentioning that content is one of the features that are used in SEO. For your website to be highly optimized, it has to have the right content organized in the right way.

Harness Online Video Power

Videos are among the top most marketing tools the modern marketer has at his disposal. Online videos have been used in the last few years and they have become a must-have for any serious websites. In case you haven't still employed the use of these videos, then probably you may be lagging in this stiff competition.

Multi-Channel

It is no longer prudent to spend all your time only on one channel, however perfect you may do it. Today, you have to express your ideas on several channels. Ensure that you advertise your ideas and products through the websites that your potential customers visit the most such as numerous social media websites. From here, you can direct them to your site.

Get Social

As mentioned above, you have to get into social media marketing to get the best out of your Digital Marketing Strategy. Create a page on the website, Twitter among other social media and have a link that will direct the users to your website. There are so many people visiting social websites today. It is, therefore, easiest to create a network and direct it to your website through social media than by any other means.

Add Some Rich Snippets to the Google Search Results

Rich snipes are credited for giving standout results with a great percentage of audiences having a likelihood of clicking the site. The use of a professional video hosting service to post a video on your site is the easiest way you can generate the rich snippet to the Google search results.

Focus on Top Quality Backlinks

High-quality backlinks play an important role in giving you're a greater score in listings within the search engines. Without using these, you may end up losing quite much. Ensure that as you create a backlink to your website, it ought to be from a website that is highly visited or that which is of high domain authority.

Implementing Sign up forms On One's Website

Sign up forms will help you identify your visitors. From these, you can be able to contact the frequently with newsletters, coupons, discounts among other features that may end up attracting a good number of them back to your website and your business.

A meager 2% of web visitors will convert on their very first visit to any site. Together with sign up forms discussed above, web owners will need to use ad retargeting to remind the visitors of the products they once viewed but took no action about them. Ad re-targeting works through the use of cookies to track the website visitors and possibly redirect them back to the site. After leaving the site, they will keep on being shown the products they viewed through ads on the other sites they visit.

Social Media Marketing: A New Era of the Booming Online Business Industry

You need new and inventive ways to connect with your customers and prospects. Social media is currently a very powerful tool to reach the masses. There are many ways to utilize social media. A highly utilized method is through influencer advertising. If you think it won't work, just look at the thousands of companies that are having successes with it. Every organization and business is now connected via social media.

Having owned Physical Therapy clinics in the past, I wish I had known social media marketing strategies as I have now. Looking back on what was accomplished with conventional marketing, (advertising in local papers, radio, bringing lunch to doctors, distributing flyers and business cards, etc.) I would have grown my private practice better with this powerful tool. Being a business owner opened my mind to self-sufficiency and to always seek out better ways to position myself towards my lifestyle goals.

What is Influencer Marketing?

The best advertising method of all time is word of mouth. It costs nothing for someone to tell someone else about your products or services. Another advantage of word-of-mouth marketing is that it keeps you on your toes. You must ensure customer satisfaction for them to refer your company to others. Influencer marketing goes along the line of a friend telling a friend about an experience with a product or a service.

First, you start by identifying strategic individuals within your target market. These people are going to influence others. The idea is unpretentious- instead of Taco Bell telling you how amazing their new Taco is, a spectacular review from a famous food critic can do more. The food critic is the influencer. In this hypothetical scenario, Taco Bell uses them to generate influencer marketing.

One example of influencer marketing is a company called Fab Fit Fun. This company sends out monthly box subscriptions to those who love their products. Now, you never know what is in these boxes. It could be anything from a scarf to a throw, and even some makeup and perfume. Many people are leery about monthly subscriptions that charge directly to their credit cards monthly. These boxes automatically ship whether you want it or not. So how does this company overcome this hurdle? Well, they get celebrities like Rhianna and Tori Spelling to do influencer advertising for them. A simple video of Tori Spelling opening her box subscription, going through each item enthusiastically and then sharing it on her social media network just made this subscription system a hit.

Another company came up with an idea. The Younique cosmetic company came up with a product, a mascara that gave a dramatic lift to the eyes. Now, there are more companies out there who have the same product. How did they step up their game? Their Moodstruck 3-D fiber lashes look great on just about anyone.

To prove their point, they gave out free mascara tubes to the general public. All these recipients had to do was to post a video of themselves on social media using the mascara. What happened next was history. The company had so many orders that they were on back order for six weeks. Every woman wanted to increase their lash volume. By showing how well this mascara does, the company created a hype. The demand was overwhelming.

Now, I kind of went all girl here. Mascaras and Fab Fit Fun. However, this is just a few of the many creative ways that companies conjure to move their products on the market. What made their strategy work?

It was providing VALUE. By providing more value than the other companies and being talked about on social media gave them an edge over their competitors.

The Power Of Social Media

We have heard of ordinary people posting simple funny videos on YouTube, Facebook, Pinterest, on Instagram which goes viral by simply being shared multiple times on all social media networks. This just proves that people are watching. They are hanging out on social media. They see products, events, and they share it on their social media circles. This is very powerful.

It is no wonder that during the past few years, big online retailers like Amazon, Wayfair, and the rest have utilized social media advertising. Even brick and mortar businesses like Best Buy, Target, Walmart, have gone online to expand their market. It is sad to contemplate that it is also due to this era of online advertising that many companies have to close their doors. The competition has become rabid. Those who do not step up to the plate lose. The most recent one closing, as you might have heard, is Hhgregg.

Finding A Key Player

What if you can be the influencer in your online business? Yes, you can be the Key Player in this success. Yes, it is more than possible. This is how many online entrepreneurs have positioned themselves as the experts, coaches, and founders of online business systems which has created wealth for themselves and others they have mentored.

How many times do you see pop up on your Facebook page "sponsored" ads of webinars, free E-books, free courses, free videos or free reports? This is the power of social media at work.

The new era is here. An average entrepreneur can leverage his advertising budget by effectively using social media to his advantage. This is because customers hang out on social media networks. This is a very effective way of reaching out to prospects and introducing your product or services.

Moreover, if your ad also comes with an added value, customer response is overwhelming. It is going above and beyond what everyone else offers. This has been proven many times by local businesses offering products and services. A free dental cleaning coupon from a dentist can end up in a 4-5k sales in orthodontics or other dental services because of the one free offer.

Online coaches and online business experts who offer free webinars have been known to make thousands of dollars from memberships or purchases made by participants in one webinar alone. I sure have attended some of them, and although I have never really purchased a product or a system initially, it had opened my eyes to the possibilities. There are ways to earn income online and work your way to passive and residual income.

Whether your goal is just to make extra income to supplement your current one or to make it a full-time occupation, there are multitudes of systems and programs that you can get started online. Many have plunged into online businesses full time and never looked back.

The key is to find your niche, find what feels good and right for you. Explore your passion, your talents, and your goals. Then act on it. That first step is always the hardest.

Most successful online entrepreneurs not only "engage" in their business; they also "live" it.

After all, it is up to us to explore all the possibilities and take advantage of the opportunities presented to us. With the onset of the Social Media Marketing Evolution, the future of digital marketing is here.

In previous years, digital marketing has been an important aspect of business innovation, and the year 2015 should be no exemption. If you have a website and aim to make it more profitable this year and the coming years, here are 3 digital marketing strategy recommendations you should highly consider investing in:

Instagram and Twitter Engagement

It's not enough that you have social media pages for your business. Of course, you have to maintain their posts so you can consistently engage with your audience and even invite a higher following online. Your Twitter account can be used to create product hashtags and make them trend worldwide. You can also use it for tracking the performance of your competitors, through following their pages, for example, or re-using hashtags that are already popular in your specific industry.

Aside from Twitter, you should also have an Instagram account. Although it's just a photo-sharing app, you can't ignore the fact that such a social media platform has a total of 200 million active monthly users (according to expandedramblings.com)! This is all thanks to the younger generation of today who log in to Instagram several times a day. Go ahead and share your brand content in IG to be one step ahead in the digital marketing game.

Facebook Lookalike Audience and Re-Marketing

Facebook certainly has a lot more to offer than what meets the eye. Page likes, shares, and status posts aren't the only reasons your business should be active in this social networking site. If you haven't tried or heard about the Facebook lookalike audience, 2015 can be the perfect time to start including it on your digital marketing strategy plans. This feature lets you set up another set of audience that may have similar interests to your main audience. By clicking Custom Audiences, you can choose other people from different countries and reach out to them through the ads that you post.

Re-marketing, on the other hand, works with the help of a Salesforce website tracking cookie. In a layman's term, once a customer visits your website, exits from it, and logs in to his Facebook account, he can see an ad about your website. This ad then serves as your website's re-marketing campaign, and do you know what its huge advantage is? Your website's bounce rates will still return possible profits from FB's display advertising!

Email blasts go a long way in grabbing the attention of your audience. Just make sure they contain compelling content and graphics. How many email blasts do you send every month? Consider doubling them. Increase your email marketing campaigns this year to have more constant communication with your target market.

Most importantly, you should never give up on creating high-quality content for the web. Through well-written blog posts and effective SEO strategies, your website will always be on top of the digital marketing competition. So, let the right professionals do these crucial tasks for you.

Opt For Digital Marketing Solutions to Promote Your Online Business

Reaching a target market over has been changing and \is not only limited to broadcasting and print but has also reached the Internet. How the browsing and shopping behavior of consumers have also affected the marketing strategies of online business. Thanks to digital marketing solutions, your online business can attract a market share in the big virtual commerce of the worldwide web.

It does not matter if an online is a small or big business. The strength of enterprise or big investment are not prerequisites to being into online business. The virtual market place has done the leverage in promoting products and services by online marketing campaigns readily offered by some online marketing companies. They dedicate themselves to creating, managing, and channeling qualified business leads to your website. This, in turn, will help in your online business promotion and possibly close deals. You will have to synchronize your business needs with its services to achieve your planned goals.

For most online companies, they choose to hire outsource or consultant services to be able to grab hold of the endless means of marketing on the Internet. These companies usually called integrated marketing company usually employs digital solutions to reach a larger specific audience that can appreciate what your online business can offer. Digital marketing solutions can involve lots of marketing digital mediums to hold the attention of their preferred customers. These channels can be e-mail, SMS, banner ads, social networking sites, digital outdoor displays and many more means that are driven by digital technology.

There are two branches of approach for digital marketing solutions. The "push" model puts a deliberate attempt to push their advertisement across their targeted audience. One classic example is email, SMS, or newsletter. They contain the brochure or product description that a potential buyer can be interested in and delivered right to them directly. All the necessary information to get hold of the products they like is available for them in one click making it easier to draw lots of order requests. Posting comments at social sites can also reach potential customers in a very friendly way that can also help the little push to make them want to avail of a product or service online.

Although some argue that some end up as spams, they can still yield a considerable attention towards your website. Another approach in digital marketing solutions is the "pull" model. They find ways to prompt the possible customers to buy the products or services you offer by exposing digital campaigns. An example would be banner ads and outdoor digital displays. that can advertise interesting products to the viewer and so they click it tom find out more about it.

Promoting your online business has been a lot easier with the available digital technology that can be integrated with the Internet. Trends right now are vastly changing so you should expect some untried channels to come up any time. One example is the digital telephony campaign where digital phones are being used to make outbound calls to possible customers. You will never know when the right one for your online business company can deliver you the revenue you never dreamed of at a fraction of a price.

Conclusion

Social Media Marketing is a field where professionals and amateurs in advertising can come across and put their ideas and plans to implement their techniques. There is no Social Media Marketer university or college degree, this knowledge that should be acquired by extensive research, it needs to be constantly employed and tested in the desired field. It is a revolutionary strategy that has taken down the old TV advertising tactics shifting it to the online market. The percentage of people that prefer to go online on a computer or capable device versus people that watch TV grows steadily every single day. Statistics show Social Media Marketing in a lower impact percentage compared to the legacy ways for advertising, but the potential it has and room for growth is in no doubt overwhelming and could be much more improved and interactive than TV has been for the past decades.

Whoever engages in Social Media Marketing is bound to find himself pulling on very many strings at the same time. Assessing, understanding the campaign's environment through research and pre-dive learning is a must. Although the marketing process might seem similar to the real-world thing, the Online Social Experience entails mastering every stage with even more precision, because you can never see or analyze real-time behaviors, except for what the prospect writes from behind his monitor, should it be true or false. A Social Media Marketing Strategy is simply the result of the conjunction of human competences and web tools that allow social interaction, interchange and sharing to the profit of a brand. It is a two-way traffic by which the seller has an on-spot obligation of being a psychologist, sociologist or an ethnologist. Be reassured you do not need to be these actually because you're a human being who is supposedly used to human social codes in general.

Sign up for my newsletter by leaving us your email, you will be informed about new promotions and new book releases:

Click Here https://mailchi.mp/e136f3ee924a/stephan-anderson

Stephan Anderson

SOCIAL MEDIA MARKETING FOR BUSINESS 2020
Book 2

The Ultimate Guide to Boosting Your Business Through Social Media Marketing on Facebook, Instagram, Pinterest And Twitter!

WRITTEN BY STEPHAN ANDERSON

Table Of Contents

Introduction

Chapter 1: Understanding Social Media Better

- A Brief History of Social Media
- Social Media or Social Network?
- When Social Media Marketing Makes Sense
- Picking the Right Social Media Network

Chapter 2: Getting to Know the Platforms

- Facebook
- Instagram
- Pinterest
- Twitter

Chapter 3: Crafting A Winning Strategy

- Study All Platforms to Create Your Social Media Mix
- Understand Your Brand
- Research on Your Competition
- Know Your Target Audience
- Define Your Social Media Objectives
- List the Actionable KPIs
- Create Optimised Profile and Pages
- Plan Your Content Calendar
- Publish Content with the Right Calls-To-Action
- Track, Evaluate, Tweak
- Trend Watching, Social Media Listening, and CRM
- Tips to Expand Reach

Chapter 4: Facebook

- Who Should Use Facebook, and Why?
- Leveraging Facebook in Your Marketing Strategy
- Marketing on Facebook in 2020

- Monetizing Your Facebook Page
- The Future of Facebook

Chapter 5: Instagram

- Who Should Use Instagram, and Why?
- Leveraging Instagram in Your Marketing Strategy
- Marketing on Instagram in 2020
- Monetizing Your Instagram Page
- The Future of Instagram

Chapter 6: Pinterest

- Who Should Use Pinterest, and Why?
- Leveraging Pinterest in Your Marketing Strategy
- Reaching #1 in Search Results
- Making Your Pins Go Viral in 2020
- Monetizing Your Pinterest Page

Chapter 7: Twitter

- Who Should Use Twitter, and Why?
- Leveraging Twitter in Your Marketing Strategy
- Marketing on Twitter in 2020
- Monetizing Your Twitter Page
- The Future of Twitter

Chapter 8: Common Mistakes to Avoid

Chapter 9: Reaching the Online Marketing Plateau

- What is a Plateau?
- What to Do Then?
- Letting Go

Final Thoughts

Introduction

Are you someone who wishes to get the word out there online about your business and needs an outline for your strategy so that you do not stumble in 2020? Well, this book was written for you!

Social media is a dynamic place with something new popping up each day. Running a business is already hard enough and the dynamism of social media shouldn't increase your workload. Instead, it should help your business. Isn't this what everyone wants?

Fortunately, there are a few underlying principles and tricks that you can use to propel your business further. In this book, we get to the heart of the matter for platforms like Facebook, Instagram, Pinterest, and Twitter. It will tell you just what metrics to measure and how to put together a winning strategy for more customers and more profits.

In Social Media Marketing for Business 2020, you'll find:

- How to use social media platforms to supercharge your marketing
- How to develop a winning content strategy for your business
- Which social media channels to invest in and which to run away from
- How to engage your customers and create a community around your products
- How to stop your competition and how to grow further
- How to always have a trick up your sleeve
- How not to make the obvious mistakes and tips to win

This book is the distilled version of all the information out there and presents to you the best practices in a step-by-step manner. After reading this book, you'll be breaking down the processes in simple steps and will be able to craft a winning strategy for your social media marketing that boosts your online business organically.

To gain the most out of this practical guide, read it chapter by chapter. Do not jump through things as they are said in a specific order that makes the next things possible. Go deep into research as it will bring up insights that are vital for your business and your social media strategy.

We begin by giving you a brief about *The Rise of Social Media*. This is important as it will tell you the core need for social media and will keep you from going astray during the planning or content creation stage.

Next, we talk briefly about the social media networks highlighted in this book – Facebook, Instagram, Pinterest and Twitter – sharing their audience and what makes these platforms unique in terms of features, demographics, functionality, etc.

We have dedicated an entire chapter on *'Crafting a Winning Strategy'* as it is the most crucial part of any social media plan you'll create. In 11 steps, the book will guide you to understand how a plan should be designed and how it should be executed. Here, you'll not only learn about planning but also your own business and how to turn it into a brand that customers love to associate with and follow. You'll understand what makes a business stand out from the rest and how you too can be one such business. From finding your voice to designing graphics and optimizing campaigns, this chapter will teach you all.

We'll go further beyond this by telling you the important tools that can help you automate these steps. However, do not forget that no tool or software is better than a human mind. So, while you use these tools and gain information about what is happening on your social channels, use your understanding of your business, competition, and audience to come up with real insights.

Next, we move on to discussing *Facebook* at length. We explain if Facebook is a good idea for your business and if it will make sense to pursue it with all your energy. Here you'll also learn how Facebook's unique features can help your business and what Facebook has in store for you in 2020. You can sneak a peek inside the new features coming in 2020 and stay a step ahead of your competition by planning to leverage these features right away. Towards the end of the chapter, you'll find what is next in Facebook and why you should continue to invest in it.

Our next platform is the kin to Facebook – *Instagram*. Should your business be there on Instagram? This chapter will answer that for you. Here you'll also learn the various innovative features that this platform offers and how you can leverage them for your business. We also talk about what happens on Instagram in the year 2020 and what lies ahead. It is a great platform to show off your business and you must be ready with a complete understanding of which areas you can benefit from it. We discuss that towards the end of the chapter with *The Future of Instagram.*

After this, we discuss yet another great but understated visual platform, *Pinterest*. It is a wonderful platform, but should your business be there? Does it help in SEO? How much time will it need initially, and can I go viral on Pinterest? Will virality help my business? This chapter will answer all these questions for you and tell you how you can make the best use of Pinterest. From pinning frequency to boards to descriptions to analytics, this chapter is your holy grail when it comes to Pinterest.

We last focus on the microblogging platform that is used mostly by the journalists, opinionated people, and VIP – *Twitter.* We explain if Twitter is a good idea for your business and if yes, how you should go about it. There are a lot of unique features that Twitter offers other than the ability to interact with your customers in real-time. This chapter sheds light on those features and how they can be leveraged for promoting business and building a brand out of it. What do 2020 and the future have in store for Twitter? Well, read this chapter and you'll know.

As we come close to the end of the book, you'll learn of the common mistakes most marketers make when they start and go on with social media marketing. We warn you about these and share how not to make, and if you have done that already, what you can do to salvage the situation and turn it around in favor of your business.

Right before we leave, we will discuss the most dreaded thing in any marketing – reaching the plateau. What is it, how to deal with it, how to move forward and if you should let it go – the last chapter has everything.

Armed with the best-of-industry insights and knowledge, you are now ready to accelerate your business growth, income and reach with social media marketing. It is up to you to take this information and change your life.

Let's go!

Chapter 1: Understanding Social Media Better

Humans have an inherent need to relate, to belong. Humans who think alike or believe in similar things have often stuck together. So, social media has existed since times immemorial.

A Brief History of Social Media

Social media that we now know began as early as 1950 with the arrival of telephones. At that time, they were way too expensive. So, individuals who were intrigued by how these devices worked, tried ways to invade the telephone's framework. They tried innovative methods to find a route around the expensiveness. This brought together various groups of people who would hack the telephone lines to hold virtual gatherings.

In the 70s when computers were introduced to the public, social media got a great boost. Now, a computer connected with a telephone using a modem could bring more people together. This advanced social network allowed individuals to talk, play games, transfer documents, and so on. The only drawback was that PCs weren't mainstream or considered an essential household item and so, the usage was still limited to those with access to a PC.

Even in the 80s, social media remained an underground marvel. Part of its blame also goes to the purposes it was used for – sharing adult content, personal programming, hacking, infection codes, etc.

It was the 90s where social media lived up to its name and became *social*. The internet became more and more accessible and developers created websites where social media was to be used for networking and sharing normal lives. However, it still eluded the masses.

As the internet became cheaper and vital for everyday life, people embraced technology, started opening and sharing their day-to-day life events.

Today, social media takes the spotlight in our life. We are always on it.

So, to answer why we need social media, we must understand its role:

- Meet, interact and hold virtual meetings
- Sharing content and information

As you mix these two, you will understand the true essence of social media – *discovering stuff.*

Social Media or Social Network?

A social network is a digital space where people create content, communicate and engage with each other. It is a space where you socialize. Now, this networking will be around common themes and shared interests, like politics, photography, books, etc.

But is this different from social media?

Yes. Social media is a platform that makes social networking possible. Examples of social media go beyond Facebook, Twitter, and Instagram. A blog is also social media.

When Social Media Marketing Makes Sense

Social media is a great way to engage your potential customers, generate traffic online, influence their consumption habits, and display your business' offerings. Since people use social networks to share their information with their friends, family, acquaintances, etc., it makes a great business sense to hang out where your audience is. It is the right channel to encourage users to rate your services and leave positive reviews that will further attract more potential customers to your business.

Interacting with your consumers will not only give you a different edge but will also create a connection and you'll be able to build a community around your products and services. This will ensure a sustainable advocacy channel, organic promotions, and creating a brand for yourself.

Additionally, it will give you a great deal of information to focus your campaigns and promotions around your audience and what they are looking for.

So being on social media is not optional anymore. It is a must-do.

Some of the common goals social media marketing can help you with are:

- Brand management
- Customer management
- Sales achievement
- Reputation management
- Community building
- Website traffic

We'll discuss more social media objectives later in this book.

Picking the Right Social Media Network

In this age, the consumer is not a drone anymore who could be coerced into purchasing something. The present consumer thinks thrice before leaping.

You already heard that Facebook is essential for your company, or that to show Instagram products is the best, or that if you want more website traffic, invest time in Pinterest. It is not that simple!

Internet today is divided into many communities which that their unique thoughts, philosophy, culture, language and way of functioning. A person active on Facebook will behave completely different when using Twitter. An Instagram influencer will act very differently than a Pinterest top user.

A good marketer knows this conceptual difference between these platforms and crafts her message in a way that resonates with their unique behaviors. A good marketer adapts. Thinking that the top-performing or most-talked-about platforms will work well for your business is nothing more than foolishness. So, how to choose?

Step 1: Study all social media platforms

Step 2: Know your target audience and market

Step 3: Research on your competition

The first three steps are discussed at length int his book. So, we will elaborate on why planning the logistics of social networking makes sense.

Can you manage a YouTube channel if you cannot produce high-quality video content at a desirable and *profitable* frequency? It does not even make business sense!

Chapter 2: Getting to Know the Platforms

There is a wide array of platforms you can use to market your product and services. This does not mean that one must settle for anything. The trick is to know which will work for you and your business.

Similarly, it is ideal to create a mix of social media channels, because hey, why put all your eggs in one basket? But which ones to pick and which ones to chuck? The answer relies on your social media marketing objectives. So, here are a few questions to help you gain clarity:

- What purpose does this social media platform serve?
- Which audience does this social media platform target?
- How much time investment will this social media platform need?
- What kind of content do I have to share with my audience?
- What technology and legalities would I have to deal with on this social media channel?

To help you make a valid choice, here is a brief look at the top social media networks to use in creating an ideal social media mix:

Facebook

It is one of the most popular platforms and is used by audiences of all age groups and geographies. This diversity can help you greatly in expanding your reach and getting more word-of-mouth, organic brand mentions.

Purpose: Helps businesses build a good reputation and promote brand loyalty.

Reasons to be on Facebook

- One post can get you a wide reach.
- It encourages organic conversations.
- The platform offers an opportunity to drive website traffic.
- Selling on Facebook is simple.

Audience: All age groups

Things to keep in mind

Facebook is a giant. If it was a country, it would be the world's third most populated country, after China and India. Therefore, it has an extremely varied user demographic which makes it difficult to get their attention.

The only way to fight the formula and attract users to your brand rather than your competition is by using a water-tight segmentation of the audience. You need to know exactly who your target audience is and what their triggers are.

Instagram

Instagram is hands down the best platform optimized for mobile devices with an even distribution of genders and a very active, highly visual community of young users.

Purpose: It is an excellent platform to share visual stories and generate quality interactions.

Reasons to be on Instagram

- Ideal for visually-striking brands
- Great indexing using targeted hashtags
- Delivers high interaction due to its visual format
- Ease of shareability of content to other social media platforms
- Endless opportunities to stand out due to constant innovations

Audience: Largely below 30 years of age

Things to keep in mind

Instagram is a treasure trove for content creators. With so many kinds of formats, from images to videos to going live and starting your own IGTV channel, it can help you manage the complete brand image. So, plan extensively and do not shy away from sharing less-than-perfect pictures.

On Instagram, authenticity drives traffic and business.

Pinterest

Pinterest is primarily a bookmarking platform that contributes massively to the "discovering stuff" part of social media. With the benefits it offers, its role in social media marketing has been colossally underrated and belittled.

Purpose: A search engine-like platform that serves inspiration rather than debatable hot topics

Reasons to be on Pinterest

- Converts browsers into buyers
- Contributes heavily to website traffic and SEO through inbound links
- Potential to be found organically
- Has an incredible brand support
- Integrates well with your other social media channels

Audience: 250 million users, all age groups

Things to keep in mind

There are many things to keep in mind to do well on Pinterest. We'll discuss them later in this book. However, be there because once it takes off, your business is going to get loads of hits and traffic each day. Make a huge effort once and it will sustain forever itself. It is an investment!

Twitter

Twitter is known for a consistent flow of information. There is always someone commenting on something or reporting something. This means that engagement is higher, and the audience will see you more often even as you share only a few bits of information.

Purpose: Showing quick updates, breaking news, etc. to deliver prompt reactions

Reasons to be on Twitter

- Great indexing using targeted hashtags
- Enables quick tracking of information
- Generate a dialogue between real people in real-time, thus, propelling brand loyalty
- Allows increasing website traffic

Audience: Young, 18 to 39-year-old

Things to keep in mind

Many brands use Twitter as their query redressal platform. Existence and care are the two pillars of any brand's presence on Twitter. It can help you strengthen your positioning through real-time interaction with followers. You can build long-lasting relationships with them, personalize your interactions with them, and create an identity of a brand that listens to its customers and cares for them.

Chapter 3: Crafting a Winning Strategy

Making social media work for you

Currently, countless articles and blogs are floating around the internet sharing all kinds of information on how you can leverage social media for your business. Unfortunately, most of them either have outdated advice or state strategies that are yet to be verified for their efficacy. What you need are strategies that help you grow rapidly with no time to waste in testing.

The easiest way to flop your marketing plans is to social media without having a sound understanding of your business, your audience, and your strategy to reach and engage with them. So, look at the big brands that are doing well. Evaluate what they are doing and how it is working out for them. Also, look at the brands or businesses that are a bit ahead of you. Understand what they are doing and how well it is working out for them. Find the areas of intersection, and those are the things that are most likely going to benefit your business.

As a marketer, you must have an objective, a product or service, a specific audience for them, and a reason to promote. If you think you have already figured it out, then cross-check that with the pointers shared here as creating a winning strategy is probably the hardest part of social media marketing and many marketers get it wrong.

The 11 sacred steps to formulating a winning social media strategy are:

Step 1: Study all platforms to create your social media mix.

Step 2: Understand your brand

Step 3: Research on your competition

Step 4: Know your target audience

Step 5: Define your social media objectives

Step 6: List the actionable KPIs

Step 7: Create an optimized profile and pages

Step 8: Plan your content calendar

Step 9: Publish your content with the right calls-to-action

Step 10: Track, Evaluate, Tweak

Step 11: Trend watching, Social media listening, and Customer Relationship Management

Step 1: Study All Platforms to Create Your Social Media Mix

While we have already discussed briefly all social media platforms, this table will help you understand more about the audience that hangs out there:

	Facebook	Instagram	Pinterest	Twitter
Number of users	2 billion	800 million	100 million	350 million
Suitable for	B2B, B2C	B2C	B2C, B2B	B2B, B2C
Demographic mix	56% males, 44% females	26% males, 74% females	30% males, 70% females	50% males, 50% females
Popular in	Urban and rural population	Urban population	Urban and rural population	Urban population

Once you have shortlisted your platforms, it is time to understand how their algorithms work so that you can tailor your content creation and publishing strategy.
Algorithms are the mathematical formulas that the platform uses to understand what a certain may appreciate in her feed and deliver her exactly that. If the formula says that a certain user does not like the kind of content you are publishing, it is less likely to show it to her. So, do not take them casually if you plan on relying only on organic means of dissemination.

Let us take Facebook's Edge Rank for instance. It uses the following three parameters to circulate organic publications:

- **Affinity:** the likelihood of users interacting with your content based on how they consumed it in the past
- **Performance:** the number of engagement (likes, shares, comments, reactions, etc.) your publication generally receives
- **Type of content:** text, image, video

Step 2: Understand Your Brand

- What is your brand?
- What does it stand for?
- Do you have a mission statement?
- What are your beliefs as a business?
- What is your tone-of-voice?
- What do you think?

These are some of the questions you need to answer yourself because your customers are going to wonder those too. So, when they do not give a damn about what you do, you'll know where you went wrong. Let us get back to the basics – Your customers want to associate; they want to belong, and they want to feel that your brand is reciprocating the same.

Answering the above questions will humanize your brand and give you a feel of who it is for the customers.

Finding your business's mission

If you have been keen on the internet, you should have noticed that almost all businesses have mission statements. Why are these mission statements significant?

A mission statement is a statement that helps a company to remain focused on its goals. Your mission statement will, therefore, keep your head focused on the marketing goal that you have on social media.

Besides the social media strategy that you have in mind, having a mission statement is vital. Yes, you have all those goals on how you will increase your audience by a certain percentage or how you would boost your engagement. But you also need to have a target.

"An archer will never shoot blindly without having a goal to aim" – The main idea here is that you need to have a sense of direction.

Don't fall into the trap where most business owners waste their time and money on social media just because it is a cheaper form of marketing. Cheap is expensive. You should have known that by know. Make use of social media as a marketing tool because you understand that it is an essential tool for achieving your business goals. So, a mission statement will act as a roadmap to guaranteeing that your social media use is a success.

Your mission statement should answer the specific results that you want or anticipate for your business now that you plan to use social media as a marketing tool. Also, an appropriate mission statement should detail where you will be focusing your efforts on the marketing campaign. And most of all, it should outline the primary reason as to why you opted to use social media as an ideal choice for your marketing demands.

Now, while content matters, the presentation is also vital. To inform them about your business, you cannot go ahead with a business pitch. You need to walk up to them like a peer, who is knowledgeable and can offer some valuable things, but most of it, this person (your brand) is their friend. So, this friend will have to know the audience's language, tone-of-voice, their general lingo, and will be relatable. Before this person can claim authority on the subject matter, he must be believable and trustworthy.

Defining your brand's beliefs

The belief that you have about your brand would form the perception that you would be creating in the minds of your prospects. What do you want them to perceive your company or business? Do you want them to think that you are a friendly company? Alternatively, you might want your audience to believe that you are a valuable company. All these ideas define your brand's beliefs.

Research tells us that consumers on social media pages are often after honesty from a business. It is worth noting that most consumers dislike snarky attitudes from businesses. The point here is that it is worth understanding the tone that matches your business' beliefs. The tone that you are using to communicate to your audience over social media should run parallel to the beliefs that your business advocates for.

The advantage of maintaining and reinforcing your brand's beliefs in your communication attributes is that it creates some ross a snarky attitude in your conversation, they would question themselves whether they are interacting with the right brand. Recognizable actions such as these define you. It helps you in creating a unique social identity among your audiences. Undeniably, it is one of the winning ways to distinguish yourself from the competition in the industry.

Finding the right brand voice

Every content creator in the world has a distinct voice. They have a unique way of saying things and putting things in perspective. If you find your competitors saying the same thing in the same way, they are just lost in a big sea and the chances of a customer switching from their business to another are enormous. So, do not follow suit. Do not be a faceless business. Stand out with your distinct voice. Have a face, a voice, a style that the audience finds interesting and gets attracted to.

- **Start by creating a word cloud:** Jot down the words you would use to describe your business. Now, add the words that others would use.
- **Categorize:** Divide the words into two sections – rational and emotional. The rational words will be like best, free-of-cost service, 24-hour delivery, etc. The emotional will be professional, smart, friendly, etc.
- **Write:** Get down to putting these words into speech. Use the rational elements (24-hour delivery) as your business proposition, but in a way that the result comes across as a friend proposing. So, it will sound something like this – We'll get it done within 24 hours. So, put your legs up and enjoy your favorite show.

At first, you will struggle a bit to come up with the right words. You might even want to try to be everything for your customers. Do not do that. Know your limitations as a business. As a friend, you can anytime guide your customer to some other business if you can't help them in some way. This is what friends do – they try their best to help their friend; but if they can't for any reason, they find the next best person to resolve the issue and introduce their friend to him.

If you can't come up with all the right words, begin with what you have. A brand voice evolves with time and that will sharpen naturally. Forcing it will make you sound desperate and fake, and you run the risk of losing their trust. So, take your time and let your customers also have time to get accustomed to your voice.

The example we shared above (We'll get it done within 24 hours. So, put your legs up and enjoy your favorite show.) also has a lot to do with the tone-of-voice. Do you want to sound like an expert? Or an authority? Like a friendly neighbor? Or an experienced veteran? Let us try to understand what tones work and why you should go for one.

Finding the right tone-of-voice

Informal: Many people stay away from someone who comes across as friendly right off the bat. Why? Because our minds are conditioned to be wary of them as they might have some vested interests. So, it is not a good idea, to begin with, a casual tone. Adopt it over time. As the customers get more and more familiar with you, they will welcome the move and appreciate the tone more. However, do maintain your authority simultaneously. Being over-zealous will harm your business and make you seem laid back and callous. An informal tone is great for connecting but not that great for selling your services. A good mix of both is what you should go for.

Promotional: While you are going to use social media to market your products, saying that right in the face of the customer is not the best approach. Nobody likes that person who arrives at the party and talks about himself or starts peddling his business. Advertise your business, but only when you have established a good connection and trust. Presentation plays a huge role in promotion. If you make your offer graphically captivating, the customers are bound to notice it. Like we said before, keep a healthy mix of friendly and promotional messages and deliver them wrapped beautifully.

Formal: Most businesses begin with a formal tone-of-voice and they are bang on right for doing so. Your first introductions are formal, professional, and to-the-point. A formal tone conveys that you are there to do business and you know what you are doing. It suggests your authority on the subject matter and draws those interested in your proposition. Embrace this tone for a few starting weeks and slowly shift gears to casual and a bit of promotional.

Step 3: Research on Your Competition

You might have made a wild guess on what you should be doing here. Concerning content, your rivals can be a great source of inspiration. Hence, instead of being jealous of their performance, you can use them to gain inspiration on the right content that will entice your audience. What are they posting? If you are dealing with the same products, you might want to ask - which group of clients is they focusing on? The most vital question is of course whether they are making conversions.

Often, we have come across the phrase "learn from the best." Truly, the last thing that you should be doing is paying attention to competitors that are not in your league. Try to emulate the big players in the market. I mean, that is where you want to be, right? Thus, find out what they are doing, and you will fill up the gaps in your social media content strategy.

In as much as you wish to stand out in your market, watching your competitor's actions is crucial. This is not to copy their strategy but learn from it and understand how you can differentiate.

There are numerous tools and strategies to do that. Here is a list of how you can go about it:

- Begin with Google search
- Put tools to good use. Try Google Alerts, Google Trends, and Spy Fu.
- Subscribe to reports. Industry trends will be quickly picked up by the researchers and they will predict what is going to happen by seeing what is currently happening. Armed with that knowledge, you can pre-empt a war on your competition and win.
- Ask your customers and your suppliers. They will not surrender to the information readily. So, offer incentives and anticipate your competitor's moves. Use the information to formulate your social media strategy and create counter moves.
- Check out their social media and try to get a grasp on what they are doing and how they are doing it. Study it closely to see if people are liking what they are sharing.
- Get into conversations at informal places, like forums. It is in these places where you'll get to understand what your customers want and how satisfied or dissatisfied are, they with your competitor's services.

This knowledge is valuable to your business as you'll know what your competitor's strengths and weaknesses are and how you can use them to your advantage. We know this is a lot of business and marketing stuff and a book on social media should just focus on social media. However, in the current times when people spend 80% of their free time on social media, merely having a page there wouldn't cut. You need to be in your best form because social media is the new-age battleground.

Step 4: Know Your Target Audience

- Do you sell to businesses (B2B) or individuals (B2C)?
- Are your services confined to a geographic area?
- Do you cater to an extremely specific set of needs (niche)?

Answering such questions for your business is essential to know who you are selling to. This will help you fine-tune your social media marketing strategy by creating an audience persona.

Defining the audience persona

Your audience can not be everyone. Even if you sell soap, you won't be selling to the entire world, all income groups may not find your soap as per their liking, and it may be more suitable for someone working in a job than those employed in others.

An audience persona tells who your ideal customer is, where he lives, what he thinks, how he behaves, how he reacts, and where he works, etc. So, to create your audience persona, think of the following:

- His age
- His sex
- His job
- Where he/she lives
- His interests
- His lifestyle
- Her personality

This description will humanize your customers. They are not some zombies with pockets full of cash who will die without your product. This exercise will paint a clear picture of your customers' needs and expectations making it easier for you to adapt your voice, your strategy, and help you create content that truly engages them. After all, you do want to reach your business objectives fast. This is just a bit of groundwork you need to do before starting strong.

Step 5: Define Your Social Media Objectives

After doing some in-depth research and learning from your competitors, the next thing to do would be to set goals that suit your specific type of business.

As a businessperson, you know that social media is merely a channel of promotion. It is not your goal, because if it is and you are doing it just for the sake of it, you should not be doing it at all. Therefore, think about what business goals social media can make more achievable and how.

- What business goals can social media help with?
- Will it be as effective in the short term as it will be in the long term?
- What are your strategic goals?
- Do you want to be discovered by those who haven't yet checked out your business?
- Do you want to inspire people to have business with you?
- Do you want to build your brand?
- Do you want to sell more and get leads?
- Do you want to remain at the top of the mind of your customers?
- Do you want to manage your reputation and attend to your customers' queries in a quick and better way?

A big mistake that most business owners make is copying everything that they see their rivals do. Do this, and you will fail terribly. The goals that you will set here are content-performance goals. It is worth noting that your content goal should be related to your social media marketing objective. If your Facebook objective is to increase the reach, the parallel content goal would be to increase the number of shares over a certain period.

It is likely that when you arrive at social media, your customers will associate with you there at completely distinct stages of their buying journey:

- Awareness
- Exploration
- Interest
- Conversion
- Loyalty

Regardless of where your customers discover you, you can use social media to reach your goals. For awareness, you can advertise; for convincing them, you can use hashtags, share videos that break through their apprehensions; for generating more sales, you can use social media store options and convert them right there on social media; and to build a loyal following, you can offer after-sales support, remarket them, ask for reviews and recommendations, and run a referral program as well.

It is important to make your goals quantifiable if you wish to attain them. Unless they become measurable, you will not be able to know how far long have gone or if you are going in the right direction.

Goals that are quantifiable become your Key Performance Indicators or KPIs. Once you know what value they were at in the beginning and how have they changed during your publishing and marketing, you can understand where your tactics are going. These KPIs will tell you if you need to tweak your efforts a bit and where. They include:

1. Scope
2. Traffic
3. Interest
4. Channel growth
5. Vanity metrics

Scope

The scope is called by different names such as reach and impressions. It indicates the number of users your post has reached. However, these users may or may not have interacted with it in any way.

Traffic

A particularly significant role that your social channels will play in your marketing funnel is the acquisition of leads and guiding them to the desired landing pages and websites. This is the traffic in question and if your social media is not bringing you any traffic, then there is something wrong with your approach.

Interest

Interaction or engagement is another term for interest. This metric will tell you exactly how many people have interacted with your post. This interaction can be in the form of likes, comments, shares, views, etc. If they are growing organically, you are thriving with an attractive strategy!

Channel Growth

The more people following your profiles, the more your reach will be. That is true. However, sometimes this number is deceptive. You may have thousands of followers, but only a handful of them are interacting with your content. This means that most people do not like what you are posting or are just bored with it. So, once you achieve your desired fan base, stop focusing on this.

Vanity Metrics

Now that we are talking about things that do not matter overall, we should also talk about vanity metrics. These are those numbers that are there for the sake of your happiness. Their presence does not make you feel guilty. So, no one left a comment, but you got 5000 likes? Congrats! In times when liking a post is another way of acknowledging, "Like" becomes a vanity metrics – It is good to have, but it does not add any real value to your insights! Therefore, take them into account, but do not waste your time and resources mulling over them as they will not help any of your future decisions.

Performance indicators of organic growth:

- Size of your community
- Scope of your publications
- Commitment (like share, comment)
- Clicks

- Messages or calls

Performance indicators of your paid advertising:

- Click-through rate
- Conversion rate
- Cost per commitment (like share, comment)
- Cost per click
- Cost per call

Step 7: Create Optimised Profile and Pages

Just like Google, social media platforms also favor businesses that have optimized profiles. This means that if you want better visibility, you must set up a profile that is well worth the attention. Below are a few tweaks you could begin with:

- Pick the right niche
- Choose a username
- Use a recognizable logo or brand photo

As soon as you sign up for a page, the first prompt is the niche. Are you a business or a service? Are you an artist or a writer? Are you a magazine or a blog? At times, it is straightforward, but sometimes when you have different plans of expansion, it gets tricky. Do not panic. Just pick that you are currently. You can change your niche later or create a new page for that.

Next comes, choosing a username and name for the page. Here, most people go with the name of the business. That was easy. However, if you have a difficult name, a unique spelling, or an exceedingly small name in a foreign language, remembering it would be difficult for your audience. So, pick something easy to remember and tag. These brand mentions will go a long way. Pick username wisely.

These profiles that you are creating on social platforms are like your storefront. You would want it to look presentable and leave a positive impression on the visitors.

You must always approach the topic of your profiles and pages with this intention of making the best first impression possible. This way, you are looking at them with the perspective required to ensure that they are sending the right message and encouraging people to follow you, trust you, and buy from you, rather than driving people away or leaving them confused or uncertain.

Every single social media platform has similar features in what is available for you to customize on your profile. Typically, you can brand your profile pictures, header images, a tagline, your username, and your wall or your feed. These areas can be branded to leave an extremely specific impression of what your business stands for so that people know as soon as they look at your profile who you are and what they can expect.

In the past, it was enough to write a basic tagline and use images that showed your logo and a professional headshot of you, depending on what your industry was. These days, this type of generic approach is not enough to capture the attention of people and leave them thinking about you and your services over anyone else. Instead, you need to do something that sets you apart and caters directly to your niche, so they see you, remember you, and willingly come back for more. This is where knowing your niche is useful: you know what type of customizations and features they would appreciate. This way you can brand and customize your profile accordingly.

For example, if you are a realtor who focuses on the niche of first time home buyers that are also families with children, you might make your profile picture a professional headshot where you are standing in front of a nice home that is in a family-friendly neighborhood. You may also have evidence of children in the background, such as a nearby park or playground, or some children's toys in the front yard of the home.

Getting the right energy into your pictures, as well as your description, username, and captions are crucial to set yourself apart from other people in your industry.

Step 8: Plan Your Content Calendar

Once the algorithm is mastered, you are ready to feed your pages strategically. Now, the important thing to understand here is that while the goal of social media is to promote your business and talk about yourself, doing do will produce disappointing results. Put yourself in your customer's shoes and think about what she would want to hear from you.

Creating Your Social Media Content Calendar

If you already have an editorial calendar for your blog, you are already one step ahead. Although, the editorial calendar for social networks is a bit different since it includes several types of content. That is possible with a good editorial calendar.

1. Choose the format that works for you
2. That's right, this is one of the most important steps. Whether by payroll or in a notebook, you need to do what is going to serve you and make it scalable according to the growth of your strategy. Be it through a calendar downloaded from the internet or an Excel spreadsheet Document everything you do!
3. Think of yourself again
4. There is not how everything on social networks is related to you. After all, it is the reason for everything you are doing. And now you need to have a redoubled attention with your habits within social networks. What time is it most present in your networks? How often do you check your networks? All this will guide your days and hours of publication, essential elements of your calendar.
5. Use your creativity
6. Have you seen any social media agency that did not have creativity as a requirement? And that is true: whoever works in the area must succeed and know how to face any situation, and the editorial calendar is one of them. Create interesting content for your person in addition to what your blog offers, create small content videos and advice on your profile. One way to diversify your post is through small infographics that give a preview of what the text will show. But only enough to arouse the curiosity of our readers.

Coming up with Content themes

If you have already started to manage your strategy, you can have difficulties in knowing what kind of content to produce specifically for your social networks. In the end, what does your person like to talk about and read about? A map of themes will guide you in the production of content and will help you understand what issues your audience wants to see in your networks.

1. Make a healthy mix of trending and evergreen content
2. Focus on relevance to your business and your customer
3. Talk about the industry and current affairs
4. Inject the special days and observances gently wherever appropriate
5. Occasionally, give your audience something worth sticking around for

A word of advice

Do not compromise on the quality of the graphics you are sharing. They show your commitment to quality, attention to detail and professionalism. You wouldn't want to come across as someone who doesn't care for what is shipped to its customers, right? So, invest in good graphics that your customers feel proud of while sharing.

When in doubt, return to this check-list:

Create quality content

Talk about what interests your persona

Generate conversations

Bet on a superior graphics quality

Adapt your content to each platform

Use engaging formats

Put yourself in ephemeral content

Enjoy user-generated content

Adopt good dissemination practices

Plan your publications

Publish at the right time

Use advertising

Optimize your publications for conversion

Use influencers

Encourage making contact

Content and social networks

If you have a content marketing strategy, you also already invest in social networks. In the end, they are essential for the propagation of your content. But coherently aligning both strategies calls for planning and consistency. Thinking about digital marketing strategies, your blog must adopt good practices to be shared on social networks.

Here are some of them:

- Produce specific images of your blog posts with your keyword in the creation, this helps your readers to immediately understand what they can expect when clicking on social networks.
- Update the title of your publication on social networks, always thinking about how to get attention to make your post more interesting.

- Plan an attractive description that will appear as a description of your post, this serves to prepare the reader for the content.

Besides, it is interesting to think about publications that will perform well on social networks, such as lists, news, texts on some subject of much debate in the media, quizzes, and infographics.

You may ask yourself: Shouldn't I just share the content I produce for my website?

Despite being an important part of your strategy, this is not the only thing that should matter to you. In a hypothetical scenario, in which your blog produces 3 weekly texts, what would you do with your social network the other days of the week? Would you leave them without any publication? Probably not, so you need to think a lot about how to manage your content strategically.

Step 9: Publish Content with The Right Calls-To-Action

The moment of publishing the content is as important as planning. It is the moment where important decisions are made. In addition to ensuring that everything goes in order such as the publication schedule, correct links, and other details, it is time to create calls-to-action or CTAs.

Call-to-action

Calls to action help in conversion, be it a micro-conversion like a comment or a macro-conversion like a sale. It is the goal of your entire being on social media. If your goal is for a user to access a link, your conversion will be that of a user on the social network for a visitor to your website.

It is wrong who believes that social networks exist only to give visibility to a company. Increasingly we see what we call social selling gaining strength. It works to manage the relationship with your consumers resulting in sales.

Increasingly there is the opportunity for users to advance in the process through the sales funnel through the social networks themselves. Whether it is to share an enriched material, to enroll in

webinars or even by hand-raised, that is someone who wants to contact a consultant.

All this must be taken into consideration for the construction of a call to effective action and that will help you to perform one of the main functions of social networks, the acquisition of opportunities.

Publishing schedule

A bit of known advice in the world of social networks is that of 3x3x3, this says that you must republish your content 3 times, on three separate times and days and with 3 different cells. That is important because it guarantees that more people have access to your content, as they will be linked at times that normally reach different audiences.

Constancy is more important than the frequency as well? Quiet, it seems confusing, but it is not. What we want to tell you is to keep a pattern in your calendar. If you usually publish 5 times a week do not change sharply to 10 times.

Although your audience has become accustomed to a minimum of publications and you want to increase your results, you need to be cautious to do so.

Using tools

With Buffer, you will save time managing social networks for your business. It also makes it easier for you to schedule posts analyze performance and manage all your accounts. So, you can schedule publications on social networks considering the time where your potential customers connect more often to social networks. So, the success of reaching your customers will increase dramatically. Therefore, once the publication calendar you have set up is established, the rest will be automatically happening.

CoSchedule is another great tool that can be integrated right in your blog's dashboard and will also take care of your social media publishing.

Step 10: Track, Evaluate, Tweak

Your work does not end with publishing and pushing the content out to your audience. You need to make sure that it is working for them. If it is not working, meaning that it is not moving your KPIs, then you need to assess what is going on and why your content may not be performing.

After that, you need to go back to your whiteboard and tweak your strategy based on your learnings.

Social media networks need to move with the world. Just as the world around them is constantly evolving, your strategy needs to follow suit too.

Therefore, have the flexibility to change a schedule publication if a story arises, or even cancel a content that may suddenly involve a controversy. This is necessary and is very rigid with your calendar is not going to take you anywhere but have discipline with it.

Step 11: Trend Watching, Social Media Listening, and CRM

If you want to stay on top of your game, these are the three vital activities that you must perform religiously.

Trend Watching

Keeping an eye on trends allows you to serve your audience with fresh content and keeps you relevant. As soon as a story is out, you can produce content around it and tap into the outspoken audience. Who knows, you might start trending organically!

You can use tools like Google Alerts, to begin with. Later, you can advance with paid tools.

Social Media Listening

You must know what your customer is talking about – that is called social media listening. Just like other forms of conversation, listening is vital to the success of marketing over social media. Where do you start to listen? You might say that you should listen to your customers first. Well, we disagree.

You must begin by listening to yourself. Take time to listen to what you are telling your audience about the products and services that you offer them. What have you promised your audience regarding your brand? But most importantly, ask yourself which audience are you talking to? Which channels are you utilizing (Facebook, Twitter, or Instagram?) Are you using the right tone?

After that, listen to your target market over social media. What are they looking for? What are they saying about your brand? While doing this listening, you should not forget to listen to your rivals. Listening to them helps in evaluating the competition that is directed to your brand.

You must be wondering how best you can engage in social listening. Here is how. Find social mentions directed to your brand. While doing this, you should identify common terms associated with your brand. Maybe people are saying that your brand is the best. Others could be saying that your brand is out of this world. Social mentions will help you understand your clients and how they relate to your brand.

A recommended practice when engaging in social listening is to react. Do not just sit there and watch as your clients talk about your brand; you must react. Think of social media listening as a vehicle that you are driving to get to your most-esteemed clients. Yes, it is possible to use it to get to your last stop faster. However, you are the one to steer the wheel. Hence, the best way to listen is not just to listen but to also react. Respond to the mentions and make appropriate comments where necessary.

Active listening also requires that you establish the rush hour. Find out the most active times when your audience is engaged on social media. Doing this warrants that you are always on time to listen to them.

Your customers expect that you carefully listen to them. Never be quick to assume the issues and negative comments coming from your audience. Respond to them accordingly to develop a trustworthy brand in their eyes. By knowing what is that thing your customer is engaged with, you can gain an edge over your competitors. If they are slacking, you can just dive right in and offer them a better service and those customers will be yours.

This also means you will be the first one to know when they complain about your business. You can then again jump in the conversations and salvage the situation much before it gets worse.

There are plenty of tools for this such as Meltwater, Keyhole, Twitter Counter, Hootsuite, Digimind, Klout, Zoho Social, Simply Measured, Buffer, etc.

Customer Relationship Management

This is part of the after-sales support and does not end at just taking the feedback of whether they liked it or not. CRM also means staying in touch with them, getting regular updates, offering valuable advice whenever required, and turning them into your advocates.

The cost of acquiring a new customer is four times of maintaining an existing customer. There is also an established trust between the two parties, so the transaction becomes easier.

BuzzstreamCRM is a great tool for this purpose. It is a Social CRM with double functionality: the construction of links and the management of communication in social networks. Its utility is to automate and monitor tasks that should otherwise be performed manually.

1. Research people who are Trending automatically. You can discover contact information, social profiles and site metrics for you. It is easy to prioritize the most important and influential contacts.
2. Keep a record of all your conversations. BuzzStream automatically saves your emails and tweets. This allows you to set reminders for tracking. You will never lose track of a conversation or project.
3. This tool generates a centralized database that will help you to work. You will be able to know useful data for your promotional campaigns and link locations through fully customizable reports. Invest your time in creating more links since with the help of BuzzStream you will investigate prospectus, monitor links and help you to have a great reach.

With all the information on social media monitoring and listening, it is worth questioning why this activity is of great importance to your business. One of the main benefits of social monitoring and listening is, of course, the gathering of information.

Listening is undeniably a good way of enhancing your business. In line with monitoring, it involves the process of monitoring conversations that touch on your brand. However, today data is quite overloaded over the internet. It makes it even harder to find out everything about your brand.

Luckily enough, there are monitoring tools that make it easy to know when one mentions your brand. Therefore, monitoring and listening tools help in gathering essential information about a particular brand.

Monitoring and listening on social media also ensure that consumer engagement is enhanced over time. How is this possible? When a business owner goes through their mentions over social media platforms, they discover ideal ways of dealing with their audience from a personal level. For example, business owners would have an opportunity of reacting to client's issues. This gives followers a positive image of the brand. Customers would gain the perception that the business truly cares about their needs and preferences. Eventually, consumer engagement is significantly improved over time.

The constant changes in the competitive business environment that we live in makes it challenging to adjust and counter competition. Luckily, technology has made it possible to find time to work on certain things such as product development. With the help of monitoring and listening tools, for example, business owners get extra time to design and implement to design and implement improvements to their brands.

In the end, a brand is continuously developed to match the needs and expectations of clients. All these would not have been possible without the help of social media monitoring and listening tools. In essence, numerous benefits can be obtained through social media monitoring and listening. Nonetheless, the main advantages of social media monitoring and listening include:

- Gaining access to an unlimited number of conversations
- Comprehensive data analysis
- Prevents social media crises
- Enhancing client relationships
- Genuine feedback from the audience
- Realizing new sales prospects
- Effective control over online brand perception
- Learning and adapting to improvement trends

-

Tips to Expand Reach

Whether you have a small or large business, extending your reach helps tap into more potential customers and grow your business further.

1. Host events

Take your business offline. Meet your customers face-to-face. Interact with them in the real world. These events can be transactional or just a fun evening where a few customers can get to know the business better.

1. Reward your customers

You can also host contests and do engagement activities online that reward your loyal customers. It can also be a referral where both parties get a certain discount.

1. Stay consistent

Whatever you do, staying disciplined and consistent with it is important. That way, the customers know that they can expect certain things from you. This goes a long way in building trust for your business as your audience will feel that they can count on you and this will eventually lead to trust in transactions.

1. Humanize your business

It is great that you are producing high-quality graphics. However, occasionally, let your customers in on the behind-the-scenes action. Use stories, for example, to share such things that may be crafted instantly, but they lend your business the authenticity. It is at these times customers will get to see the real you that has certain imperfections.

1. Get conversational

It is extremely important to talk to your audience. Host a Live AMA session or encourage them to drop in their comments and questions which you can answer later.

Chapter 4: Facebook

Facebook is one of the longest standing platforms out there. It came over in 2004 and is still growing in quality. Over the years, it pivoted to serve both the personal connections as well as business connections. This widened the used of this platform and today, it is considered essential for promoting your business.

These days, Facebook offers several glorious options for people that are desperate to promote their business online. To diversify its platform and create opportunities for businesses and individuals, Facebook has introduced options like business pages, advertising formats, Facebook stores, and groups.

Who Should Use Facebook, and Why?

When it comes to getting your business online, everyone needs to be on Facebook in one way or another. Because of this platform's design and its reputation, everyone can benefit from being present on Facebook.

Do not be surprised by how people have moved on from searching business on Google to searching on Facebook or Instagram. They are not the new-age search engines. It is just that people are now increasingly interested in the personality of the business and the image it has established for itself. Finding you on a social media platform gives your followers a greater opportunity to not only find basic information about your business, but also more personalized information about your business. More importantly, they are going to identify whether or not you are reliable, especially if they are a part of your target audience.

Having your own Facebook page will ensure that whenever anyone visits Facebook to look you up, they can find you. This also means that you need to maintain your page in a certain way. You need to give them something worth their while to look at and form an opinion about you instantly.

Even if you want to have Facebook as a landing page, you should post at least once a week so that it appears updated and has enough content to impress your audience. This will also save you from creating an image of an inactive or inconsistent brand which could lead to a lack of trust and loss of interest.

When using Facebook as a landing page, you can direct your audience to the platforms you are more active on. This way, you increase the chances of getting more sales while focusing your energy on 1-2 primary channels for communication.

Leveraging Facebook in Your Marketing Strategy

Using Facebook as a primary platform or a landing page is basic. There are so many features there that you can use to propel your business's success in 2020.

Fill out each single a part of your Facebook page with info concerning who you are, what your business is all concerning, what merchandise and services you must supply, and wherever you will be situated.

You can even sell your merchandise and services right there on Facebook or provide a booking feature so folks will book a service along with your company. The amount of options that are accessible on Facebook is large, thus, making it a wonderful platform for those who need to sell their merchandise.

As you learn to figure Facebook into your marketing strategy, your best chance is to show it either as a "hub" of where the audience can visit and transact. Or, you can turn this into a hub where people interact with your business in any approach that they want. You can take a call on the proportion of how interaction and transaction you would like to have on Facebook.

Marketing on Facebook in 2020

Is your goal in 2020 to come on top with your Facebook marketing strategy?

Then, you will have to go beyond the usual and basics. You must acquaint yourself with each part pf your Facebook page. The most effective way is to get yourself familiar with the various tabs and features so you know precisely what you can do to set your page up for success.

Customize the Template and Tabs

Facebook offers 10 template options: standard, video page, shopping, restaurants & cafes, services, politicians, nonprofit, venues, business, and movies. Choose the most relevant one for your business as this template will further show you the tabs accordingly.

Next, you customize your tabs as per your business needs. You may not require all the tabs offered in a certain template. So, remove the excess retaining only those which will have enough content for the audience to nibble on.

Make sure you give your customers the best navigation experience. Do not confuse them or make them look for information on different tabs. Everything must be straightforward and right in front of their eyes. With online searching, convenience and look is everything.

Once you tailor your tabs, return to the homepage and browse through the tabs like your audience would. Get a feel of the page and note if it was easy and intuitive enough to find what you were searching for. If you face difficulty, evaluate and tweak the flow in a way that makes it look enticing and feel useful.

Monetizing Your Facebook Page

Monetizing your Facebook comes from funneling individuals through your page to a sales page where they will purchase your product or services. The key to trying this on Facebook is by building a presence that garners engagement and creates loyalty.

Recently, Facebook decided to return to its roots of giving organic, authentic, pleasant relationship affiliation between friends, family, and people of a community. This has resulted in Facebook demoting posts where publishers ask (or incentivize) their followers to *like, comment or share* their posts with their community. In short, this is not an ideal way to get engagement as per Facebook.

So, try to boost engagement by being authentic and relevant to your niche. Share journal posts or articles that are relevant to your business. Upload videos or memes that make sense for your business as well as your audience. Build trust organically by focusing on truly share-worthy posts.

This way, your engagement will go up and your ad expenditure will go down. This multiplied exposure will pique people's interest in your business, which can end in you having a bigger probability of getting more eyeballs and leads.

You can additionally improve your chances of discovery by running ads. Straightforward pictures with a sentence or two which appear as a click-bait will no longer be effective. Instead, share things that reflect your page positively. Additionally, you can boost your top-performing posts.

There are a lot of articles on the internet with templates of high-performing ads and all you must do is copy and paste it in your advertisements. No matter how tempted you are to do that, stop yourself. Just draw inspiration from those articles, customize them for your business and its audience and use your creativity. The goal is to stand out and not get lost in the sea of me-too ads.

To use the search feature, add a store tab to your page. Now, visit the tab and write a custom description of what your search offers. From there, transfer your entire inventory of products, their descriptions, and costs into the Facebook search tab. When your audience arrives, they can view your products right there on Facebook and shop instantly.

The Future of Facebook

Ad space to spare

75% of people with access to Facebook use it regularly. This implies that it is worthwhile to invest your time in Facebook-based advertising and you can continue to do so even beyond 2020. Target an individual group or an entire market, Facebook has enough data to make both possible.

Bots

Bots are a recent trend that Facebook has adopted. It is increasingly allowing companies to create their bots. Bots are automated lines of code that can function within the Facebook Messenger app. They allow users to do various activities like finding out the weather and even buying things.

It is a straightforward interface, but they respond just like a normal person would. You feed it with a list of responses that guide the customers towards a certain direction. Therefore, you should not be surprised that unlike human handling such a conversation, these bot-led conversations rarely go off the topic.

More usage of video

While there is no denying that both watching and sharing video is extremely popular on Facebook. The site is currently working to ensure that this is an even larger part of the overall experience. In

fact, it is now possible to stream live video from any device, even a wide variety of drones.

Evolving algorithm

Facebook came up with facial recognition way before Snapchat did. Very soon, it will be able to tell what else is there in your pictures, much like Google Lens does. So, you will soon be able to perform general searches on Facebook regardless of the tags. This technology is based on the same deep-learning software that powers Google Photos which means this service might be coming to Facebook sooner rather than later.

Now imagine this happening in your videos – you can shop from there. This will skyrocket the entire influencer marketing space taking it to newer heights.

Facebook VR

Oculus Rift is owned by Facebook and that goes on to show how heavily invested it is in the virtual reality space. It also owns a portion of the Gear VR, developed by Samsung for smartphones.

VR was introduced in 2015, but it did not take off as expected. However, that should not discourage you from exploring this space. Mark Zuckerberg has already indicated that he pictures virtual reality to be something that people use to socialize with each other like never before. The Oculus group is already working on a wide variety of ways to help make socializing in a virtual space feel more realistic by using high-tech cameras to study the body language of an individual who is moving through a virtual space.

While you may not see people using Facebook to purchase items much now, the Facebook shop button is expected to see a widespread rollout in early 2020 so it will likely become far more common this year. As the name implies, this addition to the Facebook business page tab will allow users to sell a wide variety of items directly from the page which promises to make directing traffic to your wares a more straightforward experience than ever before.

This makes it even more important to have a good idea of not only what your homepage looks like but your collection page as well. Finding one instance of missing pictures or placeholder text is enough to ruin the brand message you are working so hard to cultivate. What is worse, you run the risk of missing potentially viable SEO optimization options.

It is also possible to integrate your Facebook shop with a variety of existing online stores including BigCommerce, WooCommerce, Magento and Shopify.

Chapter 5: Instagram

The pace with which Instagram has grown to become one of the most powerful marketing platforms, especially for small and mid-size businesses, is awe-inspiring.

Today, it offers some of the best features to create organic marketing posts for a B2C audience. With more than a billion monthly active users, it is a wonderful platform for those who want to grow their brand and create a strong presence online.

Having bought by Facebook in 2012, Instagram is like kin to Facebook that has beautiful integration features. You can leverage this connection to create a seamless journey for your customers and win them over.

Who Should Use Instagram, and Why?

Just like Facebook, Instagram does not discriminate based on who can use it and leverage it for success. Most modern influencers are using Instagram to connect with their audience. A huge contribution is the visual foundation of the platform which allows them to leverage graphic marketing strategies to forge deeper relationships, which in turn bolsters their productivity.

It is not necessary to be on Instagram, especially for B2B businesses. They can skip it. Nonetheless, it is an extremely valuable platform that can offer your business with an incredible advantage with its built-in visual marketing approach. Utilizing this, you can easily demonstrate how your products work to give your audience a visual idea of what they will receive, and even share insights on the diverse ways your products and services could be used. Instagram also offers opportunities to feature customer-generated content on your profile which again, boosts your visibility, increases brand recall and credibility, and allows your business to tap into a larger audience for free.

Instagram will prove to be the apt choice for businesses that operate primarily online, marketing to sales. This is because by not being on Instagram you are losing out on an ocean of opportunities to forge better connections with your audience and offer a seamless shopping experience. Just like Facebook, Instagram also has a booking, buying, and contact options that allow your audience to connect with you with just one click.

Leveraging Instagram in Your Marketing Strategy

Truth be told: Adding Instagram into your social media marketing strategy 2020 will bring a steep learning curve to your life. Thanks to the enormous number of features loaded on this platform. However, this also means infinite ways to customize your customer's experience and offer them more value.

When creating an Instagram marketing strategy, your primary goal should be to align these features in a way that together they give rise to a seamless experience. After all, you would not want to confuse your audience and make them leave because they could not understand how to reach you.

So, begin by jotting down what goals you want Instagram to render achievable for you. With your marketing goal in mind for Instagram, pause and consider what the best possible experience would be for your audience that would help them reach your goal. Then find the features that would help you get there. Now use them intuitively to guide your customers on the right path. For example, if you want more people to land on your website and learn about your company, you need to ensure that all your Instagram features driving people to your website. Alternatively, if you want people to land on your page and shop with your company, you are going to need to encourage people to browse through your posts.

Some of the best features that you can use on Instagram include:

- Instagram stories
- Story highlights
- IGTV (Instagram TV)
- Your URL
- Customizable buttons
- Free business account
- Social platform integration of other business pages
- Shopping directly from the images

Marketing on Instagram in 2020

Using Instagram's features as a part of your 2020 marketing strategy is a fantastic opportunity for you to grow your business, reach a larger audience, and make more money from your Instagram page.

It is important to note here that Instagram has features for everyone. This does not mean that all these features will work for you. Having too many features will increase your work and leave your customer bamboozled. Plenty of people are not using IGTV, stories, or shopping features and they are still enjoying remarkable success with their businesses online. So, use only those that make complete business sense to you and help make your customer's experience on your profile memorable and worthy of returning.

Instagram stories

Instagram stories can be leveraged to build suspense and make your customers feel like an exclusive part of your business. These days the strategy most people are using is transparency and authenticity, and Instagram stories make that possible.

Use them as if they are a small television series. They will stick around only for 24 hours unless they are saved to a highlight, which means that you can use them to share "programming" throughout the week with your audience. So, each day becomes an episode of a grand show that your business is keeping your audience engaged throughout.

You can have separate themes for each day, for instance, Making Monday, Technique Tuesday, Wise Wednesday, and so on. You can also turn them into hashtags and ask your audience to participate. Additionally, people can follow these hashtags and will find your feed organically when you are making your mini-episodes.

Story highlights

When it comes to making highlights of your stories, you can take your favorite clips of each of your daily episodes and upload them into your highlights. For example, say for #makeitmonday you take your favorite 1-2 clips each Monday and upload them into your #makeitmonday highlight reel. This way, people who are new to your page can catch a glimpse of your highlights from the past which helps them build a connection with your brand while feeling like they are getting exclusive insight into the best moments of your past.

IGTV

IGTV Instagram TV, or IGTV, works much like stories. This feature allows you to upload up to 10 minutes of the pre-recorded film to your Instagram profile, and unlike stories, they do not disappear after 24 hours so your followers can go back through your IGTV uploads and view your previous content. In a way, it works like a built-in YouTube experience, offering you your very own channel to feature your videos on.

When you are using IGTV as a part of your marketing strategy, the best way is to treat it like stories, except with longevity. Create videos that are 1-10 minutes long in a way that makes them interesting and enticing, and that follows some form of consistency.

You can even tie your IGTV in together with your stories marketing strategy by creating longer episodes on your IGTV and sharing the highlight reel of those in your story feed. Then, you can share the highlight reel of your story feed into your page's actual highlights.

Since IGTV requires more time and effort to make, it is ideal that you only pick one or two days per week that you are going to upload a fuller video onto your profile. Attempting to upload a new video every single day can get overwhelming quickly and may not be sustainable which can lead to you not being as consistent as you need to be to have success with your videos.

So, start modest and work your way up to grow your channel effectively.

Also, make videos that build interest in your products or services. Always make sure that you market your actual products or services in your videos so that when people for a reason, that reason earns you money.

Since people are already curious enough to watch the video, they are also going to be curious enough to view your products and services and potentially purchase them. Use that curiosity to your advantage in marketing to boost your sales, rather than wasting it by having them lose interest after your video leaves them with nothing to follow up on.

Customizable buttons

Converting your profile to a business profile will allow adding one customizable button to your page. This button will allow your audience a quick way to interact with your business, ideally leading to a booking or a sale.

The customization options include, "Reserve," "Book," "Email," or "Shop Now." You can choose the one most relevant to your business model and then follow the step-by-step process to configure that button for your business. This way, people can act immediately and that will get you more sales.

Shopping feature

This feature is particularly amazing for businesses. Although it is not brand new, it is new enough to be a strong part of your 2020 marketing strategy, especially if used effectively.

Steps to set up your Instagram shopping feature:

1. Link your Instagram business account to a Facebook business page. Make sure this Facebook business page has a "Shop" tab.
2. Upload your products to Facebook.
3. Tag them in your Instagram post using the pictures edit screen.

Now, your audience can tap on the images and the products will pop up. Tapping on them will take directly to the product page where they can purchase it.

If you are running a business where you are selling products online, especially if you are a smaller retailer such as a home business or someone who is selling on Etsy or Shopify, this is a great opportunity to increase your sales. It makes use of impulse buying as it offers a fast check-out experience without having to hustle through your store's link in bio and then scrolling until they find the product of their choice. And who knows if they get distracted in the process by something else? You might lose out on a purchase.

Monetizing Your Instagram Page

Having dealt with all your useful marketing features available on Instagram, now you need a strong funnel that guides your audience through the sales process to the final conversion stage.

The most crucial step in monetizing your Instagram page is creating posts that pique people's interests and leave them wanting to learn more. With infinite scroll, you need to make a post that is worthy of stopping by, tapping into your picture, and then viewing your profile to learn more about your business. Otherwise, people will scroll past you and will never actually discover you.

People want to see is something that is high quality, interesting, and soul-capturing. They want to feel like you have spoken to them from your heart and that everything about you and your brand is a work of art. Your products, images, and everything you write should all be a part of your artistic process as you cultivate your social media profile and she content with your audience.

This does not mean that you need to be some form of a professional artist to sell yourself on Instagram, but it does mean that you are willing to take down the mask and show parts of your real self to your audience. That is what today's audience is looking for — authentic connection!

The Future of Instagram

Vertical video

As soon as Instagram introduced vertical videos, platforms like Vimeo and YouTube also gave in and now the vertical format is here to stay. This means it is your time to learn to create such videos and edit them in a way that capitalizes on this trend.

Use apps like InShot or Stereo and add more production quality to the Instagram stories you make. There are a few choices when it comes to creating an acceptable vertical video, and you can trim down video shot horizontally.

There is not much science to shooting a vertical video. However, editing can be painful. If you have vertical video, and you can trim down video shot horizontally so it looks as though you were savvy enough to hop on this latest retro trend.

Instagram stories with AR Filters

Augmented reality and virtual reality are going to be the next grandiose thing on social media in 2020. Being new, everyone is curious about how it is used and what results it will deliver, even your audience is. Many filters often allow viewers to try out a filter that their friends are using which means that AR Filters on Instagram stories are created to go viral.

Getting in on these options and becoming comfortable with them as soon as possible is sure to pay dividends in the future. Not only are the face filters that Instagram offers a forward-thinking example of how AR can be used in traditional scenarios where you display the usage of your products. So, head over to Facebook's AR Studio, Spark AR, and create your very own unique variation for your brand. This is the best way to future-proof your brand.

Offline events viewed Life

While creating an offline experience can be a lot of work, it can be an excellent way to gain lots of followers quickly while also generating sales at the same time. In essence, it is word-of-mouth for today. For those who cannot be there physically, streaming your event Life can do the trick.

When a customer has a positive experience that is also worthy of an Instagram post then it is far more likely to end up on their page where all their friends can see and interact with it themselves.

Ads in Instagram Stories

Ads in Instagram stories have already taken the internet by the storm. Around 400 million people watch Instagram Stories each day which is ideal because it currently offers a far greater return on investment than a similar Facebook ad.

As this is still a young form of advertising, it is important to take as much advantage of it as you can before the price increases to accurately reflect its usefulness. This is the perfect time to try out a variety of different formats for your ads to ensure that your game is on point by the time even more people start paying attention.

Remember what people expect while tuning in to Instagram Stories – Casual content, nothing higher. This means that your ad aesthetically looks casual so that people tap and watch it, instead of swiping past it. Here, keep your keywords organic and remove filters from your videos.

Chapter 6: Pinterest

Unlike social media where users usually share about an experience, Pinterest is about the future. Most of its users pin the things they want to do, learn or achieve, and not something they have already done.

The platform is like a search engine like Google. The only difference is in the results it throws at you – they are graphics.

59% of Millennials have discovered products on Pinterest! This means Pinterest is on par with Instagram in terms of product discovery. 90% of weekly Pinterest users use the platform to plan a purchase. This means Pinterest boards are becoming are moving away from being a mood board to being a shopping list. For businesses, which is a piece of great news because they now have access to an audience that is waiting with their credit cards to make them buy.

You may ask: Planning a purchase is fine, but are people buying from Pinterest?

In a recent survey, 50% of Pinterest users affirmed to purchasing after finding a promoted pin. Moreover, 66% of users look at their saved pins while out shopping in brick-and-mortar businesses.

Pinterest drives 33% more referral traffic to shopping sites than Facebook and Twitter combined. Because this platform does not shove cat memes and other distractions in your face, people welcome the ads. Also, the unique placement of Pinterest ads makes them worth their while. Unlike Facebook, the ads do not compete with your entire News Feed; they show up only in the search results. This means that only when an interested user searches for it, will the ad show up.

Who Should Use Pinterest, and Why?

Pinterest is for everyone! Regardless of your business's niche or your profession, Pinterest is a valuable marketing tool for you. It is so versatile that it works for everyone. You can understand that by just looking at the variety of content that is pinned there - from podcasts to products, from décor ideas to crochet patterns, you can promote anything on Pinterest.

So, if you are wondering whether it is worth the effort or not, here are a few reasons why you should go for it:

1. It is free and does not ask for any subscriptions. So, it is free for your customers as well.
2. Pinterest for a Business profile is 100% free. You can turn your profile to your business profile with just a few clicks.
3. It is easy to monetize. You can run Pinterest ads.
4. The analytics are easy, free and transparent. You can get invaluable insight into the analytics behind your results such as impressions, click-through rates, pin performance, and monthly views.
5. It requires less content and less effort than its competitors.

6. Pins, although seasonal, have a long shelf life. This means you do not have to continue to create content for Pinterest. Some pins go viral even 6 months after they were first pinned!
7. It drives sustainable traffic to your prime web locations.
8. Like we mentioned before, Pinterest users shop at the platform; this means that it has an enormous potential to take off your sales.

Whether you are selling garden furniture or psychic readings, consider Pinterest your new marketplace. So, go get your website confirmed successfully.

Leveraging Pinterest in Your Marketing Strategy

To get started with Pinterest, you need to do the basic – Create Boards.

Create Boards

Think of your business and the many ways your products can be used. Based on that, create boards. Use your boards to tell the story of your brand from start to finish.

Be careful with the titles. For example, do not title your board "Dream Holiday" title it, "Singapore Travel Ideas." Instead of "delicious recipes", add keywords such as "Vegetarian Dinner Recipes." Give them a nice description by inserting the keywords which your target audience will be searching for. Also, make sure the descriptions sound natural and not forced. Select a relevant category.

Now, do not jump to making it public yet. Keep it secret until you have enough content on your board to share with your audience, which is at least 50 pins.

Rinse & Repeat

Now go on and create as many boards as you want. If you have a lot of content on one topic, make a separate board for it. Otherwise, keep it generic and make a more specific board whenever you have enough content.

Create a "Best of" Board

While your other boards will have and should have pins from all around the internet, this one board will be completely yours and will be dedicated only to your original pins. Think of it as your portfolio. Now, based on your other board categories, you can repin this board's contents to others. This will ensure that your original pins get as many shares as the other pins on the internet.

Rich Pins

As per Pinterest, "Rich Pins will pick more details from your website and add them to your pins". So, before you start pinning your content, enable rich pins to give them an extra boost in rankings.

This is a vital step that many people forget to do or do not know how to.

There are four types of Rich Pins:

1. Recipe: With rich pins enabled, info such as ingredients list, cooking time and nutritional info will be added to the pin.
2. Product: Additional info such as price, product description from your website & stock levels can be shared.
3. App Install: This will take users to the app store to download your app promoted in the pin.
4. Article: The headline, title, author and meta description of the post will be shared.
5.

To rank on top, you need to study those who are ranking on the top currently.

Begin by running a search on the keywords that best describe your business and based on which you are going to describe your boards and pins. Now, analyze the results on these four parameters:

- **Image:** Style of imagery, colors, photographs, etc.
- **Text:** Wording, phrasing, fonts, colors of the fonts, etc.
- **Description:** Keywords used, number of hashtags, which hashtags, calls-to-action (if any), etc.
- **Author:** Who created the pin? Are they an expert in this field? Are they a competitor, or could they be a potential collaborator?

Once you have gathered these insights, you can now use them to do better with your pins. think hard about what they are currently missing, what other hashtags you could use, what rich pins they have, and if you can use a more captivating image with a snappier headline.

- Can you offer a freebie?
- Can you say that you provide local services?
- Is there a way to show that you the more knowledgeable than your competitor?
- Are you an "insider" or a local expert?
- What makes your pain better? Is it quicker or cheaper?

SEO for Pinterest

Now that we are done with aesthetics, it is time for the juicy stuff. What is the point in creating beautiful, eye-catching pins if no one is going to find them? So, invest a bit of your time in optimizing your pins for Pinterest's search results. Welcome to SEO for Pinterest!

Unlike Google, Pinterest's algorithm is fair and simple. All you need to do is find the right keywords to be inserted in the boards' and pins' descriptions. Now, there are four ways to find those high-quality keywords:

1. The search bar

Enter your keyword in the search bar on Pinterest. A drop-down of more keywords relating to your original search will open. Note them down and use them wherever possible. If you click on one of such suggestions, even more, keywords related to your niche and audience will show up along with some colored boxes that help narrow down your search. All these are the keywords that will help you rank better.

1. Your social media marketing plan

Yes, that is where you will find your most effective keywords. Go back to the word cloud that you prepared for your business initially. Pick out the words from both the rational and emotional categories and use them in your descriptions.

1. From your competitors

After searching for your initial keyword, analyze the first 5 results. What keywords are they using on their pins? What keywords have they included in the pin descriptions? Note these down as it is these keywords that are helping them rise ranks and will help you too!

1. From your website

Here, open your Google Analytics and pick those keywords on which your website and products are already showing up. They will help your SEO even on Pinterest.

Making Your Pins Go Viral in 2020

The moment you optimize your pins for Pinterest's search, you will automatically witness a jump in your analytics. But who does not like their pins going viral and enjoying a little bit of confidence boost?

So, here are some steps for strategic pinning so you too can experience some viral pins.

Step 1: Use stock imagery

Not everyone is a professional photographer and although you may prefer to use your images, chances are that you can find better ones, for free, that will appeal to a wider audience.

Step 2: Use unique, emotive titles

There is a word limit on the description of the pin. So, maximize your efforts by using emotive words like "you need," "your dream" "you will love" etc. along with some facts and figures to make them more click-worthy.

Step 3: Tell Pinterest your pin is viral-worthy

Description, context, and quality are three parameters which tell Pinterest that a certain pin is viral-worthy. With keywords and enabling rich pins, your description is taken care of. For context, you need to pin your pin to a high-performing, high-quality board from the same niche. For quality, Pinterest runs a visual search on the image graphic and based on the scan, it groups it with other similar pins.

Together, the pin becomes high-quality and valuable for Pinterest users, so the SEO automatically favors it and the pin goes viral.

Step 4: Get Engagement - ASAP!

Engagement within the first 60 minutes is vital for Instagram and Facebook. It is the first hour where the algorithm decides if your post is going to make it or not. A series of likes, comments, and shares within the first 60 minutes of posting tells the platform that it is high-quality, and the platform further boosts it.

Pinterest works analogously. The only difference is that the duration is of a few days. So, push it as far as possible in the hope it will gain traction. Repins and comments tell the algorithm your pin is useful and enjoyed by your audience, so it will boost it in rankings.

1. Facebook Groups: This is one of the most popular but also the most time-consuming. All participants (usually 50-100+) in the thread repin everyone else's pin in that thread. This gives your pin the initial boost which tells Pinterest that it is a high-quality pin. Although this is a very time-consuming task, it has given desired results by maximizing your pin's initial exposure very quickly.
2. A "Collab post": Collaborate with other bloggers or businesses to create one post. Now, ask them all to repin the pin for that article. This shares the post with 25 more audiences than our original pin would have.
3. Your Newsletter: Send your brand-new pin in your newsletter. Ask your subscribers to pin the pin to read later or pin it for reference. Even if you have 1000 subscribers and only 50 save the pin, which is still 50 more audiences that will potentially see your content.
4. Embed the pin in a blog post: Above your pin, there is a pencil icon and an icon of 3 dots. Click the three dots, then "Embed" this will give you a code to paste onto your site for the pin to feature within in your blog post – allowing users to pin it from the post.
5. Time your pinning: If you publish at night before going to bed, no one is going to see it for another 6-7 hours and by the time they wake up, the pin will be buried in their feed. So, pin either on a holiday or during the morning commute when more followers are likely to be online. Use a scheduler if you cannot pin at those times.

Step 5: Use Group Boards

Group boards are like any other Pinterest board except more than one pinner can add to the board. Every group board has certain pinning rules. For instance, if you pin one of your pins, then you must repin 3 from that group board to your boards. This exchange allows everyone to win. However, recently group boards have turned into a dumping ground where people pin theirs but do not repin any other from the board.

Step 6: Pin Consistently

Pinterest likes pinners who show up and give as well as take and those who do so consistently. If you pop on once a month when you have a new product to launch and go on a mad pinning spree, you are not the Pinterest's type. So, check-in for 15 minutes each day and pin a handful of pins. Very soon, you will be rewarded for being an active user by getting an organic boost to your pins.

Also, being on a pinning spree may get you blocked as spam. So, avoid that habit.

Step 5: Timing is key

We have already touched on this; however, this special mention is for the trends. Head over to Pinterest's blog and insights to find what trends at what time of the year. Mark those days on your calendar and schedule that kind of pins in advance. For example, New Year Resolutions are best pinned in November, rather than in January.

Visit Pinterest and find the "Pinterest Planner" for your region and the year 2020. Create your calendar today and get ready to trend in 2020.

Step 6: Hit the numbers

Pinterest rewards you for pinning consistently and pinning lots of them. While we ask you to avoid going on a mad pinning spree, try pinning 25-30 pins a day. This does not mean that you must create that many pins daily. Pin 1-2 yours and make the rest of them as repins of other's pins.

Tailwind is a third-party scheduler that will not only find the times where your audience is most active but schedule your pins to only be posted at these times. Tailwind is one of the few third-party schedulers which are endorsed by Pinterest.

Product pins

Launched in 2015 as Buyable Pins, Product pins allow users to purchase things they found on Pinterest without leaving the platform. Usually, the social media platforms work to redirect the user to a separate landing page to complete the purchase. However, with Product pins on Pinterest, they can see the product's dynamic information, which means an updated price and inventory amount in real-time. So, if your product's price has changed due to a discount or if it is not in stock, the users will be able to see.

Now you can upload the entire catalog of your products and let the in-app sales flow in with this streamlined way.

Lens

Very much like Google Lens, Pinterest Lens is a visual search technology. It is a natural progression to the platform that was designed for visual inspiration and discovering of stuff.

Now, you don't need to type and hit *Search*. You can just click a photograph for your inspiration and get a curated list of products that match the one you just clicked. Imagine if your business has some high-quality pins of your products with rich pin enabled, and it shows up in a search – the user can directly purchase from the platform!

Taste Graph

A personalized curation tool that helps Pinterest serve its users with better recommendations of pins in their feed based on their previous searches and repins. The more they search; the more fine-tuned Pinterest's recommendations get for them. Taste Graph connects millions of users with billions of ideas that may further inspire them.

You may ask: How will this benefit my business?

Well, for starter, if your pins are what users want and have been searching for, they will show up in their feed organically. You can also target users based on their interests which are over a thousand currently, with more being added each week!

Businesses that have used Taste Graph for their ad targeting have witnessed a 50% jump in the click-through rate and cost efficiency of over 20%!

Pinterest ads

Pinterest came up with ads relatively very late when compared to other social media platforms. Even today, it shows ads only when a user searches for something. This is because it gives more importance to the experience of its current user base which is highly engaged and active. Pinterest does not want to hamper this experience or invade the user's privacy with the introduction of ads in their feeds.

We will have to see how this takes off in 2020. Nonetheless, if your pin has got potential, don't shy away from promoting it for the right set of keywords. Remember, this highly engaged audience is a more frequent buyer than those found on any of its peers!

Video ads

With the introduction of video ads, Pinterest has witnessed an increase in sales of direct-to-consumer businesses. These businesses previously relied on Instagram and Facebook but with moved to Pinterest as it offers a higher click-through rate and more conversions.

Chapter 7: Twitter

Twitter has been a highly controversial platform in the past, with many claiming that it is becoming "irrelevant" or that it is too challenging for smaller businesses to use. Some have even gone as far as to claim that Twitter is not ideal for certain industries discriminating against companies that have younger, older, or more eclectic audiences than the average company.

Who Should Use Twitter, and Why?

It is a common myth that was passed around for much of 2018-2019 is that Twitter is only beneficial if you are a politician or a white-collar businessperson. Many believed that its sole focuses were stocks, politics business, and relevant news articles. Believe it or not: none of this is true and knowing this may just make Twitter your best tool for growth in 2020.

Twitter has been proven to be one of the most effective platforms for businesses to get on, offering a whopping 80% click-through rate, where 80% of visitors on your profile are going and visiting your URL, too. People on Twitter are highly active, love to check out new businesses, and believe that if a business is on Twitter, it is a business worth knowing about. In fact, in 2019 a study showed that 85% of Twitter users said that they believe a business must be on Twitter, particularly so that they can offer customer support.

Twitter is an incredible tool for business, no matter how large, small, or niche your business may be.

Leveraging Twitter in Your Marketing Strategy

Getting on Twitter in 2020 is crucial, no matter who you are. In the past five years, many influencers and small to large businesses have harnessed the power of Twitter by getting on in the conversation and being available to offer support to their clients as needed.

Adding your business into the mix, whether you are retail or service-based, or if you are an aspiring influencer yourself, is crucial. You need to get involved in the conversation and start growing your platform in 2020 if you want to harness the power of this underrated beast. As a small business and with a smaller reputation, will have a tough time. This is truly the key to getting your foot in the door.

As your audience begins to grow and your business begins to grow as well, you can start targeting a large audience by engaging in national and international trends. This way, you have a larger built-in audience that is already going to be communicating with you through their timelines, which will improve your odds of being seen in the trending topics by people outside of your existing audience.

Knowing how big of an audience you can speak to is crucial in helping you get the word out there and grow your platform more rapidly. As you begin to grow your business, you can begin to grow your reach, too, allowing you to get even further out there.

If you are a business that deals primarily with a certain audience, such as a local business that deals primarily with local people, or a global business that deals primarily with global people,

following the aforementioned strategy is still important for you.

Even though you might not be targeting your exact audience at all points, you will be growing your popularity and visibility which means that your target audience will be more likely to see you. The larger audience, even if it is outside of your typical sales audience, will increase your perceived value, making you more likely to sell products or services while also making it easier for you to sell your products or services at a higher price tag. This way, you can leverage your audience for improved profits, not just for improved visibility and discoverability.

Marketing on Twitter In 2020

When it comes to marketing on Twitter 2020, you are going to want to first identify the size of your existing audience. If you are brand new on Twitter, chances are you do not have an exceptionally large audience (15000+ followers) and so you are to need to start off targeting smaller audiences.

If you have been on Twitter for some time and you are looking to upgrade your strategy, you may already have a decent-sized (5000-15000 followers) audience. This counts for organic, active followers, and not followers that were purchased through a platform like Fiverr or Upwork. Once you have identified where your audience size lies, you can begin applying the following techniques for marketing with your Twitter account in 2020.

Modernize the branding on your profile

In 2018, branding was centered around an incredibly lean and polished appearance, complete with stock images or images that looked like stock images. These photographs were created to give a clean, professional, and modern look into what your company offered or represented and was said to be appealing to the eye.

This is, in fact, true, and supported many businesses in growing through 2018 and 2019. That being said, trends are changing for 2020. Although the audiences do want to see images that are high quality and professional, more and more people are wanting to get away from the stock image appearance and start seeing something more personal, artistic, and inspirational.

As you create the imagery for your profile, you are going to need to create with the idea of being more personable in mind. You want your profile to have character, to represent a brand that stands apart from the generic click-and-build brands of 2019, and to be worthy of earning people's attention. That is when they will follow you and engage with your content. This means that your pictures should continue to be high quality and with a clear focal point, but that they should be personalized to feature characteristics that are representative of your brand.

Furthermore, these characteristics should be of high quality and artistic in a sense. If you are not the artistic type, a quick browse around other Twitter profiles can help give you an idea of how other people are customizing their profiles, simply pay closer attention to the ones that are more personalized and authentic.

Focus more on verbal marketing

That is how Twitter is – it is still very much a micro-blogging platform. So, avoid having "busy" images that are going to take away from the quality of your profile. Attempting to be artistic whilst creating images that are too busy for your audience to know what they are looking at is going to minimize the quality of your profile, and therefore the number of people who find you and follow you. Instead, find a way to be artistic while using details sparingly in your images.

Brand your bio and your link

80% of the people who land on your page are going to visit your link, so having a relevant and high-quality link that leads people directly to an opportunity to purchase or work with you is important. This way, you can take advantage of that 80% of people and drive more traffic to your website, another platform, or an affiliate link where you are going to earn more money than you might on Twitter.

Creating your bio on Twitter in 2020 needs to be simple, filled with personality. One-liners are still incredibly popular, with brands creating a single sentence that summarizes their entire brand, including its personality, in just a few words.

You can also add a sentence to discuss any upcoming points of interest that you may have to share with your audience.

Remember that you only have 160 characters to write out your bio, so you need to choose something that packs a punch and gets the message across as quickly as possible. This way, people get an immediate feel for who you are, what your brand represents, and what they can expect to find on your page. When you are done, add a link to your bio area so that people can find that, as well.

Pay close attention to the trends

Twitter is one of the most well-known platforms for spotting and following trends online. It has an entire page catered towards highlighting trending topics that are collected from the platform itself, as well as news platforms and gossip columns. Using Twitter specifically to learn about trending topics is a fantastic opportunity for you to grow your platform. This way, you also gain insight into how you can grow on other platforms – You stay relevant and your audience is more likely to keep up with you and pay attention to what you are posting.

Remember, you want to focus on trends and topics based on what proximity is going to be most reasonable for your audience size. If you have a smaller audience, look to find the trends that are currently growing in your local area so that you can get on board with talking about those trends, or even incorporating them into your products, services, or sales.

For example, if you have a local celebration going on that celebrates something in specific, you might consider creating products, services, or even a special sale to celebrate with your local area. This is a wonderful opportunity to get more local eyes on you, helping you expand your reach and grow your audience.

If you have a medium-sized business, focus on national trends, and if you have a large-sized business, focus on global trends. Continue paying close attention to the trends relevant to your business size, while also playing around with trends that cater to other audience sizes from time to time, too. This way, you are always marketing toward an audience that is going to be large enough for you to grow in, but small enough for you to get found in.

Using these trends is not only going to help you tap into your audience and choose a marketing strategy, but it can also serve as a guide for how you run your business going forward. For example, if you find that your local community celebrates a specific day every year, you might begin to prepare for that day in advance in future years, allowing for you to stay ahead of the curve. So, not only will following these trends help you reach out to your audience now, but it can also prepare you for having an even more impactful reach in the future.

Although the trend following has always been a popular marketing strategy on Twitter, it is growing even more popular in 2020. Therefore, following the approach of using the right proximity for your audience size is so crucial, as this is how you are going to leverage this feature in 2020 to get in front of your audience.

Previously, it was believed that just marketing to your industry was enough, but as Twitter continues to grow it has shown that this may not be the most effective way to grow your profile. You do still need to have a primary focus on your industry, but focusing on your industry, niche, and appropriate proximity is going to help you grow faster. This applies no matter how large your existing audience already is, and no matter how long you have already been marketing on Twitter.

In addition to creating a strong profile, leveraging your bio and URL, and taking advantage of trending topics, Twitter also offers you the opportunity to market by creating a way for you to converse with your audience. This platform has always been centered around real conversation, and it continues to maintain this focus going into2020.

That being said, we are starting to generate an even deeper understanding of what this means and how it affects businesses going forward. The primary key is realizing that, no matter what size your business is, Twitter can be used as a powerful opportunity to improve your customer service and offer an even better shopping experience with your brand.

First, you need to start getting involved in organic conversations with your appropriate target audience on Twitter. This means that the same trends you are posting about, also need to be the trends that you are conversing about on other peoples' posts. Showing that you are willing to get involved in these conversations, particularly in a meaningful way, really helps display your brand and get your name out there. People love seeing brands that partake in meaningful conversations and share their opinion in a way that engages and moves the conversation, rather than just sharing a generic sentence or two about the topic.

Although it will take more time to genuinely engage in these conversations, doing so will offer you the benefit of showing that you care, while also giving your potential audience insight into who your brand is. This creates that opportunity to have the deeper and more meaningful connections that you know are a cornerstone for all marketing strategies in 2020, which is why it is so important on Twitter in the coming months, as well.

When you do engage in these conversations, make sure that you are still being mindful of what you are talking about. In the past, many brands clung to generic responses because they made it easier to avoid looking ignorant, misinformed or otherwise sharing an opinion that may deter your audience from wanting to follow you. In other words, they were playing it safe to avoid losing their audience over something they said.

Especially on Twitter where we have seen many businesses at the forefront of scandals for various unprofessional displays on the platform, it can be easy to be concerned about how your responses may be taken. Still, none of this means that you should be sticking to the safer, generic response to avoid stirring the pot. Instead, you should offer genuine, authentic, and polite responses that offer your opinion. However, you need to do it in a way that ensures that your responses are educated, polite, and considerate toward the people you are talking to, as well as anyone else who might be reading your posts and responses. In other words, you can and should offer authentic and thoughtful responses, you just need to make sure that you are positively representing your business while you do it.

Make Twitter your news station

If you want to take advantage of your Twitter account for marketing, you should use Twitter as your own personal "news station for your brand. Because Twitter has gained popularity for being a professional platform that is largely focused on news and trending topics, you can leverage this reputation in favor of your brand. To do so, you can promote your Twitter as being the "first place" for people to learn about important news relating to your company. For example, this might be the platform where you announce sales, new products, or other exciting and relevant news regarding your company. This way, people want to follow your platform because they know that this is where they are going to get the first wind of anything that is going on with your business.

Monetizing Your Twitter Page

Go forward as a team in conversations

Make sure you use outward marketing terms, such as "together," and "we" as this is the right vocabulary to get your audience's attention. Apart from that, you also need to make sure that you are using the right strategies to earn money with Twitter.

The first and possibly most obvious way to monetize your account turn into part of the sales funnel. Because Twitter does have such a high click-through rate, you can feel confident that people who land on your page are going to also click through, take a look at your website, or whatever URL you have linked. Take advantage of this by organizing your page and posts in a way that encourages people to visit your profile. The key here to be sparing how you are doing this avoid making look like every single post just trying draw traffic your website.

Creating too many posts that are attempting to drive traffic to your profile or website is going to lose your audience's attention because they will feel like you are just attempting to capitalize on them. Again, although your audience understands that you are a business that wants to make money, they want to feel like they are more than just number your bottom line. Instead, they want to feel like they matter, and like you have truly given thought to how they perceive the experience.

So, make posts that encourage people to visit your page, posts that are relevant so that when people find your posts, they are more likely to click through to your profile to see if you post anything else they might like. This is a natural behavior of people on Twitter as they want to learn more about the people they are following and ensure that they are following people that they will resonate with.

A healthy mix of conversation and promotion

In 2020, rather than creating overwhelming "buy this!" posts for your Twitter, you can simply focus on having an organic, enjoyable conversation about relevant topics, trusting that this is a strategy that will draw traffic to your profile.

Once you have accumulated a healthy number of non-promotional posts, you can begin to post the occasional promotional post that features obvious promotions. The key here is to make sure that these types of posts never become the primary form of a post that you are using on Twitter.

The general rule of thumb in the past has been to use an 80/20 approach, which is still the most effective strategy as long as you are using it properly. In 2018 and 2019 it has largely been promoted that this 80/20 approach should be used on a day-to-day basis when in reality it is better to focus on using this as a part of a week-to-week approach, or even a month-to-month approach. In other words, instead of posting 4 non-promotional posts and 1 promotional post per day, you should focus on posting a promotional post 1 or 2 times a week, or 6-7 times a month. This way, you are posting enough that you are getting attention on your specific promotions, but without seeming like all you can talk about is what you are promoting.

The best part about using this form of the 80/20 approach in 2020 is that it offers more room for a greater number of promotional posts closer to special launches. So, rather than posting 2 promotional posts and 3 non-promotional posts per day, which would reflect the

60/40 rule on a day-to-day basis, you would post 2-4 times per week, or 12-14 times per month leading to launch.

This offers you a far more promotional room, without coming across as spammy during important launches. Remember that in addition to these posts you can always leverage paid advertising on Twitter to help get the word out there, even more, ensuring that your promotions are seen, but not to an overwhelming degree.

Begin with pre-roll ads

This is another terrific way to monetize Twitter in 2020. Take advantage of their pre-roll ads. Launched in 2016, these ads are becoming increasingly more popular as more people are uploading video content to Twitter now.

Going into 2020, monetizing your profile with these ads is relatively easy – all you have to do is join Twitter's Media Studio platform and begin creating, posting, and sharing videos from here. Twitter will automatically add promotions to your creations and pay you for those promotions.

Unlike other platforms which are requiring a certain follower count and level of popularity to monetize your videos, Twitter is now allowing anyone to monetize their videos, meaning that you can begin earning with Twitter right away.

That being said, if you do begin to add advertisements to your videos right away, people may not take your page or brand seriously. They may think that you are just attempting to monetize your profile, which can lead to them feeling like there is no strong reason to pay attention to or follow your platform. This can not only stunt or permanently sever your growth on Twitter, but it can also lead to incredibly low earnings due to no one watching your videos.

Instead, you should wait until you have a much larger following of 15000-25000+ before monetizing your videos so that your audience is already committed and engaged and know that the content is worth watching the advertisement first.

The Future of Twitter

Twitter bots and fake news

Researchers from MIT released a study that looked at how false information was spread throughout the internet. Their primary takeaway is that misinformation is likely to spread about six times as quickly as true information.

From a marketing perspective, this can make it easy to wonder if there is enough fake information already floating around on Twitter to make the possibility of getting any latest information out there extremely difficult. Luckily, it will remain possible to make a profit from Twitter, as long as you keep the following tips in mind.

Before deploying a new strategy, it is important to understand the current state of Twitter to avoid making common mistakes while you still have time to pivot your primary strategy. Twitter is without a doubt one of the most commonly used platforms by advertisers looking to get the word out about their products or services. Unfortunately, Twitter has been dealing with several issues lately that need to be dealt with effectively to ensure the process is as effective as possible.

Perhaps the biggest issue at the moment is the bots that have taken over aggressively. About 15% of all the users on Twitter are currently bots. These bots automatically tweet or respond to individuals who use specific words or phrases in their tweets. While a well-designed bot can be a boon to your brand, using one that is even a little off the mark is going to cause issues these days as so many people are aggressively fed up with them that even the hint of one is enough to make them swear off your brand completely.

As Twitter is hardly the leader when it comes to monthly users, the fact that 15% of its registered users are bots cuts down on the number of potential people you will reach with any marketing content which is why it is important to adjust your marketing projections accordingly.

Bots also make it difficult for a real message to get through as they commonly carry links that claim to go in one direction while sending those who click them someplace far less safe. Studies show that about 60% of all the links tweeted out on a given day are done automatically as opposed to by human beings.

While Twitter is trying to crack down on bots, many people remain skeptical that this will ultimately end up doing much good in the long run as there is so much false information being regularly spread on the platform. This is because while it may well be possible to stop bots from spreading false news on the platform, stopping real people from doing the same thing is much more difficult. Thus, the Twitter marketing strategy of the future will need to look for ways to counteract the spread of bots, the middling user growth and the deliberate spreading of false information by real people.

While it may be difficult, like any strategy, it can be used successfully if you take the time to focus on ways to play to its strengths while minimizing its weaknesses.

Be more direct

With two-way Twitter communication becoming more and more common, it is becoming an increasingly normal thing for a potential customer to tweet at even a mid-sized brand with a question that isn't readily available on their site and expect a response. While it might seem like a waste to answer individual questions in this way the truth is it is a fantastic way to invest in the long-term growth of your business.

The fact of the matter is that sometimes individual customers need some extra attention and giving it to them could help transform them into true supporters of your brand. If you do this regularly enough, then you are likely to develop a reputation as a brand that hears about its customers which is one of Twitter's greatest strengths.

85% of Twitter users believe that it is important for a brand to provide customer service on Twitter. Being responsive on Twitter adds a level of transparency to a given brand that helps it seem more approachable and helpful, and this trend is only going to continue. A splendid example of this case is Dove, which increased its overall market sentiment score by nearly 5% in just three months by doing nothing more than taking a more active response to potential customers on Twitter.

While the right type of service to provide on Twitter is going to vary by company, there are a variety of strategies you can try to generate a better response. For starters, it is important to always request a DM when sensitive information needs to be discussed. Depending on the types of questions that you find your brand being asked, this is one of the few scenarios where a bot can be used without drawing fire.

A good example of this is Patron Tequila which offers up a bartender bot that offers up cocktail recommendations based on the provided information. While this might sound silly, it increased the click-through rate of specific tweets to their website by more than 40%.

When the individualized touch is required, however, it is important to start by gathering as much useful information as possible as a means of fully understanding the situation. This may include information the user provides directly or, through the use of chatbot behind the scenes. You could set up a hashtag for things like orders that will be completed accordingly.

Depending on the size of your brand it may even end up making sense to create a secondary Twitter handle that is responsible exclusively for dealing with these types of customer service issues. Private messages are another increasingly popular means of resolving issues on the platform, and the link for doing so is included directly on every tweet.

It is important to ensure your account is set up to accept these types of messages, however, as this is not always the case. This can be confirmed by going to the Settings tab and selecting the options for Safety and Privacy and checking the box to receive direct messages from anyone. With this done you can now add URL with your Twitter ID into any tweet to ensure the send private message button appears, letting your users know they can send you private messages.

Create video content

As with every other social media platform, if you want to see a greater level of engagement in the future, then you need to take the time to create more video content. While sharing videos on Twitter is hardly a new idea, Twitter is always working on creating new ways that videos can be generated and shared with the Snapchat sharing tool on the way as well.

If you do not decide to create video content, then you are likely going to be at a disadvantage because by the end of 2019 video views on Twitter are anticipated to grow more than 200%. The reason for this is the perception that video is more likely to cut through the host of false content generated expressly for the platform.

Videos are harder to fake which is why they perform better and reach more people when compared to GIFs, images and links. What is more, video on Twitter is more effective than video on Facebook now, with the former outperforming the latter by nearly 40%.

One of the ways that Twitter users are going to judge the quality of these videos is by the number of views each has received. While this is hardly a true verification of authenticity, it is enough to provide users with a general idea of how many people think the video is worth the effort to watch as well as how far it has spread which makes it easier to determine if its source is likely legitimate.

To rack up as many views as possible, it is important to understand what Twitter counts as a view. In this case, a view is Racked up after two seconds of playtime as the video is taking up at least half of the available screen. These standards are not high, clearly, so it is important to make a big splash early with your content and go from there.

For starters, this means you are going to want to keep things short and sweet with about 45 seconds being considered the ideal length. It is also important to ensure you regularly use content pillars which are the core types of content that your brand creates and that your videos fit in with the overall theme you are working to create. Common pillars on Twitter include both inspiration and education. Videos will begin to play as users scroll over them, the first three or four seconds are going to be the most important, overall.

What is even better, for those who are using video content regularly, Twitter recently introduced the Video Website Card to make videos that are posted as effective as possible.

Essentially, the Video Website Card looks like a normal post until it is clicked on which then causes it to open in full-screen mode with a copy of the relevant tweet beneath it. The post then also includes a tag at the bottom of the video along with a header and a link to the website in question. When the user clicks on the video again, it then plays in full-screen and they are provided with a new experience as well. This can include things like having a landing page appear or opening the website directly.

Forming connections

While Twitter has always been about forging new connections between users of all shapes and sizes, this becomes more and more difficult as time goes on. This trend is only going to continue as the future unfolds thanks to two key issues: verified accounts and bots.

When it comes to bots, the issue is endemic in a system where the value of a given user is represented by the number of followers that a person has. Is it any wonder, then, that public figures of all shapes and sizes have stooped to using bots to increase their presumed reach and thus improve their actual reach in the process?

As there is already an entire industry devoted to buying and selling followers it can be difficult to determine a clear course of action moving forward. A good place to start is with Twitter Audit which is a free service that anyone can use to see an overall quality score for a given Twitter handle as well as a verdict as to whether or not the account is real or fake. Another good way to determine the quality of a given account is to look closely at the number and frequency of their tweets.

According to user data logs, the average number of tweets is less than 72 with that number making an account appear as though it may be a bot. If the account hits 144 tweets per day then in most cases the account is being filled by a bot.

Chapter 8: Mistakes to avoid

As social media marketing begins to mature, we are starting to learn more and more about how effective this marketing strategy is. We are also learning about what needs to be done to make it work, and what types of strategies are preventing people from experiencing any success through social media marketing. We know that you want to make sure that you are using

only the highest quality approach so that you can achieve 2020 growth right now in 2019, which is why we want to highlight mistakes that you must avoid if you are going to succeed with social media marketing right now.

Many of the mistakes are incredibly subtle, and therefore incredibly common. Brand new businesses, or brands that are not yet experienced with successful social media marketing, seem to make these mistakes regularly and find themselves struggling to get ahead in marketing their business as a result. The reason why these mistakes are made often comes from a lack of awareness that they even exist or need to be avoided in the first place, which is why simply knowing about them is going to set you so far ahead in the first place. Take time to acquaint yourself with these mistakes and to understand what they look like in use so that you can avoid making them in your business, allowing you to bypass many rights from the start.

Common Mistake #1: Losing sight of why social media exist.

These websites were developed to interact and network. However, if you keep pushing out content and never try to engage with your audience or respond to their initiatives if you do not participate, you are going to perish. You will end up feeling as if the platform was not fit for your business which will contradict what your initial marketing plan showed. Therefore, continue to make efforts to keep your audience engaged and if you find that they are not interested in your content, figure out why.

Go back to the whiteboard and chalk out a fresh content plan. Create and test, create and test, create and test.

Common Mistake #2: Taking your brand's voice callously.

A lot of loyal followers have stopped following popular brands because they were embarrassed by what the brand had started preaching. Or how the brand had started talking. The last thing your audience wants is getting associated with a brand that they don't agree with or find repulsive. Keeping your audience is daunting and faking who you are not will only make it harder.

Being robotic is also going to harm you in the same way. Followers on social media enjoy the intimacy of communication with other people and not with a robot or a square profile that only responds with "yes" or "no" or pre-recorded phrases.

You must add a touch of humanity to your profiles and messages. If you reply to a comment on your profile, then do not answer with the classic phrases like "we have received your comment and we thank you for the attention ...."

Be yourself on social media is as if someone speaks to you in real life! Stay authentic to who you are from the beginning and keep at it.

Common Mistake #3: Not having a Customer Relationship Management plan in place.

The first rule for online stores on social media is to listen to your community, engage with them and respond to them. When you are active on social networks, you can analyze the comments of your customers, meet their expectations and show, at the same time, to all other Internet users, that you are familiar with the new techniques of Web Marketing and the listen to the needs of your customers.

It is important to set up dashboards to monitor discussions around your product or brand on social media. You can also use the Tweet Deck tool for Twitter and Mention in the free version to monitor the web, in general.

In the same vein, being unresponsive when someone shares your content on social media is blasphemy. You need to respond effectively, express gratitude, and seize that opportunity. It is a real boon to create relationships and find ambassadors. This strategy is worth investing in to increase the reach of your brand and generate content on social networks. Also, it takes you little time, so enjoy it!

As a business, you will eventually make a mistake. It's inevitable. Sometimes the customer might just act irrational and lash out. At times, it will be your fault as well and saying sorry will not cut. The customer expects more, and you have to give her that. So, have a team ready with a plan who will deal with a crisis like this.

Even if you are managing it on your own, have a strategy in place to escort the customer to an amicable place and solve the situation gracefully.

Common Mistake #4: Not being personable enough

As you have noticed, one of the overarching trends in this very book has been the importance of how personable and authentic you are being in your marketing in 2020. Naturally, that is because this is going to be a foundational element of marketing going forward. We have already given you plenty of excellent tips on how you can be more personable, so now we want to point out what you need to avoid when it comes to being personable online.

The best way to get a feel for what not to do when it comes to being personable online is to get on social media and take a look at some accounts. Pay attention to small-to-medium businesses that are not growing well, ones that are, and larger businesses that are thriving on social media. You will quickly notice how different these businesses sound from each other. Businesses that are not thriving will sound completely different from those that are growing and those that are thriving. The ones that are struggling to grow will either lack personable communication altogether or will sound as if their personable communication is fake or generic. This type of language can only be spotted by reading the content that people are sharing, as you will quickly get a feel for whether they are being genuine.

Studying the difference between genuine and generic posts will help you notice the subtleties of what sets success apart from failure online. You will notice the nuances and phrases used by companies that are forcing their personability, versus the natural flow of language used by companies that are genuinely being personable with their audience. Through this, you will get an unobstructed vision of what to do, and what not to do when you are sharing your updates with your audience.

Common Mistake #5: Thinking you do not need a strategy

One of the biggest flawed mindsets we have seen in the day of social media marketing is the idea that you do not need a strategy. Business and strategy go hand in hand, and just because social media marketing can be incredibly easy does not mean that this platform comes without the need for strategy.

The first mistake on social networks is to get started without having developed a marketing action plan. You must determine. upstream, your strategy, your objectives, the periodicity of the posts, the tone employed, etc. It is important to build precise editorial planning to be as effective as possible in the publication of your content.

If you attempt to get online without any clear strategy of what you are going to be doing online, you are going to find yourself struggling to make any type of impact with your business on social media. It is extremely apparent when businesses have failed to make a strategy before getting into the world of social media marketing.

The tell-tale signs include a business that does not seem to have any clear direction in what they are posting or sharing, one that seems to constantly be behind on trends and, ultimately, one that is struggling to get in front of its target audience. More often than not, if your numbers are not growing consistently it is because you have failed to make a strategy, or you have failed to make a strategy.

In this book, you have identified several strategies for how to market your business in 2020, and how you can turn all this knowledge into an actionable strategy. We strongly advise that you do not overlook the part of turning it into a real strategy if you want to grow your business rapidly and successfully in the coming months.

Common Mistake #6: Not targeting your audience effectively

As you begin marketing your business online, it can be easy to be fearful of what might happen if you attempt to be "too" specific in who you are talking to. Many new businesses worry that if they speak to an awfully specific audience, no one will pay attention or want to engage with their business. They feel that they will be irrelevant, or that they will completely miss the mark with a larger audience. This leads to them making the huge mistake of not being clear in who they are talking to.

The truth is, when you do talk specifically to your audience, you are going to be irrelevant or unlikeable for many other audiences. That is the point. When you are marketing on social media, you want to be talking directly to the people who are more likely to purchase from you, while also avoiding the people who will not. This way, you are not wasting your time trying to cater to an audience that is never going to purchase from your business.

When you begin marketing your business on social media, get clear in who you are talking to, and keep talking to those people. Do not be afraid to be your authentic self, and do not be afraid to speak your opinions that are relevant to your business. The more relevant that you can be to the specific audience that you do want to sell to, the more likely they are going to pay attention to you and, more importantly, buy from you.

Worry less about the people who are not going to appreciate what you have to say, and more about the people who will. Leave the larger audience for the massive corporations that have millions of dollars to invest in talking to a larger audience than you can reasonably talk to in your business.

Common Mistake #7: Improper management of negative feedback

If you are in business, you are going to receive negative feedback. Period.

Every single business experiences some form of negative feedback or criticism at one point or another, both from people who have done business with you and people who have never experienced your business before. This is completely normal. People online like to have opinions, and they will share their opinions about everything. It is important that when you do come across people with negative feedback or criticism, that you handle it properly to avoid destroying your business reputation alongside that negative feedback or criticism.

When it comes to negative feedback, there will be two types of people offering it: those who can have their minds changed, and those who cannot. You can sort through who is who quickly by saying something simple like: *"We're sorry that you feel this way, can you please message us with your concern so we can help you resolve it?"* This type of comment shows that you are willing to support the person offering negative feedback.

Those who are willing to change their minds can then communicate with you so that you can resolve their concerns and hopefully, earn a loyal follower who respects your business. Those who are not can simply be ignored, as they are unlikely to have anything kind to say toward your business, regardless of how polite you are to them.

When it comes to business taking the high road in sticky situations is always the best choice.

Common Mistake #8: Using promotional tools in a poor manner

The more that social media matures, and social media marketing evolves, the more tools are being provided to businesses so that they can make marketing online even easier.

The selling feature for many is based on passive income: the more that you can automate or simplify your processes, the more time you have to do other things while your business stands by making money for you around the clock. Wanting passive income or time freedom is certainly not a terrible thing, but you must take the right action in turning your business into a passive income stream if you are going to be successful with it.

If you want to have success with online marketing, you always need to be able to remain personable and approachable. This means that if your business is too automated, people are going to catch on and they are going to lose interest in and respect for your company. As well, automating your business too far into the future can lead to you being irrelevant, or uploading content that does not effectively serve your market any longer. You need to use these tools effectively if you are going to have any success in reaching your audience through your social media marketing efforts, otherwise, you are just wasting your time.

When it comes to automated posters, make sure that you are always uploading relevant content, that the content still sounds incredibly personal, and that you are not uploading too far in advance. Do your best to only create enough content for one week to one month at a time to ensure that your content continues to remain relevant and personal for your audience. This will not only help your content remain meaningful and valuable, but it will also make it easier for you to make necessary adjustments in your approach or include important pieces of information along the way.

If you automate too far in advance, it can feel like a hassle to make any changes or shift your approach because you will feel like you are wasting a massive amount of time that was spent creating unnecessary content.

Another type of automation you need to be cautious with is bots. Bots can be incredibly useful, but they can also work to the detriment of your company. Many businesses have created bots for platforms like Instagram, only to have their bots sending out messages or comments that make no sense, or that come across as spammy by posting the same comment on far too many different profiles.

If you do choose to use a bot in your marketing strategy, make sure that the comments are authentic and genuine, and that they are not being over posted. It also cannot hurt, to be honest in your message by introducing your bot and letting your followers know how they can get in touch with a real person for support or inquiry if they want to. This way, while you are getting the benefits of a bot, you are also not losing parts of your audience who may prefer more personalized attention.

Common Mistake #9: Posting low-quality content to meet quality goals

Content calendars are in about every blog post and marketing book these days, and they have long been seen as a tool that is necessary to help keep you consistent with your posting.

Since consistency is key, this tool was designed to help people who are not used to posting regularly get their content out there consistently enough to be recognized by their audience. Unfortunately, for many people all these calendars have done is to place an incredible amount of stress on the shoulders of new social media marketers who are trying to produce more content then they are used to producing.

Following a marketing calendar can be effective, but it is not worthwhile if you are going to be attempting to post content that is low quality just to meet your content calendar "needs." At the end of the day, no matter how consistently you are posting, if the content is low quality, people are going to perceive your brand as being low quality and they are not going to want to follow you or do business with you. It is much better to skip a post here and there and wait until you have something more inspired or meaningful to say than it is to attempt to come up with something to say when you are not clear on what it is that you want to say.

Instead of following a content calendar day by day, set the goal of uploading a certain number of posts per week, organize what the goals of these posts need to be based on how you want to be marketing your business, and then go from there. This way, rather than attempting to push yourself to post when you are not inspired, you can simply post later when you have something more meaningful to say. Trust us on this one, your audience is not going to abandon you because you did not post anything on Tuesday at 2 pm.

Experts say you must publish a lot of content and all the time! Yes but no, regular display of content attracts attention and makes your media an active medium, but if you do not have creative or interesting content, publishing a lot of content just to publish may have the opposite effect and so attract negative attention.

Common Mistake #10: Not focusing on your analytics

Creating a strategy is virtually pointless if you are not going to focus on how your strategy is holding up. When it comes to running a business online, you must pay attention to your statistics and analytics and use them to determine what is working, and what is not working.

Using your analytics to serve as a guideline for what you need to do to better serve your audience is the single most crucial step in reaching your audience effectively. Reading your analytics is simple: you want to review your analytics consistently, ideally weekly, bi-weekly, or monthly. Then, you want to use the information you gain to identify what marketing trends or strategies are working, and which are not.

The ones that are working will have higher engagement ratios, while the ones that are not working will have lower or virtually non-existent engagement ratios. Naturally, you want to nurture the ones that are working and adapt or let go of the ones that are not.

Common Mistake #11: Promoting yourself more than 25% of the time

The main mistake of merchants on social media is excessive promotion. These platforms are primarily dedicated to the discussion and not to advertising.

Social media...everything is in the word "social". This is primarily the place to chat with your community, build relationships and manage your e-reputation. It is through your animation and your commitment that you will generate sales for your online store.

Many e-businesses spend little time on social media. A powerful e-commerce strategy with a real return on investment takes time. In general, one hour a day is enough to liven up your community. But be aware that for some brands it is a full-time position!

Doing your promotions in over 25% of the time will downgrade your value in the eyes of the audience. Because people use social media to enjoy and have fun all the time, they do not want to receive promotions from their Facebook page or Twitter account.

Therefore, the promotion of companies and brands must be done subtly and should be within 25% of the time spent on the network. For example, if you post four messages a day on Twitter, you need to promote only one brand or company.

Common Mistake #12: Use vulgar language

Use vulgar language in real life if you wish but keep it for yourself. A website or social media must be in good French (or any other language of your choice). The vulgar language is synonymous with aggression even if it is used for jokes and this will not push potential customers to trust you. So, prefer simple language, with short sentences and be courteous with all your followers even those who are not happy or who insult you directly.

If someone has posted a vulgar comment for you or your business, and you wish to respond, the best is to answer (without vulgarity always) with a touch of humor. In general, some people are more likely to write negative comments than others They can spend more time on the site, like many topics without saying anything, but as soon as they see an article that is not even a tiny bit away from their thoughts, they leave a negative, vulgar comment on it.

So, take the time to read these negative comments and respond to a relationship of trust between you and your customers (or potential customers). Either do not respond at all, or in the worst-case scenario where you cannot hold yourself from replying, use light humor and turn the conversation around its head. The person who provoked you will not have a suitable answer and you will also establish yourself as a smart, witty and composed person (or business).

With around 1hour and 16 minutes spent daily on social media, they represent an excellent communication tool for e-merchants and other advertisers. Nevertheless, there are diverse ways to use them and some practices can hurt your online business. It is for this reason that it is essential to know the right actions to undertake. This article highlights the most common mistakes of online merchants on social media and especially tells you how to avoid them!

Common Mistake #13: Being present on all platforms

Your online store must be present on Facebook. And Twitter. And YouTube. And Pinterest. And Instagram. And Tumblr. And Google+. False, completely wrong!

Your e-commerce store does not need all these channels. First, you need to know where your target audience is. Also, each network requires time and commitment. Depending on your objectives and your resources (financial and human), you need to focus on the most profitable for your e-commerce to avoid wasting time. Also, each social network has its codes and allows to achieve this or that goal. It is up to you to define which ones are most relevant to your business.

Common Mistake #14: Focus only on your brand

E-commerce stores rarely respect the community spirit of social media that wants to be "social".

You must know your audience. When you animate a community, you are part of it. It is therefore important to understand everyone's interests. For example, if your products are used in sports, health, and fitness, you need to create content around these topics. But also, to know the events to come or to share your point of view on the problems related to this theme.

You need to take a global view of your products and services. Your content must be divided according to the 80-20 principle. That is, 80% of your content must come from other external sources (curation of content). The remaining 20% remains content creation by you. Your community expects you to be an expert on your subject.

For the first time, you must be relevant. In the second time, useful. And in the third time, to stimulate the sale.

Common Mistake #15: Have a purely ROI focused vision

On social media, many e-merchants foci on poor indicators of sales. As we have already mentioned, social media is, primarily, an e-reputation engagement and management platform for your brand. The mistake to avoid is to focus only on the number of sales generated via your posts on social networks. The return on investment of these platforms is much broader.

Common Mistake #16: Using only the photo format

The photo is good, but the video is a format that arouses much more interest!

Unfortunately, many e-merchants are not taking advantage of this opportunity to create engaging and dynamic content. On many social networks, you can stream short videos to highlight your products. With the quality of today's smartphones, you can easily and quickly create an immersive video to display your services and products. You can use this format to distribute the backstage of your online store, the manufacture of your products, and do so much more.

Common Mistake #17: Using a bait-and-switch marketing technique

When you are trying to maintain a consistent brand voice, it is not wise to try out the bait-and-switch selling technique. It is a technique where a brand advertises its products or services at a considerably low price. However, when a customer visits the website to purchase a product, they realize that the discounted product or service is not available.

Customers that have depended on your product or service more than once will feel as though they are being tricked. Therefore, there is a high possibility that trust issues would be raised if you employ this selling technique over social media channels.

Chapter 9: Reaching the Online Marketing Plateau

Just like with any other field out there, online marketing can be like a ladder. As you learn new things and develop new strategies for constantly evolving platforms like Instagram, you slowly go through the ranks, get the hang of using what you learned, and proceed to the next big step on your venture.

But, as with any other field again, there comes a time when you reach a peak in marketing and, suddenly, there is no longer any growth or development. This is what is called a plateau and it can be one of the most precarious places that any online marketer could find themselves in.

Why is this so? Because what follows after a plateau is a slope and, if you are not careful with your next steps, everything will go downhill from there.

Is there a way to get out of this lull? Yes, there is. It all boils down to what you can do to keep the momentum alive until the next big thing in marketing is announced.

What is the Plateau?

The "plateau" is a rather vague concept in marketing. You won't find it discussed thoroughly in an academic setting. Even industry experts have never even established a proper definition for it.

To make things easier for you, here's a scenario: Imagine that you are a fan of a certain movie franchise. After seeing the main character endure hardship after hardship in every past entry, you are now in the final movie where he is ready to face his ultimate adversary.

It is now the climax of the movie where both characters clash and the hero won. The ending is seen. The credits roll. Suddenly, you are hit with this realization: What Now?

This is a personal plateau for you and the same is true for your business. Once every strategy has been learned, every trick has been deployed, and every trend identified, you feel that nothing can faze your brand now. There is no need for improvement anymore. Your place on social media is secured and your customer base is large and happy.

But, unlike natural plateaus, marketing plateaus are one of the most dangerous places to be in. In most cases, threats can come there in two forms:

1. Becoming Complacent

Your success in one strategy gets you pumped up to create more strategies that eventually became successful themselves. But, with enough wins, you start loving that "fight" in you. You and your brand feel that brand recognition is now enough to generate leads for the business, so your staff starts creating mediocre content. And, suddenly, a new standard in marketing pops up or the platform comes up with a massive change in their algorithms which affects businesses.

All of those strategies that you have learned and mastered are now deemed ineffective, bringing you back to square one. This is what exactly happened to those businesses at the dawn of the Internet age who did not bother to learn how to venture into the then-new market. By not learning how to do online marketing on social media, all of their mastered skills and strategies from the brick-and-mortar world became obsolete and they lost business.

2. Stagnating

It is possible that you are not exactly reckless or that arrogant to think that your brand is untouchable. You are paying attention closely to the changes in the market.

But, all of a sudden, your strategies are no longer yielding the engagements they once generated. Soon enough, your ventures in the online world start becoming expensive and ineffective for you.

This is what stagnation looks like. Your online venture, in its current form, has stopped performing well for your business. In most cases, the quality of your content has not changed. It is just that response for whatever your business is offering ranges from indifference to dislike.

Not addressing this problem has always proven to be a fatal move for marketers in the past. And it is important to note that online marketing is about to enter into a new age by the 2020s with a strong focus on personalized, intimate user experiences. Being at a plateau at this transition period will not do any business well.

What to Do, then?

The one thing that you have to understand with marketing plateaus is that everyone will eventually encounter them in their ventures. There will come a time when there will be no new developments on sight and stagnation could be seen to last for a few months, depending on the platform.

And since plateaus are unavoidable, the best that any marketer could do is to make the most of their time there. Here's how:

1. Learn where to invest more

This strategy is hugely dependent on the assumption that your content had been warmly received in the past. To put it simply, if some of your content has not been generating the amount of engagement on social media but is otherwise good, then it is safe to assume that this kind of content needs a bit of an update.

This is a rather blunt strategy at this point since it requires you to do more than what you are currently doing. For instance, if you are posting once per day, then increasing that number to 3 or 4 might do you favors. However, make sure that overall quality is not sacrificed with the increase in quantity.

2. Diversify

One other reason why reception for your content declines is the fact that you are offering the same thing over and over with little to no variation. Or perhaps you have been talking about the same topics over and over and people do get sick of hearing the same tune for months on end.

Even if the quality of your content can't be faulted, repetition does not encourage loyalty to the brand. Diversifying, however, keeps things fresh and entertaining which should drive up engagement for your business.

If you have been posting meme after meme on Instagram, for example, make sure that the next content is either a video or a quiz or a poll. The point is to never get stuck or be comfortable in doing the same thing again and again just to save effort on your part.

3. Look for a new niche

If your current audience has been giving you the cold shoulder at worst or a lukewarm reception at best, then perhaps you could find better engagement from an entirely different market. Doing so opens your brand to new opportunities for marketing as well as new topics, issues, and strategies that you could learn and master.

To put it simply, venturing into new niches of the market not only helps in expanding the reach of your brand but it could also put you in a position to better hone your skills and diversify your content while in a rut.

Of course, the challenge here is to find that new niche. Catering to the same demographics might make it hard to find an alternative audience. To make this easier for you, try to watch what demographics your competitors are targeting or have yet to tap into. Either way, it is best not to limit one's reach to segments that the brand is most comfortable catering to.

4. Go multimedia

If you had been providing too much image and text-based content, you run the risk of making people get tired of your content pretty quickly. Sure, pictures and text work great for retaining information but they do not have the impact that videos and polls have.

Highly visual multimedia content tends to generate more engagement as it targets more senses while also adding a bit more diversity in your content line-up. And if you make that content interactive, you should drive engagements for your content to an even greater degree.

And if you think that going multimedia is going to run against the point of surviving a plateau, it doesn't. Memes, for example, are cheap to create but tend to be the most shareable media out there right now. You don't even have to change a lot just to keep things fresh. Of course, with memes, the trick is knowing when and how to deliver the punchline.

5. Consolidate your presence

Assuming that you are already implementing the ideas above, the next best thing is to try improving your online presence. For starters, you can revisit your defunct and often forgotten social media pages or even features that you rarely use. You can even look at links in your content, bios, and pages to see if they still work in driving up traffic to your business.

Once you are assured that your presence is properly optimized, you can start on going back to your library of published content and retarget your niches, both old and new. Of course, there is the tried and tested method of collaborating with other creators and online influencers to attract even more audiences to your brand.

Surviving this plateau is going to be determined by your ability to adapt as well as mix and match effective marketing tools and strategies. Of course, you must not lose sight of your overall goal as your business goes through the motions. Remember the priorities of the brand while trying out new things and the business should be able to stay afloat even if everything else in the market is stagnating.

Letting Go

One of the core rules in survival is to let one of the core rules in survival is to let go of the things that would weigh you down or prove to be unnecessary in the long term. If your resources are low and the chances of success are less than likely in your marketing ventures, there is even a risk to be had in insisting that your brand operates on the same scope or maintains the same number of channels and workforce.

This would be one of the hardest decisions you would have to make but it could be integral to your brand's survival in the online world. When downsizing your marketing operations, there are a few things that you need to consider.

1. Make a list

This is basic but essential to your survival of the Plateau. Make a list of all the channels currently employed by the brand, the tools at your disposal, and the strategies and campaigns that you are currently running. This is where analytics would also come into play as you need to know how your channels are performing in terms of engagement, web traffic, and search results page visibility.

Then, slowly arrange these channels and strategies according to how well they are performing. With a set distinction between channels and campaigns that are working the best and the least, you will have a better idea as to which of them you should terminate.

2. Remain as objective as possible

Cleaning house can be hard. There might be campaigns or strategies that you and your staff have a sentimental connection to or there might be channels where you made your first steps in online marketing.

When you have to confront the fact that some things have to be let go, you should maintain an objective mindset. Try to establish the most logical reason why you are scrapping of this project so you at the very least don't devalue the efforts everybody has poured into it. Make sure that everybody else in the team knows why this is happening so they could shift their efforts elsewhere. And speaking of elsewhere...

3. Take a hit

Aside from projects and strategies, there is also the chance that you would have to let go of some key people on your staff. At this point, you must prove to your people that this downsizing is also going to affect your business and yourself.

For example, if you are going to let go of a few people, then at the very least try to make them see that you are hurting economically. A pay cut here or reduced bonuses (or better yet, none at all) for you can do a lot in projecting solidarity with your team. And by assuring them that whatever you do will ultimately help the business in the long run, there is at the least the chance that morale for your staff is not severely hurt.

To conclude

A plateau is not exactly the easiest thing to pass through for any marketing venture. More often than not, your brand will not be the same after passing here provided, of course, that you managed to survive through the ordeal.

However, what you have to understand is that plateaus are unavoidable things in marketing. If you don't hit one on your marketing, then good for you since you might be one of the lucky few out there.

If you do stumble on your marketing campaign plateau, you must be able to find a creative workaround for your current predicament. This way, your stay there would be a bit more manageable.

Final Thoughts

There is no form of 21st-century marketing technique that can beat the power of social media. Picture a scenario where a single post could be shared with thousands of people in a matter of seconds. This is how fast the news spread over social media channels. Platforms such as Twitter, Facebook, Instagram, and LinkedIn are therefore excellent marketing channels to take advantage of. You ought to commend yourself for digging deeper to filter out the best strategies to utilize in marketing your brand over social media.

Today, businesses realize that they cannot counter competition in their industries without the use of social media platforms. Interestingly, micro-companies have the same perception. As big companies are competing for their online space, smaller companies are also doing the same. After all, they say, "if you can't beat them, join them." So, companies are doing their best to counter competition by simply making use of social platforms as a way of reaching out to their clients.

From what you have learned in this material, there are numerous social media platforms that you can choose from. However, you shouldn't settle for anyone. This is a huge mistake that most businesses are making. Moreover, having a social media page on all platforms does not mean that your online presence is well covered. It is quite likely that you might be confusing yourself. The chances are that you might end up failing as you lack the expertise in marketing your product over social media.

To be on the safe side, the first thing that you need to do is to learn the art of it. How are people marketing their products on Facebook? Is it the same as how other companies are selling their brand on Twitter? The nitty-gritty aspects of marketing on social media should be on your fingertips before you think about setting up a social media business page.

The other thing that you should always be keen on is the varying attributes of the specified social media pages. Facebook is different from Instagram or Pinterest. Marketing tactics vary across all platforms. This means that having a "one size fits all" policy will render your marketing efforts useless. It is essential to gain an understanding of the different features of every social media page. These features should be matched with your marketing objectives. Doing this ensures that you work smart as you would be using a few social media pages and getting the most out of them.

Always remember to have a plan. Failing to plan is just planning to see your business go into extinction. If you do not know how to plan, learn from what your competitors around you are doing. They are investing here and there on the most reliable social media pages. But what is the secret behind it? Your rival brands have a plan, and they stick to it.

In this case, you need to take the time to audit your social media presence before moving further. Find out the platforms that generate more leads for your business. Where is your audience posting their tweets and Facebook posts regularly? Get to know what your customers want to see?

Understand your clients to delivered beyond. Delight them so much that they can't stop talking about you. And when they do talk good things about you, reward them for that.

You've probably heard the phrase "join the community." Well, being on social media demands either joining a community or forming one. Meet customers personally after meeting them on Facebook, LinkedIn, or Instagram. Listen to them. Hear with an open mind what they have to say about your products and services. Are they happy? Are they impressed by the recent changes your team has made? Can you improve upon a particular service or product that you are currently offering? Well, listening is what will win you more clients. Use their feedback and your knowledge to market your brand over social media effectively.

With regards to monitoring, always monitor your performance regularly. Know where your brand lies in the minds of your consumers. Undeniably, you do not want to be an "option B" in the market. Therefore, make use of the right monitoring tools that work for you. It is recommended that you go through different reviews about these tools before choosing any. It ensures that you end up picking the best from the lot.

Content! Content! Content! This an area that you must improve. Big brands in the market are always at their frontline in making sure that their content is unbeatable. Try your level best to make sure that your content is also relevant. Customers on social media fancy the idea of being associated with brands that post relevant content. If you think that you are not witty enough, just keep it simple. And if possible, hire an expert to do the job for you. Content is what will sell your brand out there. It defines what you are doing, and what you are offering your customers. Therefore, knowing what sells matters a lot to the success of your business.

In line with content, this goes hand in hand with knowing your customers. Without an in-depth knowledge about your customers, you will never know the right content that suits them. So, do your homework. Research about them and their online shopping behaviors. This tells a lot about what they anticipate from your brand.

Before you forget, remember to take note of what your competitors are doing. Their actions could be regarded as a blueprint for what you should be doing. This applies mostly to smaller businesses in the market. Try to stay unique. But don't be the odd one out.

Taking everything into account, marketing on social media is not challenging. It is also not easy. Therefore, a business owner should invest their time and money in learning the art of it. Getting to know more about social media marketing basics will make a huge difference to your business both in short and in the long run. A working strategy that is worth bearing in mind is that companies should learn from the best.

Why? It is the only surest way of also becoming the best on the market. Good Luck!

WRITTEN BY **STEPHAN ANDERSON**

Sign up for my newsletter by leaving us your email, you will be informed about new promotions and new book releases:

Click Here **https://mailchi.mp/e136f3ee924a/stephan-anderson**

Stephan Anderson

WRITTEN BY STEPHAN ANDERSON

Social Media Marketing 2020

Book 3

Build Your Brand and Become the Best Influencer Using YouTube and Instagram Marketing! Top Personal Branding & Digital Networking Strategies

WRITTEN BY *STEPHAN ANDERSON*

Introduction

Many people have discovered creative methods to earn money using the internet. A "money-making" technique that is currently popular today is the influencer marking through personal branding on social media.

Whether you are a writer who wants to get the attention of readers from all over the world or a person with great taste in fashion and beauty, you can create your content, curate other people's great content with your flavour and make money out of it. Yes, that is possible, and this book will help you do precisely that!

On top of it, you will be able to build a sustainable business around it. You may wish to keep it small like a source of passive income, but that is your choice because people are raking in millions with just this. However, writing a book around it means that it is not as simple as it sounds. There are certain things to learn, certain things to tweak and certain hidden secrets that only the pros know. That book will tell you all that so that your start is explosive. You know how they say – well begun is half done!

But why a simple platform like Instagram and an effort-intensive platform like YouTube? You may ask that.

That is because these platforms get maximum share and engagement. That engagement quickly turns into leads and sales.

Today's Instagram influencers are not influencers by accident. It is no coincidence that some personalities have over 10, 20, 30 million followers, while other people struggle to get a few thousand. To gain a massive amount of traction on social media these days, you need a plan! A plan which will see your Instagram account break through the noise of a million other accounts and put you right in the influencer category which everyone is so desperate to achieve.

Top fitness Instagram influencers like Kayla Itsines, Jen Selter & Massy Arias all dominate their area's by using extremely creative Instagram tactics. Tactics which keep both new and existing followers wholly engaged in their content.

This book will give you a peek inside the world of influencers. You will learn precisely how influencers create great Instagram campaigns. That will eventually make your account stand out from the rest and get you closer to becoming a paid influencer. You could have offers coming in left right and centre for companies begging you to promote their products and services. Here is a snapshot of the highest-paid Instagram influencers earned PER POST during 2019.

Kylie Jenner - $1 Million per post

Selena Gomez - $800,000 per post

Cristiano Ronaldo - $750,00 per post

Kim Kardashian $720,00 per post

Beyoncé - $700,000 per post

Dwayne The Rock" Johnson - $650,000 per post

Justin Bieber - $650,000 per post

If each of these celebrities uploaded a sponsored Instagram post on the same day in 2019, then the bill would come to a whopping $5.27 Million! And that's just one day of the year! Now imagine yourself as an Instagram influencer receiving just 0.1% of that revenue. Does not sound like a lot? It would be over $5,000 per post! No wonder that even the smaller Instagram influencers are earning hundreds of thousands of dollars and living a life which was entirely out of reach for them ten years ago.

There are no theories to learn from this playbook. Each section is an actionable exercise you can apply to your soon to be huge Instagram account.

Talking about YouTube, it can be seen as the heart of the social media platforms as its content is widely distributed throughout the other platforms. Four hundred tweets per minute contain a YouTube link, and YouTube's search bar is the second only after Google. YouTube has the benefit of having one of the most engaged audiences out of the social media platforms. With tweets flooding Twitter news feeds, and posts cluttering Facebook feeds, it is harder than ever to reach followers on platforms. However, 85% of YouTube subscribers consider themselves "regular" YouTube users.

It is recommended that if you pursue a YouTube channel that you have a professional team of producers and creators as the content uploaded should maintain a high standard. However, a lot of prominent Youtubers have started with just their mobile phone and a personality. Now, video content and a strong YouTube presence can be significantly harder to establish and say Twitter, Facebook or Instagram. But if video content were right for your brand, it would be well worth the extra step.

The following sections will reveal all from exploding your following list, to engaging your followers, to creating a fantastic content strategy — all the way through to negotiating advertising deals and getting paid to post.

We will begin with the fundamentals of personal branding and why it is essential. Then, we will move to explain the basics of influencer marketing. The pointers mentioned in this chapter will help you create an attractive pitch for businesses as well. So, please read it carefully.

Next, we share the baby steps to becoming an Instagram Influencer. We take you through the entire roadmap of optimising your Instagram account for beauty, finesse and content strategy. Content creation and curation are two essential parts of any content strategy. The chapter will explain how to create a balance between the two and create a viable content plan.

The following chapter will polish your posting basics. You will learn the different formats and features of Instagram that you can make use of and how to time your posts for maximum exposure. Analytics is a crucial part of being an influencer. So, you will also get a basic understanding of the engagement rate and how you can quickly calculate it.

Every Instagram influencer is a creator, a storyteller. Therefore, it is terrific that Instagram has a story feature. You will be learning how to create super-engaging stories and give your followers a seamless experience on your Instagram profile through highlights and Instagram Live.

Finally, you will learn the best strategies to monetise your Instagram profile. Be it Affiliate Schemes, paid partnerships or collaborations, the book covers everything. Additionally, it also shares tips on how to reach out to companies to partner with you, creation of a contract, price list, etc.

Part 2 of the book is all about YouTube and becoming a YouTube celebrity. We breakdown what YouTube's algorithm is and how it favours one video over another. That chapter is significant as it covers the tactics for explosive channel growth, from the frequency of posting to YouTube SEO.

Next, you will get to understand the basics of video production and creation and how to keep coming up content for your channel. The chapter also covers simple tips and tricks to bring in traffic initially and sustainably too.

The next chapter is all about perfecting the nuances of video creation and publishing that will turn the amateur in you to a professional. Here, you will finally be the YouTube celebrity you always desired to be. The last chapter in Part 2 explores the less discussed, but smart ways to beat your competition on YouTube. Do you want to make it big on YouTube? Do not take this section lightly.

The final chapter of the book takes you back to personal branding. No matter what you do and on which platform, you are carrying your brand; and there is not enough you can do to assert it. If you do not maintain your personal brand, it will not matter how big you started or how fast you grew; you will fall.

So, take care of your personal brand. We are sending your way a bounty of luck and success.

Your personal brand

A brand is not a product or a service. It is an idea, a design, a symbol, a behaviour and a reputation. For example, both Samsung and Apple operate in the same space of technology, but they represent technology in totally different ways. That is their brand.

A brand is a distinction between what one thing is and not the other. That is what makes each one unique. In simple words, you have a few things that others have and a few things that others do not have. That is your USP and your differentiator. That will make your personal brand!

So, we all carry our personal brand. All your life, you have shared your brand with everyone you met or interacted with. How you portray yourself defines what your brand is. But do you believe that this represents you in a complete, real sense?

What is Personal Branding?

Personal branding is similar to the branding of a product or service. However, in the case of personal branding, this product or service is an individual. Politicians, actors, artists are all known for their unique tastes and style of working, which makes them resonate strongly with a particular section of folks. That is their personal brand.P

Personal Branding is a practice of marketing yourself to a specific audience of people. It is about promoting your skills, ideas & experiences to people who are interested in what you have to offer.

Let us begin with your name. That is your brand. How your appearance distinguishes you from others, is your brand design. You have different parents, values, personality, perception and qualities from others. All these make you unique.

In essence, personal branding is all about being your authentic self.

For example, you might be fantastic at putting outfits and accessories together, which people find attractive. So, with time, you gain followers on social media who appreciate your sense of styling and deem you as a style inspiration. Similarly, you might be great at online gaming, and you share tips and tricks regarding that on social media. Gradually, you gain a following of people who are interested in gaming.

Make sense?

Importance of Personal Branding

CVs or resumes are no longer enough. In future, they will exist only as fossils. What will thrive is your unique promise. Your brand. Anyone can have a similar set of skills and qualifications as yours, and so, they can poach your opportunities. To win, you need to be indispensable. You have to be not just the right fit, but the only fit for a job. Regardless of whether you wish to pursue a career or become an influencer, it would be best if you had your personal brand to sell your skills.

Here are the steps to create your personal brand:

Step 1: Know your strengths

Step 2: Know your shortcomings

Step 3: Know your values

Step 4: Identify your passion

Step 5: Find your niche

Step 6: Position yourself appropriately

Step 7: Understand your competition

Step 1: Knowing Your Strengths

Your strengths are an essential factor in creating your personal brand. It does not depend on what you think your strengths are, but on what others believe are your strong areas.

Think of people who you feel have a fabulous personal brand. You will observe that these people have complete clarity on what they want in life and who they are at their core. They know their unique selling points and what value they bring to the table. After doing the following exercise, you will join their league too. So, let us begin.

Write down the following in a notebook to identify your strengths:

1. Your career highlights
2. Professional moments or incidents that you are proud of
3. 2-3 most fulfilling projects of yours
4. Think of why you felt fulfilled while executing them or when they were done
5. The role you usually play in a group project
6. Perception of your group members about you
7. Your techniques and thought process to overcome challenges and obstacles
8. Tools that you use often
9. Professional or personal things that bring you joy, something you enjoy getting involved in
10. Things you like to discuss and debate about

Now, describe each of your strengths in just one word. Write those down too.

Pick individuals who know you, your partner, family, colleagues and friends and ask them to share their understanding of your strengths. In the wake of doing that contrast your rundowns and theirs. Show them your list and check whether they see you in the same light as you see yourself.

It might seem obvious; however, you would be astounded by the number of people who would list down all that they have ever done. Pass on your energy and connect your strengths to gauge results. Tell your target audience about your gifts. Convey it to them adequately utilising all resources accessible to you. While interacting with your audience, recall your qualities and morals. That will set you apart.

Step 2: Knowing Your Shortcomings

We all have certain shortcomings and acknowledging them is never easy. However, we do not wish to live a life full of disappointments. Therefore, you and we need to be honest about our shortcomings. Remember that weakness is anything from being utterly uninterested about anything in life to have limited skills to do anything of interest.
Let us do a similar activity as we did for strengths to identify your weak areas:

1. List down the things about your education and career that you do not like at all
2. Note down the reasons why you dislike those aspects
3. Think hard about your beliefs on how worthy you are and if you deserve better
4. Ask yourself if you feel drained merely by the thought of performing specific tasks
5. List down such tasks that make you feel out of action
6. Make a list of all the low points of your career
7. Write reasons against each on why you think that they were the low points
8. If you are given a group task, which role would you never like to perform, and why?
9. Have there been any tasks that you have done, but that did not bring you any joy?
10. Did these tasks fail? Why was that?
11. Do you ever give up? What makes you do that?
12. In a conversation, at what point do you feel uninspired to talk more?
13. Are there any particular topics that you feel uncomfortable talking?
14. List down 10 of your weaknesses.

Be honest with yourself. Know that there is no need to waste time on shortcomings that do not hamper your professional growth. Now, establish what limitations you can turn into strengths to kick-start your career. Start learning the skills to propel your growth. If talking to people makes you nervous, become a regular at networking events and work on yourself bit by bit.

Step 3: Knowing Your Values

Do you have some principles, a code that you use to navigate through life? Those principles form your value system. They determine your moral compass, your personality, attitude, actions, reactions, and so on. Do not confuse them with your profession.

Take five minutes to visualise these people and think what their personal brand is – what do they stand for. Understand the difference between their profession and their brand.

1. Barack Obama
2. Marie Kondo
3. Pele
4. Music band, Queen
5. Mark Manson
6. Seth Godin
7. Oprah Winfrey
8. Meryl Streep
9. Anna Winton
10. Frida Kahlo

Picture it like this: Perhaps your reason for unhappiness at work is that your work is not aligned with the values you uphold. Having values, therefore, is taking a stand for your beliefs. It is critical to align what you engage yourself in with who you are at your core.

By knowing your values, you get an understanding of who you are and what you stand for. To establish and route your thoughts in a way that matches your passion, you need to have strong values. Simply put, before involving yourself in anything, ask yourself, *"Is this in sync with my values and what I stand for?"*

Finding the values for your personal brand

1. On the internet, you can find valuable resources on how to establish your values for your brand. These may be present as lists of adjectives which you can use to describe your values.

2. Pick out a list that you find suitable for yourself and by process of elimination, choose the top five words that make sense to your understanding of yourself.
3. Now, think why you chose those words specifically and define what they mean to you.
4. Use them to build your mission statement and hold yourself accountable if you are not respecting your values.
5. Communicate these values everywhere – in your CV, website, social media platforms and blog posts.

Step 4: Identifying Your Passion

Have a passion for what you do! That is the biggest secret. It might seem difficult to reconcile the idea of passion and work. But it is not impossible. Clubbing your passion and work will bring you more joy than you can ever imagine. It will keep you inspired and wanting more. That is why influencers are flourishing. They did not take the beaten path or picked a career because many people were making easy money out of it. They picked it because they felt passionate about it and turned it into a viable business model. With passion, you can do that too!

If you still cannot put the finger on your passion, recall a time when you found it challenging to wait to do something. Rewind to the day when you jumped out of your bed in the morning. Think of the things that broke you into tears of joy. Do not forget the projects that unleashed your creativity and filled your head with ideas. See, it is all about feeling stimulated and motivated to do something. That something is your passion!

Ask yourself:

1. What do I like about my current job?
2. If I were to volunteer, which charity would you choose? Why?
3. How do most of your days go and in doing what?

Now take a minute to think about the potential influencers you follow on Instagram. As you do that, answer the following questions in your head:

- What do I love about my current job?

- Which would the charity of my choice if I were to volunteer in future? Why?
- What do I spend most of my time doing?

The chances are you follow certain influencers because they create valuable content in your areas of interest. These areas of interest are also called "niches".

Step 5: Finding Your Niche

The following exercise will help you understand more about what your niche could be and how you can start to build the foundations of your personal brand. Be as specific as you can when answering the questions below. You will need this information later down the line.

1. Who are you? (Write a short paragraph.)
2. What makes you unique?
3. List all of your passions (Don't just list things you are "kind of interested in", but the things you are genuinely passionate about.)
4. What are you good at? (The skills that distinguish you from your friends and family? It can be anything. It might help to think about what people compliment you on and what do you get attention for)
5. Based on the above information, who could your audience be? (To make it easier, make a list starting with "people who are interested in".

Now you have a list of "niches" that you could become a mega influencer in before we get into the techniques needed to grow a huge following.

Step 6: Positioning Yourself

Once you are crystal clear about your values, strengths, attributes, niche, and passion, it is time to now position yourself. What does that mean exactly? It means that you establish how you would like others to see you based on your qualities, strengths, values, attributes, and passion. Do not forget – it is all about authenticity. No matter where you work, you must be consistent about who you say you are.

So, create a positioning statement for yourself. Pin it on a board. You can use this statement during interviews too. It is not going to be about a boring career summary, but a powerful and fresh take on where you see yourself. It will capture your essence and uniqueness.

Step 7: Understanding your competition

Make a list of ten mega influencers in any particular niche or industry. Take a look at how they present their accounts and the kind of content they are posting. What times are they posting? How many times do they update their content? How are they interacting with their followers? How many social media platforms are they present? Is there content same everywhere or are they creating and posting different content everywhere? If yes, what are the key differences, and how do they help these influencers?

Do not try to memorise it. Chart it. Yes, create a chart of influencers who you envy or find irresistible. Use the following pointers to fill in the chart against the name of each. Do not slack here as the chart you create now will come in handy when you create a killer content campaign for your brand.

1. Account Name: Are the account name and handle different?
2. Niche: Do they operate in multiple niches? What is the ratio?
3. Display Picture: Is it a logo or a picture? Is it generic or a decent shot?
4. Bio: Add a summary of what the account bio states.
5. Call to Action (or CTA for short): Simply put, does the bio direct followers to do something specific? For example, does it ask them to click follow? Visit a website?
6. Content-Type: Does the account have videos, images or both? What does the account have more of?
7. The theme of the content: What kind of images/videos is the account sharing with its followers? Is it short "humour" videos? Amazing landscape images? Selfies of the account owner? Product images?
8. Followers: How many followers does the account have? How many are they following?

9. Engagement: Engagement means the number of likes, views, and comments each post is receiving. Look at the last 3 - 5 posts on each account and note these down. The more likes and comments show what your audience is reacting strongly to.

10. Posting schedule: How often is the account posting? Is it once per day? Three times per day? 6 times per day?

Seeing what successful accounts are doing is one of the most effective ways to grow your personal brand account.

Influencer marketing: Understanding the Basics

Whenever a celebrity does something, it creates buzz and turns into a piece of breaking news or a topic of gossip. When a similar thing happens in business, it becomes a 'hot issue'. There are many ways companies create such hot issues, and one of them is using "Influencer Marketing".

The current day and age are filled with marketing messages and business slogans. Think of an advertisement. What came to your mind? Magazine headlines? Or TV Commercials?

In influencer marketing, it is more straightforward and more accessible. The influencer will say a few magical sentences on a short video and Voila! Sales start pouring in! These influencers with their vast and huge following can make businesses stand out from chaotic and old-school advertising techniques out there. Additionally, they will also bring massive value to your brand.

So, what is Influencer Marketing?

Before we dig deep into its understanding and insights. We first define the two words: Influence is the ability to affect the behaviour, development, decisions and character of someone, and even the impact itself.

Marketing is a way with which businesses promote or sell their products and services.

So, when combined, Influencer Marketing becomes a kind of marketing that utilises "influencers" who can influence others to buy what are they promoting or selling.

Even though Influencer marketing seems like a hot issue currently, it is nothing new. In fact, influencer marketing was born at the same time as the discovery of social media sites happened. Celebrities, Sports Enthusiast, and Thought Leaders were the first influencers of their niches and brands partnered with them to promote and sell their products and services.

So, here, we share a few characteristics of influencer marketing that make it so compelling and relevant:

Social media communication has already allowed everyone to voice out their opinions. Anyone who can speak properly and has an internet connection is welcome to create and share their content. Any smartphone user is capable of producing high-quality photographs and sharing them with the world through their social media account. Those who have the great and highest engagement will rise in status and stands a chance to become an influencer for that particular niche.

Influencer Marketing is Authentic

Indeed, it is. You must have seen those advertisement online that claim to know the easiest way to lose belly fat. Do you think those things work? Did those advertisements ever convince you that those claims might be right? Or, how about soap advertisements that promise to remove all tan or freckles in just one wash? Is that even remotely possible? Such advertisements that are full of fake promises are what give Influencer Marketing its authenticity and efficacy.

Influencer campaigns are organic and genuine than those advertisements that are scripted. Why? First, Influencers rise from the general population. In a way, they are people's champions. They are visible and had already used the product or service they are promoting. They are those role models and leaders who have gone through strict public scrutiny to build that level of trust and credibility. Therefore, invest your time, effort and money on leveraging their audience and connecting with them as you will witness much better results and ROI.

Influencers Help You with Your Brand Image

Social media can drive traffic to your business website. It can strengthen your bond with your customers, boost your overall SEO and generate organic media coverage. Influencers emerge as your "Superman" when you need a hand to increase your brand's recall and create a buzz about something on social media. Influencers will help you target the appropriate demographic, grow your network online, share ideas on how to create content for your business that and bolsters your SEO.

Influencer Marketing Is Cost-Effective

If you are tired from posting flyers everywhere that did not bring you any sales, try influencer marketing. It may turn out to be the best method for your business.

There is no fixed price for Influencer Marketing. You can either offer them a free item, pay them based on their performance, or discuss a flat rate for their services. Nonetheless, you will observe that influencer marketing will give you the best ROI. Plenty of research has proved that it is more affordable and effective than any other form of traditional advertising. Influencer Marketing is nothing like celebrity endorsements or paid gambling. It is about being authentic and unique and leveraging the genuine relationship between the brand, influencer, and their audience. That is precisely what distinguished influencer marketing from other marketing strategies.

Social Media Influencers: A Skin-Deep Industry?

While one spends hours scrolling through social media and admiring the picture-perfect luxurious life of influencers, one is bound to think that an attractive face and some luck are all it takes to become one of them. The reality, however, is often a lot different from such wishful imaginations.

So, here are the three fundamental traits of a successful social media influencer of today:

Identity

To move beyond being a forgettable pleasant face on Instagram, you need to establish a distinctive digital personality. That will require you to have a clear roadmap of content creation and how you aim to develop a reputation for being a go-to person for any particular niche.

An authentic influencer is also known to create buzz on their own and not merely ride on the trends with generic content. That means maintaining an intricate balance between the current market trends and being your avant-garde self.

Likability

Apart from looking pleasant and being creative, it is essential to have an amicable personality. When it comes to monetising the influence, influencers need to establish a healthy working relationship with brands and businesses. With the mushrooming of micro-influencers, it is a buyer's market.

So, when two influencers share the same niche, audience and almost identical influence, businesses and agencies will gravitate towards those who easier to work with than the over-the-top divas. It is common-sense to have common courtesy, especially when an influencer's critical criteria are to be likeable.

Integrity

While it is crucial to pay your bills even as a social media influencer which means business, one must not forget about integrity. It has to be your constant guiding principle. That means that the influencers must genuinely prefer a brand and its offerings to be able to 'sell' it and persuade their followers to 'buy' the content and to buy the product in question. A mismatch of influencer and brand will at best make little sales and at worst, tarnish the reputation of the influencer

Using significant persuasiveness in their niches, influencers may monetise the influence, use it to further causes that are close to their hearts or stay as an entertainer. To be able to choose these options, an individual must meet among the necessary prerequisites. While a pleasing appearance does help initially, authentic influencers are more than genetics and make-up.

Why Businesses Need Social Media for Influencer Marketing

Influencer marketing can be considered as an effective strategy to attract and engage with the potential and existing customers.

You can no longer question the significance of social marketing. Everyone is using the social marketing agency or channels for personal and professional purposes. These days, most businesses are leveraging the benefits of social media networks to expand their influence and distinguish themselves from the competition. They want to go beyond just maintaining an online presence. So, they need to stretch out their brick-and-mortar retail to digital, and here, they must take advantage of influencers and technology.

The ascent of social media has reignited enthusiasm for influencer marketing. In today's digital times, persuading the audience towards purchase is not limited to actors and celebrities. Any well-known blogger or a social media influencer can make that happen. Anyone who has established his or her credibility with a broad audience and has a considerable following online is an influencer. Their reliability, skill, and realness can convince consumers to draw in with your image. What is more, that is the reason it is recommended to set up a potential association with them and arrange your advertising exercises around them.

Becoming an Instagram Influencer

Becoming an Instagram influencer is not a sprint. It is a marathon. Growing a highly engaged following will take time but will profit you massively in the long run. Companies are competing harder than ever to seek out and partner with social media influencers. They want influencers who have excellent engagement rates and a loyal following. A good Instagram Influencer is bombarded with partnership offerings from all around the world. Let us make it happen for you!

Who is an Instagram Influencer?

An appropriate definition of an "Instagram Influencer" would be a user who has established credibility with an audience, who can persuade others by virtue of their trustworthiness and authenticity to act.

This definition tells us that an influencer is:
- someone with a massive network of followers
- whose followers share the interests of this influencer
- someone who is known to be an honest person and people's champion

Honest is the keyword here. The reason is that no company wants to be associated with dishonest people. By using this trust, your influence, they can (and will) persuade followers to buy and use the different products and services you promote (which are theirs).

In return for your influence, businesses will pay you to put their products or services in front of your followers. This, in turn, gives them the exposure they need to sell more goods. That is a form of monetisation which we will discuss shortly.

So, as an Instagram influencer, you have a responsibility, to be honest, and only promote products you believe in. If you choose to use your influence to encourage hate or negativity, then you can kiss your chances of monetising your Instagram goodbye!

When are you officially an influencer?

Technically you are an influencer the minute someone acts on the back of your recommendation. Whether an audience member buys a product you have talked about, visited a restaurant you recommended or watched a movie you raved about. The real question is, what do companies and brands look for when seeking to partner up with Instagram influencers.

Understand that all businesses and brands are different, and when it comes to partnering with influencers. They will look for entirely different characteristics, attributes and metrics. Whether it be the niche you are in, the content you have posted or your image. They all have different requirements.

With that said, most companies generally look for the same two fundamental things before they look for anything else. These are:

1. A large follower base (usually a minimum of 10,000)
2. A high engagement rate over your last ten posts (+3% minimum)

These are general guidelines. Some smaller business will be happy to partner with you if you only have 3,000 followers and a 10% engagement rate; whereas others will want influencers with over a million followers and a 1.5% engagement rate.

Again, these two points are only the beginning. Companies may then look at your content, your image, your niche, how you behave with your followers, your captions etc. Everything in this playbook works coordinated with each other and has been laid out to help you build the best Instagram account and maximise your chances in creating business deals with potential partners.

Optimising a Beautiful Instagram Account

This chapter will tell you how to create an Instagram profile which sticks out from the rest and gives you the best chances of ranking highest in the search results. Before we work through each section and maximise your Instagram account. You will need to get familiar with each part of your Instagram and understand its purpose and why it is essential.

Instagram Username or Handle

Now you will need your smartphone or device and your influencer study chart at the ready while you work through each section.

Your Instagram Username or Handle is the name which displays at the top of your Instagram page. That @handle is the first thing which makes your account stand out. It is your unique ID which everyone on Instagram will know you by. Here is some information that you should know about this @handle:

1. Only you will have the @handle you choose, no one else on Instagram will have the same @handle.
2. It will appear in the Instagram search results when people search for you or accounts similar to yours.
3. People see the @handle when you like or comment on images or videos across Instagram

To keep it easy for your audience, have a handle that is short, nice and convenient to remember. You might find that the name you wanted is not available because an account already exists by that name. In such a case, do not start adding random numbers to your handle name.

First, try some variations with dots and underscores. If that does not work, try adding words like official, yours, I am, etc. or your niche or country. Add numbers only when you have exhausted all these options and even then, use a number that is relevant to your personal brand.

To change your @handle, open up your Instagram app on your smartphone or device and head to your profile page. Click edit profile" and update the "username" section. Instagram does an excellent job of letting you know if a username is already taken so play around with it and create a username which sticks out to your new and existing followers.

Your Instagram Name

The name section of Instagram differs from the @handle we discussed in the previous part. That gives visitors a bit of extra information on who you are and what your name is. For your personal branded account, we suggest you use your name or your name plus the niche you are in. Your name will appear in bold right underneath your profile picture (which we will discuss in the next section) so visitors' eyes will be drawn directly to it each time they visit your profile.

Again, you may already have your Instagram name setup in a way which quickly identifies who you are if that is the case, fantastic! You can move to the next section. To update your name, click "edit profile" then update the "name" section.

The critical thing to remember about the name section is that Instagram search function will use it to find you when people start to look you up.

Choosing the Perfect Instagram Display Picture

Before we look at how to update your Instagram display picture, let us look at the top 5 things which make the perfect Instagram display picture.

1. Make your display picture all about your brand:

   Remember your brand is you! So, create a good display image all about you. An excellent clear headshot makes the perfect display image. Why? Because you are selling you! You are the brand; you are the influencer, you are the owner of this account, so make it clear to your followers what your account is all about.

2. Think about the background of your display image:

   When selecting a headshot for your Instagram display image, the environment is significant. It does not just add to the look and feel of your display image, but the entire appearance of your account. A carefully selected background, which matches the overall colour palette of your account, will look super professional and impressive.

3. Keep your display picture up to date:

You want people to know that you are fully active on Instagram. It does not look great if it is summertime and your display image is of you on a skiing vacation. Try to keep your display image up to date as possible. If you choose a seasonal theme for your display image, then remember to update it when that particular season ends. Again, you do not want as Christmassy display image in February!

Choosing a neutral theme means your display images can be used for longer but not too long. It is good to update your image everyone 6 - 8 weeks as it keeps it fresh and get your followers interested enough to visit your profile when they see it change.

4. Consider using props in your display image:

Is your niche makeup? Then make your picture look like you are about to apply makeup. Is your niche fitness? Then hold a dumbbell in your display image. Your image needs to capture you, your amazing personality and your niche all at the same time. If this seems a tad tricky, then at least get yourself a beautiful and exciting background.

5. Choose the right image size:

The size of your profile image is significant. Instagram displays your profile image at a size of 110 x 110 pixels. So, when you are viewing an Instagram profile on your smartphone or tablet. You will see the profile image in the size of 110 by 110 pixels. It has not very big, but big enough that you can get an indication of what the picture is about. To get the most precise display image, we suggest you upload a display image which is a little bit bigger at around 500x500 pixels.

The reason for this is because:

- This particular image size will display the most precise image, making you even more recognisable. Especially when people visit your profile and see your image in the search field and comments section.
- The image size keeps the vital image square. Instagram loves square images because it then crops your image into a circle of 110 by 110 pixels.

You can adjust and move your image before you upload it to your profile. When you do this, make sure your image is centred and looking symmetrical.

Most pictures you take on your Smartphone will be a good enough size to upload. There will be further information in later sections on how to create the perfect image size using tools such as Canva.

Creating an Instagram Bio That Sticks Out

You will find your Instagram bio sitting underneath your name, and it instantly tells users briefly about who you are. A good bio can capture visitors' attention and entice them to follow you.

As an influencer, you want your bio to sell your Instagram account and nothing else. You want to get people to hit that follow button, so they see all of your regular updates. You could take an influential approach or a funny one. It does not matter; the important thing is that people connect with immediately.

Some research suggests that you have less than 2 seconds to make an impression on Instagram. That means that as soon as someone clicks on your profile, they will click off it almost instantly if nothing immediately grabs their attention. As an influencer, you want your bio to grab the reader's attention, connect with them in some way and then direct them to take a specific action. In this case, you want them to click "follow".

Some do's and don'ts of Instagram bios

Emojis

Emojis are an excellent tool for engaging visitors. They make your bio look colourful and will break up the text nicely. However, do not overuse them as it will make your bio look cluttered. Just a few scattered throughout will be enough to make your bio look fresh and exciting.

Also, try to add in emojis which are relevant to what you are communicating. If you want to add in your bio that you are a dog lover, then use a dog emoji. If you are adding to your bio that you love make-up, then add a lipstick emoji. If you use emojis which are not congruent with what you are saying, then it could look confusing and cost you followers.

Format

You want your bio to be aesthetically pleasing and easy on the eye. The way you do this is by making sure the spacing is right. Take a look at the profiles on your chart and see how their bios are spaced.

The Instagram app is coded in such a way that it does not recognises spaces in the bio. It does not accept new lines which makes your bio look clunky and crowded. The best way to create your bio is in the notes app on your Smartphone or device. Then copy and paste directly into the bio section of the edit screen. That will give you a nicely formatted bio which will grab the attention of any new visitors and improve your chances of converting them into a new follower.

Your Call to Action (CTA)

You have probably seen the phrase "call to action" a couple of times so far. But what does it mean? A call to action is a short phrase, like Book Now or Click Here, which instructs a visitor to take a particular action. Have you ever seen a website which asks you to "buy now" or watched a YouTube video which asks you to "hit the subscribe button"? That is a call to action! So, what is your call to action?

That is all about making you an influencer on Instagram, and what do all Instagram influencers have lots of? Followers!!! That is right; you want followers. You want people who visit your profile to hit the follow button and become a new follower.

When you update your bio always make sure the last line of text has a "call to action". Some good examples you can use are Follow Me, Hit the Follow Button NOW, Click Follow NOW for Loads of Amazing Updates, Tap Follow to See More of Me, Click Follow & Send Me a Message.

Use emojis around your call to action, so it draws the visitor's eyes to it. A right call to action could be the difference between someone clicking off your profile and clicking follow.

Do not forget to experiment with your call to action; you may find some "call to actions" work better than others depending on who your audience is.

Creating the Ultimate Content Strategy

"Good content isn't about storytelling; it's about telling your story well."

There are nine types of content you can choose from when posting on Instagram. These categories will give you countless ideas on what to post to your account. The important thing is that you are posting and getting your personal brand out there and in front of people. The nine categories are:

1. The Selfie
2. What's Happening
3. Quotes
4. Humour
5. Short Videos
6. Trending Daily Hashtags
7. Behind the Scenes
8. Products in Use
9. The How-to Post

Let us look at each category in more detail.

#1: The Selfie

As an influencer, people need to see you, and they need to see who they are interacting with. So, post selfies of yourself wherever you go. Remember, that backgrounds are just as crucial with selfies so get creative.

#2: What's happening?

What are you up to? Are you out shopping and find a costly pair of shoes? Post it! Come across a fantastic statue or piece of the street? Post it! Are you just sat on the grass reading a book? Post it!

What is happening posts are not only excellent opportunities for posting exciting things, but they can turn into unique selfie opportunities too.

#3: Quotes

Posting your favourite quotes is a perfect way to engage with your followers. Quotes can be funny, serious, informative, intelligent, and people react to them well.

#4: Humour

Anything you find funny should be posted on Instagram. People love to laugh, and if they laugh at something you have posted, then they will connect with your account in an extremely positive way. Do not forget to keep it tidy and try not to post anything which makes you look like a clown.

#5: Short Videos

Instagram lets you post short videos up to 60 seconds long. Short videos are just an alternative to images so you can post selfie videos, what are you up to videos, Trending Daily Hashtag Videos, Product in Use Videos and Funny Videos. Video is becoming more and more popular, so do not be shy! Post videos as often as you can.

#6: Trending Daily Hashtags

Each day Instagram has some top trending hashtags which you should use to get maximum exposure. For example, Monday has #MondayMotivation, Tuesday has #TipTuesday, Wednesday has #Workout Wednesday and so on. We will discuss more hashtags in the next sections.

#7: Behind the Scenes

Behind the scenes posts are usually created by companies who want to show you their business "behind the scenes". It helps followers understand the who is who of their industry. For influencers, behind the scenes could be a look at their home life, pictures of their pets, their homes, their families etc.

#8: Products in Use

As an influencer, you may get asked to promote products or services. An excellent method is to post the "product in use" image. Whether it is eyeliner or a protein bar the beauty of the product in use shot is that it helps your followers envisage what it is like using the product themselves. That pleases companies who may sponsor you to promote more of their product.

#9: The How-to Post

This type of post does wonders for engagement because it gives the user free knowledge that they did not have access to before. Although not impossible, you can create a good "how-to" post using just one image but do not forget you can add up to 10 images in one post using the carousel option or post a 1-minute long video. Choose whichever feels right for you!

Curating Other People's Content

When you browse Instagram (or the web in general), you may come across a piece of content that you like so much that you want to repost it. Although you can do this, you need to know that posting copyrighted content without permission could be a violation of the law. Here are some things to consider when reposting other people's content:

1. Where possible, get permission from the content owner to repost. Otherwise, mention the name of the original creator to give due credit. There are lots of cool apps on the app store designed to make reposting easy. These apps automatically credit the creator, so you do not need to.

2. Many websites offer royalty-free images. You can take pictures from there and use them in your content.

3. Two other great sources for content are Reddit and Tumblr. People from all around the world post content they find interesting specific to certain topics. You can use that content to share on your feed.

By using the above categories, you will never run out of things to post. Do not set yourself any limits; just let the content flow freely and see what people react to. You will find that some posts do well, and others do not. Pay attention to what posts are getting the most likes and comments. As time goes on, you will be able to see what your followers like, which means you can post more of it.

Instagram Posting: The Basics

As an Instagram user, you will know how to post basic images at the very least. The following information walks you through some of the additional features Instagram has to liven up your content. You must mix up the use of these features to keep your content fresh and engaging.

In-built Instagram Tools for Posting

Boomerang

It is a free app by Instagram, which is also in-built in its UI. It takes a burst of photographs and loops them backwards and forwards into a "boomerang" video. It brings images to life and gives them an excellent 3D feel. Give it a go!

Layout

The Layout is another app created by Instagram, which lets you create funky collage images. That is great for your content strategy because it gives you more variety in your posts. Download it now and play around with it.

Select Multiple or Carousel

The select-multiple tool is another feature inside Instagram, which allows you to create a carousel of images. You can select up to 10 images in 1 post which your followers can swipe through. It is another cool feature which again gives you more variety in your content creation

All of the above apps are accessible when you click the "upload" button located in the centre of your Instagram profile home screen.

Post Captions

Adding captions to posts is one of the most underestimated features of Instagram. The word caption comes from the old French word "caption" which means "capture". And that should tell you the function of your captions. They should be capturing your follower's attention and grabbing hold of it.

A great caption will amplify the engagement of your post and boost your exposure to more followers across the Instagram platform. That is a skill all good influencers have!

Instagram captions allow you to add up to 2200 characters, including emoji. So, you have quite a big space to say what you want to say. That does not mean you have to max out the character count each time you post in fact, quite the opposite. When it comes to captions, less is more!

Now here are the top 6 things you need to consider when creating a high-quality caption:

1. Make the first line attention-grabbing.

   Remember, that Instagram allows only the first few lines, usually140 characters, of your caption openly and rest everything is tucked under 'Read More'. To read any more than that, the viewer will need to click the "more" button that appears in your caption. So, you need to make the first line of your caption stand out and grab the viewer's attention to the point they have to click more and read the rest.

2. Ask a question.

   It is a smart way to interact with your audience. Asking questions and encouraging people to answer can open up a massive conversation with your followers and potential new followers. Get people to come forward with their own opinions and experiences. Do not forget to respond to the best comments. People are delighted to see someone they admire to engage with them. That is an excellent step to creating a solid fan base.

3. Direct people to your bio.

   Adding your own Instagram handle into your caption is a powerful way to get people to visit your bio. You can create a caption telling people about the content in your profile.

4. Call to action.

   Create a caption which directs the viewers to take a specific action. This could be to "Tag A Friend Who Likes Coffee" or "Visit My Profile to Find Out More.

5. Format your caption.

   Just like the bio, Instagram is not great when it comes to formatting your captions. An excellent app to download is "Caption Writer". That great little tool is easy to use and completely free! Just type your caption in the format you want then copy and paste it over to Instagram.

6. Change up your fonts.

   Yes, you can choose different fonts for your Instagram captions. An excellent place to get cool fonts is www.igfonts.io or www.instgramfonts.com. Check each site out!

More Amazing Tools for Creating Amazing Content

Canva.com

Canva is a cool, free, graphics design site. It is simple to use and has lots of fantastic stuff which will help you create some eye-catching content.

Canva uses drag-and-drop features, so you do not need any experience in design. There are loads of templates you can use for Instagram posts and Instagram Stories too.

Adobe Spark Post & Adobe Spark Video

These two apps can help you create some stunning content for your Instagram page. They do take a bit more getting used to than Canva, but when used correctly, it can make your content stand out.

Both Adobe Spark Post & Video are available in the app store.

Adobe Photoshop

The adobe photoshop app is a professional image editing tool you can download for free. With this app, you can touch up your photos, remove blemishes, add text and change perspectives. It is awesome!

Adobe Photoshop has some cool paid features that you can make use of. However, the free version offers you more than you can get anywhere else.

Timing for The Maximum Exposure

When to post your content could be the difference between 100 likes and 1000 likes. The right time for your post to go up depends on the content your posting, your follower count, your hashtag strategy and your location on the globe.

Your account is unique, and your best time to post will be too. Data suggests that Wednesdays tend to generate more likes per post on average. However, it is only a tiny bit higher than any other day during the week. With that in mind, do not worry too much about what day of the week to post.

What you should worry about is the best time to post. Again, the data shows that the average number of likes is low during the early hours of the morning. They then start to pick up as we move towards the time when most people are waking up from their sleep and are just beginning their day.

There is a point during midday and early evening when activity is the highest. Some analysis says that Instagram gets busy during lunch periods and when people come home from work or school etc. With that information, make a note of these times and consider them when you are posting.

One great tool to use is an app called "When to Post" which is available for free in the app store. That amazing app will monitor your account and give you the three best times to post every day.

Frequency of Posting

There is no specific number of posts you should create each day to get your account out there. It differs for every account right across Instagram. So, focus more on the quality of the post rather than the quantity. However, as a general advice post a minimum of once per week and not more than thrice in one day.

This balance is vital to show your followers that you are active but not addicted. What is the point of uploading ten posts in one day, which are of average quality that make you look like a spam account?

Choose quality over quantity.

Instagram Engagement Rate

Engagement rate is something that the Instagram algorithm monitors regularly. It is a way of determining how effective a piece of content is with its audience.

The reason Instagram works out the engagement rate is that it wants to make sure its users only see the best content on its platform. For example, if you follow #adorabledogs, then Instagram wants to make sure you only see good, quality content relating to "adorable dogs". It will do this by searching its platform for any content with the "adorable dogs" hashtag. Content will then be prioritised based on the highest engagement rate.

Instagram does this to remain competitive. If they did not, then it would be full of trash content that people would not be interested in. That could result in people leaving the platform for a competitor.

Instagram automatically applies a simple algorithm to each post to calculate its engagement rate.

Calculation of Engagement Rate

Engagement rate (ER) is worked out like this:

(Number of likes + Number of comments)/ (Number of followers) x 100 = ER%

For instance, after posting a picture, you get 500 likes, 40 comments, and you have 4500 followers. The math would look like this:

500 (likes) + 40 (comments) / 4500 (followers) x 100 = 12% (ER%)

So, this post would have a 12% engagement rate which is absolutely massive. The average Instagram account has a 3% engagement rate. Anything consistently above 3%, mixed in with a high number of followers, and you are considered an Instagram Influencer.

If your math is not high then no problem, there is a simple calculator you can use to work out your engagement rate for each post. Just fill in the blanks and let the calculator work it out for you.

www.iginfluencerplaybook.com/Instagram-engagement-rate-calculator

Before we proceed to the next section, here is one thing to note: Although working out your engagement rate is a good thing; you want to focus most of your time on your content itself. Combining that with the strategies you are about to learn in the next section will naturally skyrocket your engagement rate bringing in a massive wave of new followers.

Maxing Out Your Engagement Rate

Now you know about engagement rate, let us look at the strategies which will get your content in front of millions of users across the world. We will go over the three most effective ways to boost your posts and get the maximum engagement rate. These are:

- Hashtags
- Geotags
- Social Proof

Hashtags

Hashtags are short descriptive pieces of text which categorise your content and make it easily searchable. So, let us say that you want to search for Gucci. You could type in "Gucci" in the search function, and it will bring back all the available images which have #Gucci in the caption or the comments section of the post.

People generally follow the hashtag they are interested in too. So, someone who follows "#Gucci" will often see Gucci content in their feeds. Before we find and create some fantastic hashtags for your account, take a look at some of the dos and don'ts of posting content using hashtags.

1. Keep your hashtags 30 or less in one post.

   Each post allows to use up to 30 hashtags in total so use them all! The more hashtags you use, the more people will see your content. The more people see your content, the more followers you get. If you try to use more than 30 hashtags, Instagram will not let you upload your post.

2. Keep your hashtags relevant.

   If you are making a post about working out in the gym, then you will want to use tags such as #fitness #gym #workout etc. You would not use hashtags like #catsofinstagram or #makeupartist because it would look confusing to anyone viewing your content. Keep your hashtags relevant to you, your post and your personal brand.

3. Insert hashtag in the comments section of each post.

   You can insert your hashtags in either the caption section or the comments section of your post. It is recommended that you post your hashtags in the comments section. The reason for this is that it keeps your captions looking clean for each post, so users will not initially see what hashtags you have used. Once you have submitted your content along with the caption, revisit the post and click the speech bubble icon to open the comment box. Here you can add the hashtags relevant to your post.

4. Try to mix up your hashtags.

   Some people save their favourite hashtags and copy them each time they post. There is some evidence to suggest that Instagram considers the use of the same hashtags over and over again as spam. That would be a disaster because you could end up having your account banned. Avoid being repetitive and mix your hashtags up. You will get maximum exposure this

5. There are specific hashtags you must avoid.

   Avoid any hashtags which are asking for follows such as #follow4follow, #pleasefollow, #followme, #like4follow etc. Potentially using these tags could get your account banned, which is the last thing you want as an Instagram influencer. Also, you do not want to come across as desperate for followers.

Top Trending Hashtags

The best part of hashtags is that you can literally hashtag anything! You can use existing hashtags, or you can even make them up. The idea is to use hashtags which are being used more frequently because this increases your exposure to more potential followers.

A great tool to find top trending hashtags is www.tagsforlikes.com which monitors Instagram each day for the top trending hashtags. You can use these hashtags to build your following and personal brand. The great thing about www.tagsforlikes.com is that it gives top trending hashtags for different categories too. If you are having coffee with friends, then tagsforlikes can provide you with the top trending coffee & friends hashtags etc.

When you are adding hashtags, think about what you are doing, who you are with, what your post is about, and where you are. You can even hashtag the city or country you are in! The point is you need to hashtag everything relevant at that moment in time! Do not hold back, go wild; this can be the difference between 5 likes and 5000 likes.

Daily Trending Hashtags

There is a tradition on Instagram, which means you will see specific hashtags pop up on certain days of the week. That is 100% something you need to take advantage of because so many Instagram users subscribe to these hashtags.

Below is a list of the top 79 hashtags which trend Monday through to Sunday. These hashtags are a great way to get exposure as well as giving you some inspiration on what to post. Keep this list handy and try to incorporate them on the days you post.

Monday

#MondayMotivation #MotivationMonday #MondayBlues #MarketingMonday #MusicMonday #MeatlessMonday #MaxoutMonday #MondayRun #MondayOutfit #MindfulMonday #ManicureMonday #MancrushMonday (or #MCM) #MondayFunday #ManicMonday

Tuesday

#TravelTuesday #TransformationTuesday #TipTuesday #TechTuesday #TuesdayTasting #TuesdayShoesday #GoodNewsTues #TuesdayTunes #TakeMeBackTuesday #TastyTuesday

Wednesday

#WomancrushWednesday (or #WCW) #Humpday #WorkoutWednesday #WisdomWednesday #WellnessWednesday #WayBackWednesday #WoofWednesday #Winesday #WineWednesday #WackyWednesday #WomenWednesday #WinItWednesday

Thursday

#ThrowbackThursday (or #TBT) #ThankfulThursday #Thursdate #ThirstyThursday #ThoughtfulThursday #ThursdayThoughts #TGIT (Thank God It is Thursday)

Friday

#FlashBackFriday #FearlessFriday #FashionFriday #FictionFriday #FridayReads #FollowFriday (or #FF) #FeatureFriday #FitnessFriday #FridayFun #FridayNight #FactFriday #FreebieFriday #TGIF (Thank God It is Friday)

Saturday

#Caturday #SaturdayStyle #SaturdaySweat #SaturdaySpecial #SaturdaySale #SaturdayNight #SaturdayNightFever #SaturdayShoutOut (or #SS)

Sunday

#SundayFunday #SundayRead #SpotlightSunday #StartupSunday #SundaySweat #SelfieSunday #WeekendVibes #ScienceSunday #SundayBrunch

Geotags

A geotag is another great way to get exposure from users in specific towns or cities. Instagram uses your physical location to tag your content to whichever location you choose. For example, if you tag your post to Los Angeles, California, then people following or located in LA will have a higher chance of seeing your content. Tagging a location is easy. Simply use the "Add Location" option when uploading a post and choose a location. It does not have to be your hometown, either!

The good thing about geotags is that it is not just limited to towns or cities. You can geotag in venues, bars, clubs and shopping malls. Any location on the map will be available to geotag!

Social Proof

Social proof is a potent tool when it comes to increasing your engagement rate. But what is it?

Social proof comes in many forms both online and offline, but it boils down to this. People love what is widespread, and the more popular something is, the more exciting and trustworthy it becomes. It is a form of human psychology.

Have you bought something from Amazon and observed the star rating? You probably did not buy an item which only had a 1-star rating. Instead, you went for the 5-star rating. Even if it costs a little more, that is social proof.

So how does social proof work on Instagram?

Research has shown that you are more likely to engage with a piece of content if it has a higher amount of likes and comments. People follow the social norm, so the more likes and comments you see on a piece of content. The more exciting, trustworthy and valuable the content is perceived to be. So how do you max out your social proof?

You are about to learn the top 3 ways you can max out your social proof. These strategies have helped some of the biggest influencers on the Instagram kick start their careers as a social media influencer so take them seriously.

Note that these methods are only used to gain traction in your following and not something to be used long term. When your account eventually reaches the 10k followers' mark, and your engagement is above the standard 3%. Your social proof is something which will increase each time you post.

Here are the top 3 strategies to kickstart your social proof on Instagram.

1. Tell your current following when you post.

    How do you do that? Simple! You do it through your Instagram story, which we will go through in the next section. (This is powerful)

2. Add a call to action (CTA) on your post.

   We discussed the call to action in the first part of the playbook. When you create a
   post, you should add a phrase in the first line of the caption which invites the user to
   like and/or comment on your post.

   For example, let us say you upload a post of that delicious Strawberry Frappuccino
   you have just bought at Starbucks. The first line of the caption could read "Like if you
   love Frappes!" or "What's your favourite Frappe? Comment Below!!".

   Research has shown that by adding a call to action to your posts. You can increase
   likes and comments by up to 250%!

3. Power Likes

   Power likes is a system provided by the super successful social media management
   company GoSo. They manage thousands of genuine, high-quality accounts across
   Instagram. For approximately $35.00, GoSo will deliver 100 natural likes to two of
   your posts each day for a full month. That massively boosts your engagement rate
   and social proof at the same time. Sign up today and give it a try, once you provide
   your Instagram @handle and place your order. The likes start rolling in after around
   15 minutes.

   That is a great way to boost your engagement rate instantly. As your likes start to flow
   through, your post will rank higher in users Instagram feed, meaning even more
   organic likes and follows.

Becoming an Instagram storyteller

Instagram story feature is quite possibly the most engaging and accessible form of social media at this moment in time. In fact, as of 2019, Instagram has over 1.5 billion users worldwide. Over 60% of which view and create Instagram stories almost daily. That is over 750 million people worldwide viewing and posting content!

That is a lot of people!

So, the question is, how can you make your Instagram stories stand out above the rest of the crowd?

In this chapter, you will learn,

- What Instagram stories are and why they are so important.
- The Do's and Don'ts of Instagram Stories
- What to post on Instagram Stories?
- Top 10 tips for creating super-engaging stories
- Story Highlights tactics which keep people coming back to your profile

What is Instagram Stories?

Instagram stories let you post pictures and videos that vanish after 24 hours. Your content is neatly packaged together in a slide show format, so it is almost like creating your own mini-movie.

It is an excellent alternative to posting images and videos on your feed. Not only will your story keep your followers super engaged, but it can bring them back to your profile to like more of your content.

You will find Instagram stories across the top of your feed. The most recently posted stories will always appear on the far left. The oldest ones, or the ones you have viewed, will move further down to the right.

Instagram stories are important because it is a direct portal into your day to day life. The more your followers see you, the more trust you build with them. The more trust you develop, the more influence you have, and your influence is what companies will pay you for!

DO: Post daily.

Post an Instagram story several times a day. There is no hard and fast rule around what time to post. Some research suggests that peak times are between 11 am and 1 pm then again between 7 pm and 9 pm.

DON'T: Overdo it with animations and decorations.

There are tons of fun animations you can use in your story, so it is super easy to get carried away. Avoid this mistake!

DO: Post quality content

No matter what you post in your stories, bring an element of value each time.

DON'T: Write your text too small.

That is a mistake people make all the time, and it makes your followers disengaged. Make your text nice and big. Sometimes you may want to write something which is longer than a few lines. That is fine but be creative and spread it over a few story posts instead of cramming into one post.

DO: Be creative.

Instagram Stories are a canvas for creativity. Even if it means keeping up to date on other people's Instagram stories do it! As a story artist, you will need as much inspiration as possible.

DON'T: Be negative or abusive!

As an influencer, you will have your critics. There is not an influencer out there who has not had their fair share of haters. Do not use your influence to be negative or abusive towards these people. Companies looking to pay people to promote their products will avoid anyone who is obnoxious or offensive.

DO: Use Hashtags and Geotags.

That will blow up your reach and engagement. One smart way to add many hashtags to your stories is to use them in the same colour as your background and squeeze them small. Now push them in a corner where the audience is not likely to pay attention.

DO: Be transparent and build trust.

Posting content about your day to day life will build trust with your followers which is a high-end goal to have. The more confidence you build, the more of an influencer you are.

What to post to your Instagram story?

Your content strategy for your Instagram story goes hand in hand with the content strategy for your main feed. So, the nine categories of content that we discussed in the previous chapter will work for your stories as well. Let us do a quick recap of these:

1. The Selfie
2. What's Happening
3. Quotes
4. Humour
5. Short Videos
6. Trending Daily Hashtags
7. Behind the Scenes
8. Products in Use
9. The How-to Post

There is one more additional post category you must regularly use when posting a story. That category is known as the "call to action". Top influencers commonly use the story strategy right across Instagram and one you should use each time you add a new post to your feed.

So, what is it?

This strategy involves your sharing the content from your feed to your Instagram story but with the twist of creating a secret reveal. That prompts your followers (or anyone else who views your story) to visit your profile to see the content in full quickly.

That is a super powerful strategy that will drive hordes of people to your profile. However, do not overdo it. Try to use it only for your best images and videos.

Here is how it works!

Step 1: After you have uploaded content to your feed, click the "share button". It is the icon just above the caption, which looks like a little paper aeroplane. The share menu will appear, click "Add to Story".

Step 2: Here, you can decorate the post by covering the image.

Step 3: Add your strong "Call to Action". In this case, there are two - "Tap Here to Find Out", and the "Tap Here" gif, which is animated. When the user taps the screen, it will link them straight back to the original post, and all will be revealed.

This tactic stirs up real anticipation with your followers, and they will be eager to visit your profile to find out more. You can do this with selfies, how-to posts, quotes etc. You can do this with almost all content you post, and it is a super powerful way to keep your followers guessing!

Top 10 Tips to Quickly Create super-Engaging Stories

Tip #1: Use Coloured Backgrounds

Creating colour backgrounds is a smart little way to brighten up your story post. It is simple to do, check it out!

Step 1: Open your story and take a picture of anything. (it does not matter what)

Step 2: Hit the pen icon in the top right-hand corner, so the colour palette appears across the bottom of the screen.

Step 3: Choose the colour you like.

Step 4: Tap and hold the screen until the entire background changes colour.

Told you it was simple!

Tip #2: Carve Out Images

Carving out an image is a brilliant way to get your viewers to focus on just one part of your image. It is simple too!

Step 1: Open your story and choose an image you want to post.

Step 2: Now fill the screen with colour.

Step 3: The colour will now fill the screen, but your image will still be behind it.

Step 4: Choose the eraser function across the top of the screen and start to erase parts of the screen which will display some of the uploaded images.

And there you have it! You have carved out an image.

Tip #3: Drop shadow your text

A great way to make your story text stand out is to create a drop shadow. It is simple yet extremely unique. Here is how it works.

Step 1: Open your story and choose your background. It can be an image, video or colour background.

Step 2: Write your text choosing the colour you want and the size you want. Duplicate the text by using the copy and paste function. Resize each line of text, so they are the same size.

Step 3: Now layer the text on top of each other but slightly off centre. That gives you a cool shadow background which makes your text look 3D.

You can do these 3 or 4 times for extra effect.

Have a play around with different colour schemes and fonts when trying it out.

Tip #4: Type Letters Individually

This effect is incredible, and the best part is, not many accounts use it, so it will make your stories stand out from the rest. It will take you a little bit longer, but the effect is well worth it.

Step 1: Choose your image, video or background

Step 2: Type each letter of your caption individually

Step 3: Position the letters to make your caption

Again, it is all about experimenting, but you get the idea. When using this technique, you could try different fonts, add a drop shadow, write your words horizontally or vertically. Give it a go on your next story.

Tip #5: Mix Your Fonts Up

Another great way to captivate your story viewers is by mixing up your font selection. In the Instagram story mode, you are limited to only five fonts. These are Neon, Typewriter, Strong, Classic and Modern.

What to Post on Your Highlight Reel?

Your highlight reel will evolve as you evolve as an influencer. But the list below will help you kickstart your creativity for generating fantastic highlights.

Step 1: Add A Welcome Message

A great start is to add a simple welcome message for your profile visitors! People love this. Some research was conducted, which shows that a highlight welcome message can increase followers by 67%, that is amazing! Add a simple "hello", tell the visitor who you are, what your profile offers and do not forget to add a strong call to action in there and ask them to follow you.

Step 2: How-To

Whenever you post a "how-to" story, you are providing valuable information to your followers. You do not want to lose that information because it is pure gold to anyone who follows and admires you. Use these "how-to" stories to create permanent tutorials which will be right at the top of your profile for all to see.

Step 3: Blog Posts

A highlight reel is a great tool for creating a blog! You might find yourself on vacation for two weeks in Canada. Create a highlight reel dedicated to your vacation. Show off the beaches and local landmarks, show the world what an amazing place it is. Create a highlight reel dedicated to your cat or your workout regime or your morning routine. Whatever your niche is, create a highlight reel for it.

Step 4: AMA (Ask Me Anything)

Another amazing category for your highlight reel is the "AMA" which stands for "ask me anything". As the number of your followers will grow, so will the number of questions you receive. Use any question you get asked to create an "AMA" highlight reel. Your followers will love to find out more about you which in turn can boost your engagement and your influence!

Step 5: Create Your Episode

Thanks to the highlight reel, you can create hundreds of your niche episodes. Things like interviews, products, partners. You can create a reel about your family, your morning routine, your gym routine, your dog, your cat or even progress on the guitar lessons you are having.

Before You Start Creating Your Highlight Reel

Before you can upload a post to your highlight reel, you need to upload the post to your story. Instagram has a "Save To Archive" feature which we recommend you activate. That will save your story posts to the cloud, meaning you will never lose a single piece of content. To do this simply open your Instagram app and click "Settings". Then follow this path:

Setting > Privacy > Story > Save To Archive

How to Add A Highlight Reel to Your Profile?

Adding a highlight reel to your profile could not be easier.

On your profile, you should see a circle with a "+" symbol in the centre. Tapping this icon will take you to your story archive. Here you can choose a post to add to your highlight reel. Remember that the last post you select from your archive will be the first post in your highlight reel.

Adding A Highlight Name

All new highlights will need to have a name and icon associated with it. The name of your highlight should be no more than nine characters long. So, aim to keep the name of your highlight short and sweet.

Adding A Highlight Icon

When it comes to adding a highlight icon, you have two options - Add an image from your camera or photo library as an icon. Make your icon.

We recommend the second option. Creating your highlight cover will keep the look and feel of your Instagram profile page consistent with your overall Instagram aesthetic.

Try to make sure that your icon represents the highlight reel as much as possible. If your highlight is about music, then use a musical note. If the reel is about travel, use an aeroplane, etc.

Canva is a great tool to create your custom made highlight covers. You can also find some free highlight covers using the link below:

Instagram Live

Instagram Live is a fantastic feature which allows you to live stream directly from your device your followers. It is just liked a live TV channel! It is a fantastic way to bolster trust with your followers, interact with them live and find out more about what they want to see from you.

As soon as you go live, your followers will receive a notification inviting them to watch you. If you want to stand out above the rest of the influencers in your niche, and become one of the top earners, then this tool is an absolute must for you.

How to start an Instagram Live broadcast

Starting an Instagram Live broadcast is easy. Let us walk through how to broadcast live and review some of the other features you can use when broadcasting to your followers.

Step 1: Once your Instagram app is open, click the camera icon in the top left corner. That will take you to your Instagram story page.

Step 2: You should now see a menu across the bottom of the screen — slide over to the "Live" option. Then hit "Go Live".

Instagram will check your connection before the broadcast begins. Congratulations! You are now live.

Step 3: To end your broadcast, you just need to hit "End" in the top right corner.

Instagram Live has some cool features once your broadcast begins, and you can find these across the bottom of your screen.

Comments

The comments field allows you to type comments live to your viewers. Your broadcast will be a bit like a chat room but with your live video playing in the background. Your viewers can ask your questions which will be viewed here. That option allows you to direct message to people who follow you or watch your live broadcast.

Split broadcast function

That is awesome for engagement! This option allows you to share a broadcast with a friend, followers or associates. It is excellent if you are in partnership with people in your niche.

Filters

This option lets you add screen filters which are great for entertainment.

Add Image option

This option lets you add an image to your broadcast. That will come in handy when promoting products or services.

What should you broadcast?

There are different types of broadcasts you can create to keep your followers engaged. It is a good idea to plan your broadcasts ahead of time, so you do not look unorganised. With that said, do not worry about creating the perfect broadcast. Just get out there and engage with your followers.

Use some of the following formats to get yourself started on Instagram Live:

The How-to Broadcast

That is a great way to inform your followers of something in your niche. The "how-to" broadcast brings value to your followers, and the more value you bring, the more trust you build. If people are getting something out of you, then they are more likely to continue watching.

AMA (Ask Me Anything)

AMA sessions are great for engagement and something you could do as a standalone broadcast. You could also run an AMA during or directly after a how-to broadcast.

Behind the scenes

Are you out shopping, eating or even relaxing at a friend's house? Then this would be a perfect time to broadcast a "behind the scenes" post. Show the world what you are doing and let them in on your day to day life.

Live Show or Live Events

Are You at a concert or event? Then you have another great opportunity to broadcast live. A live event is not just about attending concerts. A live show could be something as simple as a box opening broadcast. If your niche is fashion, then broadcast a box opening of those new shoes you just bought.

Interviews

Find people in your niche and interview them; this makes for a great broadcast. You can set a one on one interview or use the split broadcast function. The beauty of the split-screen broadcast is that you will get exposure to your interviewee's followers.

As you become a natural broadcaster, you may want to create more spur of the moment type broadcast. That is when you do not plan any particular broadcast, and you just put yourself out there and see what happens. Again, this is great for your followers and your engagement.

Monetising Your Instagram Influencer Profile

We will now look at the top 3 ways influencers earn on Instagram. These are:

1. Affiliate Schemes
2. Post for Product Partnerships
3. Paid Collaboration Partnerships

Affiliate Schemes

An affiliate scheme is a programme most reputable companies offer. You can usually join a company's affiliate scheme quite easily. Most companies have a link to their affiliate scheme at the bottom of their website. If they do not, then it will be a case of contacting them to request information on how to join.

Once you join, you will receive a unique link to their website, which you will use to promote. The link they give will be unique to you, so whenever a follower uses that link to visit the company website. The company will know that the customer came from your promotional work and they will pay you a commission should the follower make a purchase.

Commission amounts vary depending on the company you chose to promote. Some pay only 1% of commission others pay 50%. Most of the time, these commission amounts are set and non-negotiable. So, you need to check what the company is offering. Otherwise, it will not be worth your time and effort.

Before you decide to go for affiliate schemes, you need to understand that promoting affiliates are not generally profitable unless you have a lot of followers and a high engagement rate. That is because, when it comes to commission, most affiliate schemes pay on the lower end of the scale. So, make sure you check out what the company is offering before deciding whether to promote an affiliate.

Post for Product Partnerships

Post for product partnerships are precisely that; you generate a post for a company in exchange for the product they are selling. No money is exchanged; instead, you get to keep the product as payment and Hey get their product exposed to your followers. Simple as that!

Post for product offers can be great and will most likely be the first offer types you receive as an Instagram influencer. Lots of smaller businesses use this route as an excellent way to get their products out there. The best thing is, they are ready to make deals with influencers right now.

Depending on how much the product is valued at will determine what effort you should put into promoting it. We will discuss more pricing and contracts later in the book. However, understand that if a product is valued at $10, then you are not going to create 30 posts over a month for it. Your account, your following and your influence are worth so much more than that.

Post for the product is a great way to start as an influencer. It will give you experience in building business relationships, negotiating post requirements and promoting products. However, do not get overwhelmed when the offers start to roll in. You need to be meticulous in who you choose to work with. When you receive an offer, do your research on the company and ask yourself the following questions:

- Does the product fit my niche and what I am representing?
- Is this a product I would genuinely need and use?
- Is this product something my followers would be interested in?
- Does the company have any bad press or negative reviews from paying customers?
- Does the company have ethical values which align with mine?

Instead of losing time in wait for companies to connect with you for product offers, be proactive and look for companies which offer products you like or even buy from. Reach out and ask them to use you as part of their marketing campaign.

There is more about how to approach companies later. But understand that this is hugely effective because companies know the power of influence and are desperate for right trustworthy influencers like you.

Paid Collaboration Partnerships

Paid collaboration partnership is another way of saying "paid ad". You promote a product or service to your followers in exchange for money. That is the reason you want to be as an influencer!

If post for product suits the smaller company, then you will find the medium to large companies go down the route of paid collaboration. The reason for this is that the medium to large companies now have specific departments dedicated to social media. Within those departments comes a budget which is used to pay for promotion. Because influencer marketing is becoming an extremely effective way of selling products, a large portion of this budget goes on finding and paying high-quality influencers to promote products and services.

You need to use all the skills from this playbook to improve your chances of tapping into that budget. Just like with post for a product, companies will reach out to you, and when they do, you will need to research the company and ask yourself the same questions:

- Does the product fit my niche and what I am representing?
- Is this a product I would genuinely need and use?
- Is this product something my followers would be interested in?
- Does the company have any bad press or negative reviews from paying customers?
- Does the company have ethical values which align with mine?

Finding Companies to Partner With

As an influencer with a super highly engaged following, you will receive partnership offerings from all kinds of companies. However, it is not a recommended strategy to sit back and "wait for the offers to roll in". Finding good companies to partner with is a real hustle. But fear not, there are two great ways to find companies you want to partner with. Here they are:

1. Find influencers in your niche and see what products they are promoting.

The first reason you should do this is that the products being promoted are already in your niche. You should only aim to promote products in your niche because it aligns with your followers' needs. The second reason you should do this is that the company is already taking full advantage of the influencer marketing industry. They will have a budget ready to partner with highly engaging influencers like you!

2. Search Instagram for products that you use or products that you would use.

Are you a fashion influencer? Then look for clothing companies that sell products you love the look of. Are you a fitness influencer? Then look for sportswear, nutrition and any other companies relating to fitness. The beauty of this is that these companies are using Instagram to promote and create engagement about their brand. They completely understand the power that influencers like you have to engage people and develop sales for them.

Why you Should Approach Companies for Partnership Deals

As your follower base grows and your influence increases, you will get contacted about new potential partnership deals. However, this is what you should do – be as proactive as possible and reach out to companies about a partnership. Do not sit back and rely on them contacting you. Here is why:

1. The influencer industry is growing, so you want to let companies know who you are and what you are available for partnership deals.
2. Reaching out to companies about partnership deals will get you ahead of your competitors. (i.e. other Instagram influencers in your niche)
3. The influencer industry is growing so medium to large companies do not need to seek out new influencers. That is because influencers are contacting them daily.
4. Even if a company does not want to offer you a partnership deal now, it does not mean they will not participate in the future. They will keep your details which could turn into big $$$ later on down the line.

What if they say "no"?

Influencer marketing is still at a nascent stage, and some companies have not woken up to its true potential just yet. With that in mind, don't lose your confidence or focus when you receive a message back saying thanks but no thanks." You will get rejected by companies, and that is absolutely natural. That is a numbers game so the more companies you contact, the more chances you have of landing that first paid collaboration deal.

How to Approach Companies for Partnership Deals?

The best way to approach a company about a potential partnership deal is through, you guessed it, Instagram. There are three main reasons for this:

Reason #1

The person who makes the decisions around who to partner with will usually be in charge of the social media account. So mostly, you will be direct messaging the person who can say yes or no to a potential partnership deal.

Reason #2

By messaging via Instagram, the company can instantly view your account and all of your quality content. They will be able to see who you are, what you stand for, and why you will be a great fit to promote their products or services.

Reason #3

The company is active on Instagram, which proves they understand the power of Instagram influence.

Before you approach any company about potential partnership deals, you will need to get extremely familiar with your audience stats. That can be found in your "insights" page under the "audience" tab. That and your engagement rate are the two main pieces of information which companies will want before considering you for a partnership deal.

When you send a message, keep it friendly and professional. Explain who you are, what your niche is, and why you like their products. Then give them all the information from your audience" page including age, range, locations and gender split. Then go on to explain what your engagement rate is over your last ten posts.

You want to position your message in a way that excites the company. So, what excites companies you ask? Money!

Money excites companies so stick a dollar next to your engagement rate. For example, if your engagement rate is 3% which equals likes for 450 followers. Then explain that one post from your account could equal 450 sales! Do not be afraid to sell yourself.

What to Charge and Creating Your Price List

You can quite quickly charge $75 - $100 per image for every 10,000 followers you have. That based on an engagement rate of around 3%. That does not add in the fact that you can offer amazing videos, stories, highlights and Instagram Live posts either. We are talking a base rate of $75 - $100 per image post for every 10,000 followers with 3% engagement. Keep that figure firmly in your mind.

Each method of posting can be charged at a different rate. That is because each process will take longer for you to create and have different levels of engagement and effectiveness.

When to Charge Companies

When you start charging real money is down to you. You can start asking for monetary compensation immediately. You can also go down the route of post for the product until your confident enough to set a dollar price for your services.

Just remember that you are offering more than only exposure to potential buyers. You are offering brand awareness to a follower base who trust you as an influencer. That's 1000x more powerful than any TV or radio advertisement.

Going down the post for product route is a wise move to start with as it gets you used to negotiate deals with limited commitment. Plus, you can begin contacting smaller companies about a post for product partnerships with as little of 3,000 followers.

Creating Contracts

When you first create a contract with a company. You will need to be extremely specific about the terms of that contract. It is always good to agree the following before creating any posts for a company.

1. What content or content package does the company want to purchase?
2. Have they agreed on the price?
3. How will payment be made? Confirm when content will be posted
4. Does the company have any requirements within the content? For example, how do they want the product displayed in the content, etc.?
5. How long will the campaign last?
6. Does the company want to be tagged into the post? If so, how?
7. Does the company want exclusivity?

What Is Exclusivity?

Some companies request exclusivity when entering into a paid collaboration. What this means is that the company wants you to promote their products and no one else's products for an agreed period. For example, say a company wants to pay you $1500 to create eight posts (2 per week) over a month. They may request that you do not promote any other products or services for other companies during that month.

Basically, they want you all to themselves!

Further to this, exclusivity means they may want full rights to the content you create. When you agree to this, you allow the company to use that content in any way they chose. They could repost it on their social media pages, add it to their website or use it in YouTube ads etc.

Exclusivity is not necessarily a bad thing, and it could lead to some fantastic business relationships. However, make sure you understand what the company's definition of exclusivity Is. And do not forget to confirm how long they want their exclusivity period to last.

Disclosing Your Paid Advertising Partnerships

If you are in a paid partnership, then it is a legal requirement to disclose the fact that you are being paid to promote products or services. Some countries have strict advertising standards, whereas others do not. You will need to contact your countries advertising standards agency for advice.

If you do not have time for that, then there are two straightforward ways to make sure you are compliant with advertising legislation.

1. Hashtags

   You can readily disclose your partnership by merely using hashtags #sponsored #spon #paid #ad #partnership. These are all internationally recognised hashtags which admit full disclosure so use them all when either posting for a product or for a paid partnership

2. Tagging

   Another effortless way to ensure that you satisfy all disclosure laws is by simply tagging in the company you are partnered with.

Make sure you are open, honest and transparent whenever you are promoting a paid partnership. The last thing you want is contact with your government advertising standards agency!

There have been cases where influencers have gotten themselves banned from influencing on Instagram. So, do not get caught out. Do not be put off by disclosure either, just use the above two techniques to ensure you are fully disclosing your intentions to promote.

Introduction to YouTube

With the advent of YouTube in 2005, it became one of the most significant game-changers of the Internet. It was beneficial to video producers, entertainment industrialists, and casting agents. They could now easily find sources of talent. If videos became a mega-hit, the producers and agents contacted the video uploader to sign record deals and contracts. Since YouTube's inception, several "YouTube celebrities" have ended up becoming a worldwide phenomenon due to their homegrown talent. Many Hollywood companies and record labels have also been on the constant lookout and have partnered with YouTube for this very purpose. Celebrities have given several comedians, bloggers, and singers recognition, one notable example being Justin Bieber through Usher. Several celebrities also created channels to increase their fame.

Celebrities who were conventionally popular through traditional media also received invitations from the team at YouTube to upload videos, increasing the amount of traffic to the site and growing their target audience and followers to a far greater extent than what they obtained through their TV shows and movies.

In the year 2006, YouTube also partnered with NBC and promoted TV shows aired by NBC. Following this came the purchase of YouTube by Google, for $1.65 billion. That served as an excellent platform to market products, and advertising companies flocked the scene. Thus, marketing professionals of big companies fled from the television screen to the Internet. Soon YouTube became customer-driven and business-driven. Independent artists, singers, and comedians were able to milk the crowd with the little-to-no cost. Four big record labels came into play though they were all very apprehensive given the large amount of copyrighted content that was on the site. YouTube provided a platform to these big record label companies by creating a partnership with them. The lucrative offer was that the site served as a base to make more money for these record labels. In 2009, YouTube partnered with Vivendi and formed Vevo. Vevo was a music service video channel.

YouTube also provided a platform for several channels to increase their profits by investing $875,000 in NextUp, which was a training and tips program for prospective users of YouTube. The company also used celebrities and icons to promote the channel, hoping to get the best of both worlds.

YouTube also was a free platform to test and promote music labels. Videos were categorised as mega, mainstream, and mid-sized, which got rave reviews from target audiences. With this, recording artists could test songs before releasing them for free. That increased the number of hits. YouTube also made its policies very strict as its popularity grew. In 2014, YouTube started to block videos from labels that flouted rules and were not a part of the paid subscription, and they lead to bad reviews and loss of profits.

Today, YouTube is the creator's paradise. Let us take you there.

Beginning with YouTube

Creating a YouTube channel is the easiest of all the tasks you must do in reaching your final goal. So, let us get right to it. Following is a 3-step process to achieving this feat:

Step 1: Create a google account

Step 2: Decide a name for your channel

Step 3: Customize your channel

Step 1: Creating a Google Account

This step is relevant only to those who are yet to own a Google account. If you already have an account, you can skip this step (that is, creating a Google account).

You must note here that using YouTube is exclusive to Google users only, so you must have a Google account. Yahoo or other accounts are not accepted on YouTube. In case, you do not have an account yet, open your web browser and visit https://www.mail.google.com and click on "Create account".

Fill all the required details and choose a secure password. When you are done with all those, accept the Google Terms and Conditions and click "Finish". Once your account is made, log in on your browser and start enjoying all of Google's products and services.

To access YouTube, visit https://www.youtube.com. YouTube uses your Google username as your YouTube username by default. But before you sign in on YouTube for the first time, you will be required to supply your first and last names. These names will be used as you Identification on YouTube. So, it depends on you if you wish to use your real name or something else.

Step 2: Deciding on a Name for Your Channel

The success of your channel is contingent on the choice of name for it. It could be confusing at times to decide on what name you would use to identify your channel. There is no principle or sets of instructions that place restrictions on what you can and cannot use as your channel's name. However, a good name could be a source of the traffic to your channel (although not all the time), as well as a good description of your channel and what it represents. So, think about it thoroughly.

There are two methods adopted by popular YouTubers for naming their channels – using their real names and using their brand names.

You must be creative about this. Here are a few tips you could adopt in coming up with an interesting brand name for your channel:

Alliteration

It is an effortless way to come up with a brand name which sometimes also gives interesting and memorable brand names. Examples of such brand names are PayPal, Coca-Cola, Dunkin' Donuts, Best Buy and Charisma on Command.

Rhymes

Many famous brand names were coined using rhymes. Rhymes are quite like alliterations. However, they differ in that alliteration is characterised by similar consonant sounds while rhymes may use the consonant sounds, or the vowel sounds or both at the same time. An example of a popular channel name coined by rhyming is PewDiePie.

Single-word

You could use a single word you feel describes or represents what your brand stands for as a channel name. It could be descriptive or non-descriptive or just a word you like, anything. Remember you are at liberty to choose whatever you prefer as your channel name.

Step 3: Customizing your channel

Your channel's appearance gives off its first impression and can be a basis to keep or lose viewers. People prefer to see something that appeals to their taste, and so you must consider what would be more attractive to your viewers. The options available for you to customise your channel are:

- The Icon
- The Art
- The Description

The Icon

Your channel icon is the first crucial customisable option available to you. It is what people see beside your channel name even before they open your channel. The photo can be a photo of yourself or a logo. You could also have your photograph converted to paper art by professional designers; it is a quite popular move by YouTubers. It looks good even on people that are not ridiculously photogenic.

The Art

This refers to your banner which sits like a horizontal bar at the top of your channel page. You could have a professional designer design one for you on freelance networks for as low as $5. You can also use royalty-free stock photos from anywhere on the internet.

The Description

The description offers a summary of what your channel stands for. Although few actual subscribers care enough to read channel description, you would not want to lose subscribers because you did not do well in this area.

Here you can add links to your other relevant social media profiles, websites, business email, a featured channels section, a Frequently Asked Questions (FAQ) section and a channel trailer.

A channel trailer gives people an idea of what to expect and what they will experience on your channel. It is a visual presentation of your past channel activities. You can feature here your most popular content to deliver an impression.

Time to Upload Videos

Uploading videos is easy. After logging in, all you need do is click the upload button at the top-right corner of your YouTube page. Now, you can drag your video and drop her or click that large upload button to browse for videos on your device. You could use the import option - this allows you to upload videos you have saved to the cloud, for example, Google Photos. The scheduling feature allows you to upload your videos in advance and put them on auto-publish at a specified time in future.

Important points to note

1. People can view only those videos which you make public. If you set them on private mode, only you will be able to see them or those with whom you have shared a direct link to that video.
2. When scheduling videos, you set the time where the videos go from either private or unlisted to public and automatically the videos status changes at the scheduled time and date.
3. The maximum size of the video to be uploaded on an up-to-date browser is 128GB. If your browser is not updated, then you might be able to upload a maximum of 20GB.
4. YouTube accounts that are yet to be verified cannot upload videos longer than 15 minutes. The limit gets removed after you verify your account.

To avoid getting an error message like "invalid file format", upload videos in mp4 format. There are many video converters online that you could use to convert your video from whatever format to the acceptable format.

How to Make Good Content on YouTube

The typical YouTube audience is 13-35 years old, and they are looking for engaging content with a lot of value to offer. So, your content should be captivating and flashy. However, if you are aiming for an older demographic, these people may watch videos up to several hours in length, if they are engaging.

The King of content length, though is the ten-minute video. A ten-minute video is not too short to be sparse and is not too long to be boring. If you pack your video with exciting and engaging content, aim for a video length between five to fifteen minutes but pick whatever is best for your content. If you are making ultra-short comedy videos, these might be less than three minutes in length and if you are uploading your lectures, these might be hours long!

Here are the most popular types of content on YouTube:

Comedy videos

They are some of the most shared videos on the internet as they keep the audience pleasantly occupied. These are often fast-paced and with a high energy level. If you wish to create comedy videos, there are two ways to go about it:

The first method is to be the most extroverted and outgoing version of yourself. Its scientifically proven people are going to listen to things that are loud and things that change quickly, and these are principles you need to embed into your videos. A monotone monologue just is not going to cut it!

It is a proven fact these types of channels have a higher number of subscribers than most network's comedy television shows, which is crazy to think about.

Though the sense of humour is personal, there are a lot of comedy videos online, and you can be sure you will find somebody who matches your style. Remember, do not be afraid to be inspired by the style of another YouTuber, but add your own personality and flair to your videos.

Unboxing videos

Though this might come as a surprise, it turns out that there are lots of people interested in watching someone else remove a new product from its packing. Think about when you buy something new that you have wanted for a prolonged period, the excitement that you have when you finally open it, that great feeling of self-esteem and joy.

If you can transfer that through a screen to your followers, you are already on your way to thousands of subscribers.

Finding Stuff to Unbox

The truth is, people, do like to see expensive and upcoming items reviewed. An effective way to find these items is to type in your product name into YouTube and see if there is a market for it. In addition, if you ever see a video and think "I can do better than that" then you can. That is what finding a niche is all about.

Your product does not have to be expensive. In fact, it is counterproductive to start reviewing costly products in the beginning. But your passion is essential.

Product reviews

You can also do product review videos, and this opens an opportunity for you to make a lot of money in the future by doing sponsored review videos, especially if you have a large subscriber base.

Most people want to know other people's opinions about the products they want to buy before they buy them. Pick something you know a lot about. People will listen to you if you know a lot about something and can bring that confidence and passion across.

 If your video is positive, then they will want to make a purchase. A smart way to leverage this fact to make money is by using Amazon Affiliates. That is an incredible way to bolster your income from YouTube.

Since lots of people go on YouTube in search of reviews for the products they want to buy, try making reviews on a product that people do not have videos on. A beyond excellent way to check what people are looking for is to type the product in on Google AdSense and check how many searches it has. If a product has many searches on AdSense but no videos on YouTube, then you have struck gold.

Gaming Videos

If one niche dominates YouTube, it is undoubtedly this. PewDiePie, the biggest YouTuber, started with this niche! That can be like an unboxing video; in that, you are showing people a game that they have never played before.

 What is unique about this, though is that you inject your personality into the video to enhance the game. People want to see your unique reactions to whatever is going on. Pick a game, or a genre of games and stick to them.

Remember, the essential thing in this equation is you and your reactions. A secret technique to increase your viewers and subscribers, especially if you are a PC gamer, is to find an indie game on Steam that is upcoming and message the developer by email asking for a copy before the game is released.

Even if you do not have a lot of subscribers, if your videos are quality, then most reasonable game developers will say yes. If they say no, however, you can wait until the game is released and review it later. If the dev features your video and the game is successful, this can increase your subscribers and grow your channel like crazy.

Live Streaming

Live Streaming is also great for creating engagement between you and your viewers. That is excellent for getting donations and live feedback on how you are doing. You do not have to be good at whichever video game you are playing; however, this is where your personality must shine through.

Since this type of streaming typically involves a webcam or camera or some sort, make sure you are comfortable and confident in front of a camera. Remember, practice makes perfect.

Vlogs

The classic YouTube videos. The concept is simple. You shoot a video talking to the camera about any random topic. People want a window into your life. They want to know what you are like, all your nuances. The more you can open while keeping the video engaging, the better.

Pro tips for vlogs

1. White rooms reflect light much better than dark rooms, so try and film in a light environment

2. Good lighting is necessary. You can buy a ring light inexpensively from Amazon
3. Be positive. In life, it takes effort to be a good person and say positive things on camera, and people want to be uplifted and forget about the stressful day they have had in general.
4. Finding a niche is especially important. There are many channels with excellent video quality, but they do not have many subscribers simply because their niche is just too competitive, and they are unaware of the tips in this book.

Educational / How-to

In 2019, the amount of traffic to these kinds of videos increased by 70%, that means the views these videos got nearly doubled. Imagine how much this will increase during 2020.

If you are good at something or know how to do it, you can give tutorials on YouTube. It is simple; in fact, you do not even have to be good at something. Look at How to Basic as an example of this fact. Whether it is Mathematics tutorials (which is a hugely growing niche on YouTube) or underwater basket weaving, there are countless things that people need help on.

Other types of content include haul videos, memes, Top 10 compilations and the infamous prank videos. Of course, there are an infinite number of video types that exist, and if you do not see your kind here, do not dismay.

How the YouTube Algorithm Works

One of the biggest keys in being able to grow with any online platform is learning how the algorithms work so you can begin leveraging the algorithm

The YouTube algorithm is unlike other algorithms, which tends to favour things that have been seen or liked more than it favours viewing time. That is because YouTube is amongst the only video viewing platforms that offer full-service video watching and is entirely dedicated to video-based content. So, along with building a fantastic marketing strategy and using high-quality content, you also need to know how to work the algorithm to generate the success that you desire in the online space.

The Importance of Frequency

On YouTube, one of the most important things that you can do for your growth is to publish the latest content for your viewers consistently. Many people forget that YouTube is a social media website, which means it favours accounts that are engaging in regular sharing back and forth. The more frequently you upload to your channel and have friends and viewers engaging with your videos, the more YouTube is going to favour your content and drive you up in the rankings when it comes to people searching for your content.

You might get a lot of hits early on, but if you do not maintain your frequency, the content that you share will stop getting views. You need to keep your momentum and continue growing it if you are going to generate continued success with YouTube, which means that you need to ensure that you are consistently uploading videos.

Another massive benefit of frequently uploading new content is that you are driving new traffic to your channel consistently. That means that not only will your new videos get visibility, but you will also increase the visibility of older ones. As people land on your videos, they will hopefully take the next step and visit your channel to see what other videos you offer. Through that process, if you have plenty of high-quality videos uploaded that are relevant to your niche, these individuals will click-through to your older videos and watch them as well. The more they do this, the higher your older videos will rank and the better your overall channel will rank as well, which means that your growth rate will increase exponentially

Creating a consistent frequency is best done if you create a posting schedule and then adhere to that schedule as you grow your channel. If you look at any mature channel that presently exists on YouTube, chances are, their posting schedule is listed directly on their intro clip, or they say it when they introduce themselves at the beginning of each video. These schedules ensure that your audience knows how often to check back for recent videos and gives them an idea to how frequently you are uploading updated content. It also keeps you on a consistent schedule so that you know exactly how often you need to be uploading without falling behind or creating an inconsistency that leaves your audience constantly questioning as to when they will see you next. You should seek to be uploading at least once per week, but two or three times is preferable if you want to grow your channel quickly as this will give your viewers plenty to watch when they find you online.

What YouTube Cares About

While frequency is important in terms of relevance and visibility, there is one other thing that YouTube cares about when it comes to a ranking - number of watch-time minutes. Watch-time minutes refer to the length of video that those who are landing on your video are watching. In other words, if people are watching your videos all the way through, or at least are watching them longer than any other videos in your similar search terms, then you are going to get listed higher in the feed.

So, as a YouTube content creator, your primary objectives, aside from creating consistent and high-quality content, are creating content that encourages people to stick around and watch your videos all the way through.

The reason YouTube favours watch times is that it means that your content is exciting and that people are enjoying watching it. When your watch time is low, YouTube assumes that you are offering low-quality or uninteresting content that will bore their members and leave them, unwilling to return to watch more creators in the future.

Calculation of average viewing time

Average watch time = Total watched minutes / Total viewers

For example, you have 100 watch time minutes, and you have had 25 unique viewers. So, the average watch time for your video would be 4 minutes.

YouTube will then rank you lower than anyone who has experienced at 4:01 watch time or higher, and higher than anyone who has experienced a 3:59 watch time or lower.

Your goal is to improve your watch time to get it as close to 100% so that YouTube starts favouring your videos and ranks them above anyone else's.

Encouraging Higher Watch Times

You can increase your overall watch time by considering the importance of creating relevant and high-quality content. There are additional things that you can do to improve your total watch time, as well.

1. Offer an incentive to stay till the end of the video, such as a summary to a story that you have started, or a giveaway offer that they can gain by watching your video all the way through. When you offer an incentive like this, make sure that you mention it early on an allude to it throughout the video in order for people stay interested in what it is and continue to watch so they can learn more about the incentive or hear it all the way through.

2. Fill your videos with valuable information that is relevant to your viewers and share it interestingly. Do not create an annoying video that struggles to get to the point or that has been watered down.

3. Keep your videos reasonable in length for people not to grow bored or disinterested purely based on the duration of the video. The length of your audience's attention span will ultimately depend on what you are talking about, so consider searching your niche market and getting a feel for approximately how long the videos are. Try and stay fairly like the median length, so you are not exceeding it by too much and losing the interest of people along the way.

4. Another way to increase your viewership is by structuring your playlists. As you begin to develop more videos, you can group your videos in playlists for your audience to watch. If you arrange these videos into playlists linearly or in a sensical way, your viewers can watch your videos and continue watching them through.

5. You have seen this before, but a fantastic way to encourage further views and to retain an interest in your videos and your channel is to make use of "cards." For example, say you just showed your audience how to fix a tire, and now you want to show them how they can pack a proper safety kit for emergencies in their trunk. These two would be highly relevant to each other, so using cards to reference the opposite video when the current video ends would be a great way to encourage your viewers to move back and forth between both videos. That works almost like a - funnel on YouTube where you drive "hot leads" through a series of your videos and, based on their current interests and their retained viewership, you can almost guarantee that they will watch more of your videos all the way, too.

Lastly, make sure that your videos are being titled and described adequately so that people know what to expect when they watch your video, and they get precisely that.

Optimising Your SEO

Every single search engine that exists today, including YouTube, has an optimisation strategy that you can use to increase your ability to get found in the search rankings. It is called Search Engine Optimisation or SEO. That SEO strategy is different for every platform since the algorithms used to generate rankings will vary depending on what each algorithm is looking for.

YouTube favours high-quality content that is relevant, interesting, retains viewers, and gets consistent engagement from those who are actively watching it. You can increase the favourability of your videos in four steps:

Step 1: Creating an SEO plan

Step 2: Putting SEO into action

Step 3: Monitoring the performance through analytics

Step 4: Keeping up with the trends

Step 1: Creating an SEO Plan

Begin with keyword research

First, do some keyword research to get an idea of what people in your niche are looking for. Start by writing down a list of potential keywords that are relevant to your video that you think will best describe what your audience can gain from watching it. The best way to populate this list is to go to the search bar and type in one or two words and then look at what comes up in the recommended search list. That list will be based on the most commonly searched topics on YouTube. So, choosing potential keywords from this list will make sure that you are likely to get seen by others.

Once you have generated your potential keyword list, you can go to any keyword research platform, such as Google Keywords, and started typing in those keywords in the search bar to see how they are ranking. Ones that are being searched frequently, such as tens or hundreds of thousands of times per month, can be considered as being popular enough to warrant actual results from. Ones that are not being searched often, such as the ones that are only being searched for a couple of hundred times or less, should be ignored as they are unlikely to generate your desired results. Furthermore, avoid those with search rankings over 500,000 views per month as these may get you washed out by your competitors who may already have a better viewership than you do.

Maintain high watch time

The next part of SEO is keeping all your videos high in retention as possible to avoid having YouTube believing that your audience is not interested in watching your videos. If you are getting started, ask your closest friends and family to watch your full video to get it a high viewership ranking right off the bat.

Enhance keyword relevance

Another thing that matters on YouTube, which people often forget is that you need to say your keywords aloud while you are filming the video that you are creating. YouTube will recognise that, and this looks positive in terms of your relevance.

Promote your videos

Share your video to every different platform that you are actively on and then encourage your followers to re-share the video if they feel that it is relevant or interesting. Not only does that get you more views, but it also helps YouTube recognise that your video as popular and interesting. The more inbound likes there are out on the net directing people to your videos, the higher your ranking is going to become because it is seen as exciting and relevant.

The higher these analytics grow, the more your channel will grow, so it is well worth your time to invest in these details and nurture your growth through SEO.

Step 2: Putting SEO into action

SEO is a complicated skill that is difficult to explain. There could easily be an entirely separate book on the subject. But the fact that it is not a natural skill to master is why those who understand it can gain success on YouTube.

Here are a few pointers to tweak your SEO:

1. The titles for the videos you post on your channel should include keywords that people will search. It is not a smart idea to make titles that abandon all creative integrity just for the sake of SEO. But whenever you are creating titles for videos, it should be kept in mind.

2. Making your titles exciting is an integral part of SEO. When people search for the keywords included in your title, they should want to click on your video because it is something they want to see.

3. Tag your videos properly. Tags are keywords you attach to your video so that YouTube knows what exactly is in your video and what categories it falls under. Let us say you have a YouTube channel all about birds and you want other people who love birds to find your videos. The smartest way to get this done is by adding tags to your videos that include keywords that bird lovers would be searching for on YouTube.

Once you have begun posting and optimising content to be found by people on the internet, you will need to invest time analysing the performance of your content.

YouTube Analytics is a tool which is available, free of charge to anyone who has created content on YouTube. To access YouTube Analytics, you need to navigate to the Video Manager from within your channel. You will now see Analytics listed in the left-hand panel. Your YouTube analytics tells you absolutely everything about your videos and your channel overall, allowing you to get a better insight as to what is working and what is not. Through your analytics, you can see what you need to do to improve your viewership and get better rankings, overall.

The first thing you want to monitor when you go to your YouTube analytics is your overall retained viewership ratings because this is what YouTube cares about the most. If this number is high, chances are the rest of your analytics are going to be higher as well. Wouldn't it be lovely to know how many people watched your video in its entirety, or what the average duration of each view was? This information does not seem that interesting, but on closer inspection, it is enormously influential.

If one of your videos is only being viewed for the first 50%, what does this tell you? Are you losing the interest of your viewer or did you say something at 50% which has made the viewer turn off in disgust? Now you have these stats to hand; you can make informed decisions about how you choose to broadcast in future. Sure, it is nice knowing you have had 200 viewers on your video, but it is not so lovely knowing that half of them turned off in the middle of your video.

The beauty of YouTube Analytics is that you have this information at your fingertips and can act before it is too late. You can address such issues and ensure that your next broadcast does not make the same perceived errors like the one you are currently analysing.

YouTube Analytics also gives you a gender breakdown of your viewers. Now, this might not make any difference to you depending on what your broadcasts are about, but if your broadcasting style is on the assumption that the core of your audience is of a particular gender, you now have the raw data to back this up. You can now focus your presentation style to the gender of your audience which will allow you to attract more viewers from that gender or retain the viewers you currently have because you are now delivering content which you are more confident is relevant to them.

If you are broadcasting something of high complexity, which contains many small parts, users viewing on a mobile phone may not be getting the best experience of your broadcast due to the size of their screen. While this is beyond your control, it is worth knowing what kind of device your broadcasts are being viewed on.

When you read your analytics, make sure that you not only pay attention to your overall channel growth but to your video performance as well. The production of each video will tell you whether your strategies are working in each video, especially as your channel continues growing. As your channel grows and these numbers have a more extended history, you can start recognising the trends on your channel. That will give you a unique idea as to what your viewers like and what they do not like on your channel.

These trends will show you everything from what titles draw the most attention to what styles of videos keep your viewers watching the longest, and even what content gets the most views in general. You want to start producing more of the material that meets these three criteria:

- receives the highest views,
- with the highest retention ratings, and the best engagement ratings.

So, the videos that have many people clicking through to watch it, that have people watching it all the way through, and that have people liking or commenting on or subscribing to your channel are the videos that you want to favour.

You should not exclusively pay attention to your high-performing videos, either, as this will leave money on the table. When you have a video that underperforms or that does not meet the expectations that you had for it, take some time to research it and look through its analytics to see what may have gone wrong. Pay attention to how you may have unintentionally sabotaged the video or prevented it from growing and see if you can improve on these things or avoid them altogether in the future.

Step 4: Keeping up with the Trends

If your YouTube channel aims to discuss topical items, you are going to need to keep up to date with breaking news and viral themes. As we have already discussed, delivering content that the viewer wants is paramount to the success of your YouTube channel. So, you are going to need a way of finding out what fellow YouTubers are watching and talking about so that you can strike while the topic is still hot.

YouTube Trends is another free tool that is available publicly that allows you to see what the most popular videos currently are in terms of both views and shares. That data, as with the YouTube Analytics tool, can be dissected further so that you can see on a country by country basis what is popular. You can also break down the trend data by age or by gender, so if you have a target audience in mind, and you now have the information of what this demographic is demanding from YouTube.

While YouTube Trends give you vital information on what viewers are enjoying; you should not automatically jump away from the focus of your channel. Visiting Trends, just before you are about to record your next broadcast, is always a good tactic. If you find something is trending that you can work into your video, then there is an increased chance that your video could be shared, thus giving it more exposure.

Remember, today's trend is yesterday's news so if you plan to use trend topics in your broadcast. You need to act immediately.

Making Your Videos

Most of your time will go into producing your videos. There are two sets of tools that you will need to create your channel. First, you will need the tools that you will use make and edit your videos before you upload them to YouTube. Second, you will need a constant source of content. In the case of YouTube, content refers to events that you film and edit. Some people prefer to film themselves while others use events around them as content.

Video Making Tools

Video Capturing Device

First, you will need a camera to capture video clips with. The high-end video cameras will cost you thousands of dollars. To start, however, you could choose to buy a low-end camcorder that allows you to take high-quality videos.

If you are creating a vlog or capturing videos outdoors, you may also use your smartphone mounted on a stabilising tripod or handheld stick. As soon as your videos improve; however, you may want to invest in a handheld or shoulder-top camcorder.

Microphone

Most video recording devices already come with a built-in microphone. However, if you are creating videos with a narrated audio, you may want a microphone that will make your audio sound clearer.

To start, you may use the audio recorder in your smartphone. However, you will need to do your recording in a quiet place to make sure that it does not pick up the unnecessary white noise.

Audio and Video Editing Software

Once you have your raw video footage and audio files, you will need editing software to put them together. If you have a separate audio file to edit, you may need an audio editor to improve its quality. Some of the things that you may need to do are to remove any background noise and to improve the pitch of your voice. For these simple tasks, you can make use of free audio editing software Audacity. While it is free, it is more than enough for most starting YouTubers.

Next, you will need a video editor. That type of software allows you to create a new video by putting together your raw audio and video files. Older versions of Microsoft Windows come with the Windows Movie Maker. While old, this software is excellent for beginners.

If you have your tools, all you must do is to practice in using them to create great videos. To find video editing styles, look at your favourite videos on YouTube and try to copy their transitions, timing, and other parts of the video.

Looking for a constant source of video content

The most daunting part of being a YouTuber is finding inspiration for new video content. Vloggers can upload videos every day because they only film themselves in their rooms talking in front of the camera. Even just doing this, however, still requires arduous work. Most vloggers immediately start making their videos for the following day after creating their newest videos. Some channels post content weekly. By posting weekly, you will have more time to plan and create a video. One way to make the process easier is by creating a video post plan for an entire month. If you plan to post a video every week, you will need to prepare four videos and produce them at the same time. By planning your video's content, you will be able to avoid running out of video ideas to post.

Ideally, you want to stick to your niche when thinking of video ideas. The best YouTube channels talk about topics that other people are also interested in. If your channel talks about popular TV series, for example, make sure that you post videos regarding the most recent TV series. That will elevate the viewership of your videos.

In the end, you want to create videos on topics that you are also interested in. Jot down a list of the issues that you love and pick one channel topic from your list. You can rank the items in your inventory to decide which theme you are most passionate with.

With YouTube, you already have your work cut out for you when it comes to finding traffic. YouTube is like a social network. Millions of people are using the platform every day. It is just a matter of attracting them towards your videos.

Most of the traffic you will get will come through YouTube's own video suggestion system. As soon as a user goes into YouTube, he or she is shown multiple video suggestions. These suggestions vary per country. If the user is logged in, the recommendations will be tailored to fit his or her interests.

As an aspiring YouTuber, you need to understand how this process works. Here are some of the crucial details that you need to work on to make sure that your videos are suggested to the users:

Optimise the Text Content of your Videos

You will be getting an opportunity to add text components to your videos. These text components will be indexed by Google Search as well as the YouTube search algorithm. To increase the likelihood that your target audience will find your video, you want to include the right keywords in this part of your content.

You can add text contents in the title, description, and video tags. Make sure that you include related keywords in these sections of the video. In the title, you want to add a part that will hook the users. Here are some useful types of titles that you can use for your videos:

1. Ask a Question

   Many popular channels like TED Talks and TEDx Talks make use of questions to lure in audiences. For it to work, the question needs to be attractive to your target audience. Ideally, your video needs to have an answer to the problem. Otherwise, the users will feel disappointed with your video, and they may leave a "dislike" on it.

2. Mention a Famous Name

   Many YouTube Users also go to the platform to look up information about their favourite public figure and celebrities. Politics, music, show business, and sports are all popular on the platform. If your video is in any way related to any celebrity, include their names in the title to give your video a boost.

3. Describe an event

   If there is an exciting event that happens in the video, you can describe what happened and put that description in your title. That is the most commonly used form; however; it is useful in capturing the attention of YouTube users.

Optimising the description and the video tags

The description section and video tag allow you to add other keywords that may not have been included in your title. Only a small percentage of your users will check your video description. However, they are still an essential part of your content. For instance, this is the part where you could include links. You could use this section for your monetisation as well as for adding links to your sources.

The tags, on the other hand, are purely for the use of the YouTube ranking algorithm. You will need to add the most relevant keywords to these parts.

Use Engaging Thumbnails

Next to the title, YouTube users will look at your video thumbnail to learn what your video is about. Ideally, you want your thumbnails to work together with your title. It also works if you use engaging images in the thumbnail. People tend to be drawn towards images that they are already familiar with.

You could also use text and special symbols in your thumbnail to grab people's attention. In the past, people have used red arrows or red circles to make their thumbnails attract more attention.

Converting Traffic into Subscribers

Also, make it a habit to ask your viewers to subscribe to your channel. By subscribing and clicking on the bell button, the users will get a notification on their phones when you release a new video. To increase the chances of subscription, you could publish a video regularly and ask your users to subscribe and hit the bell button at the start of each video.

From Amateur to Professional

All that you have been doing until now is what any amateur would do. That chapter will turn you into a pro on YouTube. So, sit tight!

Make those thumbnails pop

A thumbnail refers to the small picture shown when your videos come up in a search result or are listed anywhere on YouTube's website. It may prove a random point from the video, or it can be a picture you upload that has words describing more of what happens. If you look at a few of the most admired channels on YouTube, both individual and professional, you will notice that most of the top channels have exceptionally clean and professional quality thumbnails.

While you may not want to spend all the time, it can take to create an impressive looking thumbnail. It should be noted how important it is to get many views on any video. Other than the video title, the thumbnail that represents your video is the first thing people see as soon as your video shows up in a search result or the recommended videos section. The quality, or lack of it, can make or break whether someone clicks on the video to view it.

To make great thumbnails:

1. Design it in unison with your title in such a way that will make users feel they have to view your video because it contains something amazing or unique.
2. Make the font of the words you put on the thumbnail look clean and modern.
3. Make the words you use on the thumbnail provocative and exciting.
4. Use a picture of high quality; a high definition shot in good focus that users will understand easily on any device.
5. Do not use Microsoft Paint to create their thumbnails. Use Canva or some other professional picture editing tool.

Using Calls to Action

Annotations for calling your audience to action are those little pop-ups that come up while they are watching the video. These can lead to a higher number of subscribers by including them to click the popup while they watch your video.

Many video creators on YouTube noticed increased subscriptions to their channel when they added these. You can put in a link that encourages audience members to subscribe, or you can use a graphic. If you do this in a way that is not annoying or obnoxious, your subscriptions will grow as a result. However, if you annoyingly do this, you might lose potential subscribers.

Allow People to Discover you

YouTube gives users the choice to click a link and get sent to your website. So, if you already have a website, do this as soon as possible. There is utterly no reason not to take advantage of this option if you can. Any effort you dedicate to bringing video views to your channel can be taken advantage of any time you direct viewers to your webpage.

Besides, this will make your channel a verified, authentic source for your personal brand. In your YouTube page channel settings, you can add your blog URL or website to the channel. You could also add your URL or website to the description of your YouTube channel. You can also add a subscribe option button on your webpage or blog to bring more subscribers to your channel.

Intros and Outros

The intros and outros you use for YouTube will aid you in branding your name and will help your videos have a higher entertainment value. It will give your videos a professional feel and can be used as an opening theme, like a show that people come back to and enjoy the familiarity of. In addition to this, an appealing intro ensures your audience is more involved with your videos.

To get the best of your content out on the web, you must make a lot of it, and edit it ruthlessly. Most creative geniuses make a lot more content than they show, and what we see is their best work. It should apply to your YouTube videos too. Edit them fearlessly to ensure that you are only publishing your absolute best videos.

When you try to force yourself to publish on a strict schedule without taking the time to make the videos enjoyable, your brand will be hurt down the road. Make plenty of recordings for your final cut, but only publish the best. If you are unsure of a specific take, you can always take multiple shots. If you are using Windows, Adobe Premier is an excellent program for editing your videos.

Optimising Descriptions in your Videos

Returning to the SEO (search engine optimisation) side of making YouTube content, you should never neglect the description of your videos. Your video description will allow your content to be easily discovered in a search engine while also giving your potential audience members a sneak preview of what your content discusses. However, this should not be overdone.

Putting a detailed description in your video will not make any sense because the first few sentences are the only parts that are displayed when someone loads the video. Like your video title, the keyword should be used in the video description but not overdone. You cannot outsmart search engines by entering the keyword 20 times, which will just hurt your odds of getting displayed on search engines. Instead, make it authentic and natural.

Use Meta Tags for your Videos

You can put Google's Keyword Planner to productive use by finding relevant ideas to use for keywords in your videos, then adding them to your content and videos. That will allow you to be easier to discover on both YouTube and Google searches. If you overdo this, it is not going to help (and will do the opposite) but adding in some well-placed and researched words will help your rankings a lot.

Be mindful that if you have a low view count on your videos, it does not always mean your content is not good. It might just say that it is not easy to discover for viewers. Metadata plays a bit role in allowing your content to be more easily displayed to those who are searching. Look at some videos that are well-converting and look at the meta tags they have on them to get an idea of what works. However, do not simply copy/paste these tags because that will not work.

Think about How you End them

No matter what your video content is about, you should always end videos on a high note. Like the very last bit of dialogue before a play ends, videos should end in a way that is memorable and positive. Ask the viewers watching to subscribe and like your video if they enjoyed it, and then ask them to visit your blog our website. Keep in mind that if you do not ask for anything, you will not get anything.

End all your content with a confident flourish, allowing viewers to know you appreciate them. End videos in a positive way, smiling and leaving your audience eager to see more content from you.

Think about Collaboration

You can collaborate with other video creators on YouTube. It has turned into quite a common act among video makers. Why is that? Because when you work, everyone benefits from it. Your audience benefits, the people involved in the collaboration benefit, and so do you.

Creativity is all about being constructive and viewing other video creators as your competition does not help. Instead, celebrate the success of others and see how you can join to improve each other's success. Look for successful video creators in your field and see if you can collaborate to do an exciting project. And always remember to look for what you can add to their channel as well.

It will let you connect with new audience members that you may have never reached before. The person you collaborate with will also have access to new viewers. The audience will appreciate the new value and extra content, as well. As you can see, this is an advantage for all parties involved.

Make sure you Interact with Viewers

The art of social media relies on interaction and connection with people who share your common goals and ideas. It means that the amount you care directly influences your success. When the people viewing your content can tell you care for them as people, they will return the favour. No one wants to be involved with someone who does not care about them, even when they are just YouTube subscribers. Try to interact with your viewers, paying attention to the requests they give you in comments.

You might get some anger or backslash in comments, but do not allow that to distract you from paying attention to your loyal listeners and viewers. When your viewers take the time to comment on your videos, try to respond to what they are saying. That will build more trust between you and your audience, leading them to respect you for taking the time to connect. That is how you make a loyal fan base.

Do Challenges and Offer Price

Who does not like to receive prizes or complete challenges? After you build up a loyal fan base, you can offer them compensation for staying true to your channel. A contest or prize giveaway can help you to lure in new viewers and reward those who have stood by your channel. You can give away T-shirts, a tech gadget, or a free hosting subscription. The possibilities are endless.

No matter what you choose to give away, your viewers will appreciate receiving something free and will share this with their friends. That will give you an opportunity for free promotion, but also a possibility of viral advertising for your YouTube channel. For huge giveaways, some hosts on YouTube require that their audience members must subscribe to each of their social media platforms before they can enter the giveaway, which is a great approach. The prize items should be relevant to the niche of your videos, but it is okay even if they are not.

Promoting Across Platforms is a Must

In our modern social media age, being active and present across different platforms of social media is necessary for succeeding and growing any online audience. When you are attempting to create a brand for yourself, you must be discoverable. That means being active on more than one platform for social media. Try putting up profiles on Twitter and Facebook. However, you can go further and put up Instagram and SnapChat accounts too. You can give Google and Facebook ads a try to provide yourself with further promotion. When you are visible throughout various platform online, you are making yourself far more apparent. Make sure that you are being aggressive about securing your first followers, which will, in turn, motivate you to create better content. You cannot just build a great website and expect your customers to show up right away. Use every resource you can to build up your brand. You can also share your channel with interested friends but try not to hassle or annoy them.

Keep on Trying

Experimenting and changing your methods until you find what works is the best approach anyone can take. Remember that there is never one single path to success and that what works for others might not always work best for your pursuits. Find what works for your brand and channel. That could include switching up the thumbnail, backgrounds, camera angles, and other techniques given to you in this chapter. Pay attention to the way your audience changes according to these changes, and always stay true to what your brand is about.

Making something memorable and valuable on YouTube will require lots of perseverance, time, effort, and dedication from you. However, if you stick with it and stay patient, it can work for you. These are only guidelines to get you started. Do not be scared to think creatively and come up with your methods!

If you want to use YouTube for company business, you must provide suggestions to your viewers. The fundamental way to use YouTube is just to do video clips that sell your product or service and solutions. That has better than nothing but as more of your opponent's use YouTube, just throwing video clips will not be enough run.

As more and more companies' business come onto YouTube, you need to provide more value to the industry for you to endure and flourish in your industry. The best way to stand out from your opponent is to give guidelines through your video clips regularly. That is because the majority of beginner YouTube promoters will only be concentrated on promoting their items and solutions. All their video clips will be about going to this website, blog or call this number or buy this or buy that. After a while, individuals will be fed up with that.

Provide valuable content

If you want to win in the YouTube activity for the long run, then you have to provide helpful information. Whether it is one video a week or one video every few days or even one video a day concentrated on discussing, at least one tip to your viewers that will make a tremendous effect on your company business actually, run. Not only will you get more brings and customers by doing that, but you will start to separate yourself from all the other YouTube promoters who are capturing themselves on foot by looking like anxious sales representatives looking for some fast cash. So, provide value regularly, and you will win the audience.

Use Power of Face to Face Human Touch

One of the most frustrating things I come across is video clips where the individual never reveals their face. Some individuals have YouTube programs where they display their items or discuss their solutions but never show their face. Do you know what that does to your audience?

You viewers can gradually get frustrated with you and incorrect with you!

What are you trying to hide? Why are you trying to cover something? Is something incorrect with you, or do you have some unsure business? If you want to use YouTube for your company business and build the highest possible achievements, then you have to set it off and be willing to display the experience.

Showing the experience will make a considerable improvement in your company business. Individuals usually like, link, and believe in you even more. Your company business will experience more individual to them. The more they experience they know you, the more they will purchase from you. If you are an entrepreneur, then your advantage appears in that you can provide that personal touch to your clients while the big organisations cannot as much!

So, use that personal touch to your advantage by displaying the experience in your video clips.

To do that, do face to face videos! Face to experience video clips is video clips where you only need to display the experience as if you are discussing to them on a digital camera one-to-one — no more concealing the face any longer. That is poor, uncommitted and cowardly. Just display the face and go all the way. Then this will do amazing things for your company business.

Mix Up Your Videos

You can go to the best cafe in the world. Initially, you will love it, but if you go there over and over again, you will become ill of it. Similarly, your viewers will like to see a wide range in your video clips. So, my tip is to mix up your video clips. Do not always do the same type of video clips. Do not only educate guidelines in your video clips. Sometimes, show videos clip of you while you are on holiday having a fun time.

Do not always do videos clip clips where you are at the office. Do video clips while you are at the recreation area. Do video clips while you are by the seaside. Just mix it up. When you mix up your video clips, then it will be more fun to look at and give a little wider range to your viewers.

Follow The 80/20 Rule

When you do video clips, you should concentrate on following the 80% value to 20% message ratio. An increasing number of businesses are using YouTube to introduce themselves to the world. However, most of them are just throwing their video clips. They are essentially creating a bunch of "commercials" on YouTube. Now, that is better than nothing but let me ask you something. What do you do when an industrial comes on? You like to change the routeing channel.

In this mass confusion age, you have to go the one step further to stand out from your competition. To do that, you should to do less "pitch" video clips (a commercial type of videos) and concentrate on doing "value" video clips where you share tips, how-to tutorials, or any video that gives value to your viewers. As you provide more value to the marketplace, your income will soar because funds are just an exchange of value.

So, once you create your own YouTube route, do not just throw in video clips that offer massage video clips. Create 80% of your video clips of some value – whether it is a tutorial, an inspirational the message, a simple little tip, a lifestyle video, or something that can bring value to your viewers. Then 20% of the time, offer some message type of video where you sell them your products and services.

The goal of value video clips is to have the people like/trust/connect with you because whenever someone shares with you something, you start to believe in them more and want to learn more from them. The goal of these video clips is to earn cash. The key is to provide both value and message video clips to make some money from online video marketing.

Use Exclusive Videos for Subscribers

YouTube has a choice to unlisted videos clip so that the regular community cannot look for that video on YouTube Google. The only way to see that video is to have the YouTube web link. Do not just hand out everything for 100%. Make stages of content material. Free content material can be on your route channel. But once they are in your list record, you can deliver them even better unlisted and unique material.

Once they buy your items, they get even better personal content material as well.

Create Multiple YouTube Channel

Have an active channel and some supportive ones.

It is never excellent to put all your egg in one container. Broaden your container by developing multiple YouTube programs. One YouTube route channel can have 2 to 20 video clips. Then another YouTube the route can have to 2 to 12 video clips and so forth. That way, if one YouTube route channel goes down, then you have another set of YouTube program to yourself.

Use the Multi-Platform Video Strategy

If you are serious about using online video promotion, then apply several video systems platforms. Did you know that YouTube is not the only video system that positions well on Google?

There are other online video promotion systems that you can use that can position well on. Look for engine search engines. One is Dailymotion. The best part about DailyMotion is that they are not known to take down their content material creator's programs easily. They also perform great on search engines.

Another video system is Vimeo. Videos that are submitted on Vimeo seem to position well on Google if you do the right SEO to it. However, Vimeo is not very helpful to the people in the internet marketing/affiliate marketing/business chance market, so if that is your market, stay away from Vimeo.

Having video clips in different video systems (such as YouTube, Dailymotion, Vimeo), you open up the opportunity for all those three video clips hyperlinks to show and rank on Google.

Bonus Chapter: Tips to Nail Your Personal Branding

Creating a personal brand is not easy. It is not unusual to forget yourself in the process and reach nowhere. Even when you know where to begin, you can feel lost. That is okay. Nobody gets it right the first time. The key is never to stop trying. Work with what you have, assess the output, tweak the process and reassess. Iterations will gradually build your influence. Here are ten fantastic tips that will help you create a genuinely engaging and influential personal brand:

1: Have a focus.

2: Be authentic.

3: Have a story to tell.

4: Stay consistent.

5: Accept failures.

6: Spread positivity.

7: Follow your idols.

8: Walk the talk.

9: Let people talk about you.

10: Create a legacy.

1. Have a focus.

You cannot please everyone. You can do everything or be someone to everyone. Make peace with that and maintain your focus on your key message because that is unique to you. Having a single focus will resonate with firmly with one target audience, which will make it easier for the audience to identify with you. That will also help you create better content around your personal brand.

Once you have carved you niche, carve one within it. Go deeper. Be specific. Become memorable.

2. Be authentic.

The easiest way to nail your personal brand is to be yourself. If you are finding that difficult, then perhaps you need to make peace with yourself first. You need to be at ease with who you are and what your flaws may be. People can see through drama and façade. You cannot dupe them into buying you without conveying how happy you are with yourself.

It will also make content creation easier. It will be a no-brainer. A little fine-tuning here and there and you are done. Faster turnaround time will ensure consistent content generation and engagement. But it begins with being genuine and authentic.

3. Have a story to tell.

Why? Because stories sell. Period.

An old pendant is just an old pendant worth penny. But if you say that the Queen gifted this pendant to her most loyal servant and midwife after the birth of her eldest son, suddenly, the pendant is worth millions. So, if you want to sell yourself better, you need to package your skills inside a beautiful; wrapping of a story.

Everyone has a story; the only catch is finding it. Founding your personal brand on your journey, on your story will make it unique and powerful. With a story by your side, you will no longer be boring or just someone in the sea of many. You will be a warm person who lived an authentic, extraordinary life.

4. Stay consistent.

Staying consistent and having a focus go hand in hand. If you consistently create content around one single topic, people start associating that topic with you, and you slowly become the voice for it. Having too many focus areas or not following through with your messaging or plan will confuse your audience increasing attrition and decreased engagement.

So, do not underestimate inconsistencies thinking that no one will notice them. When you are an influencer, people nibble on your content not just in comments, but in their chats and offline as well.

Even if your personal brand is fun, you can have a catchphrase at the end or a style of editing to maintain consistency. It sounds corporatish, but that is going to do wonders for you. Because corporates became huge for the same reason – they were consistent.

5. Accept failures.

It is easier said than done. It is human nature to avoid failure, and that makes us conservative. As an influencer, you need to be creative. So be ready to fail. Embrace it like a friend.

Trying new things and failing at some or all of them will give you a better understanding of your personal brand. Remember, we talked about iterations. Failures are those iterations that tell you what is working and what is not. Keep experimenting, fail fast, succeed faster.

6. Spread positivity.

Often, we hear news about celebrities who acted out in public or treated someone badly, and we instantly lose respect for them. We feel that success has gone to their heads and has turned them into arrogant snobs. However, we also hear cases of people who became humbler after tasting victory. Their stories inspire you to be better.

So, when you gain that influence and become famous, do not burn bridges with people or brands. Stay true to your personal brand and your values. Never forget to leave a positive impact on others regardless of what you are doing and where you are.

7. Follow your idols.

To learn the tricks of the trade, we look up to our idols. It not only helps us initially to set footing and distinguish right from wrong but also guides us later in management of projects and fame. Start noticing what they do and how they do it. Add your unique flavour to it and continue. They have a team of experts guiding them, but you do not. However, mimicking their mannerisms when you cannot figure out your own will slowly get you around.

8. Walk the talk.

While it seems natural to create two different profiles – one for your brand and other for your friends and family – things tend to get messy. Keeping two separate accounts is only a mechanical part. You can go ahead with that. However, even when you are interacting with your family and friends or are present on informal occasions, your personal brand follows you. You can be two different people at the same time.

So, walk your talk wherever you go to stay authentic to your brand promise and image.

9. Let people talk about you.

Always talking about yourself will make you seem like an attention seeker. So, encourage people to tag you, message you or share their views about you even when you do not agree with them. Let them tell your story.

In case you do not agree with them, give that story to your people and watch them turn it around for you. That is the best PR you can get where you will also get to know what people think of you and how they defend you. That is your community!

10. Create a legacy.

Your personal brand will live till you live. But can you make it live longer? What if you want to exit this business? What happens to your brand? Think about this right now.

Even when you are not creating content anymore or engaging in that topic, people are mentioning, tagging and pulling you into those conversations. That is your legacy. Your exit strategy. Think about what you can do now to make that happen.

Final Thoughts

As you may have understood by now, this book is populated with all of the secrets that you need to know to grow your clout on Instagram and YouTube in 2020 – whether you have been around on these platforms for a while or if you are starting this year!

We sincerely hope that by reading this book, you were able to discover plenty of great information about Instagram and YouTube and how you can encourage growth so that you no longer have to worry about creating content and delivering it to cricket. When you begin enforcing these strategies, your previously quiet or non-existent audience will start growing and will add spark to life, and you will start seeing significant growth on your influencer.

Even though these platforms are still new and evolving each day, they have several significant influencers. It might seem intimidating initially, but there is always an excellent opportunity for you to connect with your audience and grow a position of authority in your niche. Despite what rumours may lead you to believe, no niche is saturated, and there is still plenty to be gained from it.

Think of it this way: YouTube and Instagram earn money when people like you create an influential platform through them and use it to draw more attention to their platform. As you grow and start building a name for yourself, they will promote your content so that you and your audience can become even more on their platform. It not only leads to enormous growth for you but for themselves also.

By using the secrets in this very book, you can grow yourself to the point that YouTube and Instagram want to support your growth as well to ensure that you are both experiencing success from their platform. That shared investment in your growth means that no matter how old these platforms are, there will always be room for more influencers to step in and make a name for themselves.

After you read this book, I hope that you go ahead and begin building your personal brand using the strategies that you were able to learn from this material. Start by choosing your niche and creating particular high-quality videos that are relevant to your audience and their interests. Once you have made your content strategy, ensure that you properly execute it, so your content is more likely to be found by the right audience or the audience that is most likely to love them!

After you have done everything you could to leverage these two platforms through designing and SEO strategising, you will need to move over to other social media platforms. This way, you can start building a name for yourself around the web. That will not only deepen your relationship with your followers, but it will also give you several avenues to approach new viewers on for them to find you on YouTube. That way, you maximise your growth potential so that you receive the desirable number of viewers and the level of growth that you are aiming for.

Once your influence starts growing, you can begin taking advantage of monetisation features to earn you a more significant profit. Whether that includes direct marketing things to your audience, using advertisements, or using these platforms as a part of your sales funnel, make sure that your monetisation feature works best for you!

If you feel that you can logically do it, do not be afraid to leverage multiple monetisation features to gain maximum earnings through your investments. After you have mastered the process of growing your audience, all you need to do is continue to monitor your analytics and promote your growth! Through this, you will build the momentum on your profiles and achieve the ultimate level of growth through your strategies, making all of your efforts completely worth your while.

Billions of videos are being watched on YouTube every single day-name it-but that will not hinder you in doing your stuff. Just remember, you need to find what your niche is and improve or enhance it, and you have to come up with a solid marketing plan. And if you feel stuck, make use of the smart strategies shared in chapter 13 to leap past your competitors in no time. Once you have these things, you are on your way to generating great income online!

After reading all the strategies from this book, you are now equipped with all the tools you need to start doing whatever it is that you need to do to an exciting content!

Sign up for my newsletter by leaving us your email, you will be informed about new promotions and new book releases:

Click Here https://mailchi.mp/e136f3ee924a/stephan-anderson

Stephan Anderson

©

C

O

What social media platforms
are available - what do
we want to use?

What is our goals
in social media?
Why have it?

Made in the USA
San Bernardino, CA
06 February 2020